364.152
Ba   Baumann, Ed

Murder next door

DATE DUE

NO27'91 OC15'92			
DE 9'91			
DE16'91			
DE26'91			
JA 3'92			
JA17'92			
JA24'92			
FE 4'92			
FE13'92			
MR14'92			
JE11'92			

Murder
Next Door

Murder
Next Door

*How Police Tracked Down
18 Brutal Killers*

Edward Baumann
and
John O'Brien

Bonus Books, Inc., Chicago

95 94 93 92 91   5 4 3 2 1

Library of Congress Catalog Card Number: 91-73457

International Standard Book Number: 0-929387-61-9

Bonus Books, Inc.
160 East Illinois Street
Chicago, Illinois 60611

Printed in the United States of America

To police officers throughout the country whom we have known, admired and bent elbows with.

CONTENTS

FOREWORD

In *Murder Next Door* Edward Baumann and John O'Brien give us a one-way ride into a world of murder, mayhem and mysteries, like a roller coaster stretching into the next county, a jarring, breath-sucking, often terrifying trip through a nightmare land. Their style is like that of reporters of old— Fred Pasley, George Murray, Jack Lait—one that immediately captures us and takes us to the proverbial scene of the crime. We discover the hapless victims as if trailing behind the cops answering the first call, seeing the carnage for the first time as they do, sharing their shock, disgust, and wonder.

You won't find the romantic, tidy murders of the venerable Agatha Christie here, nor the offstage slayings of the immortal Sherlock venting myriad intellectual theories. Bodies, yes, almost flagrante delicto, described as they are found and, beyond this horror, the tracking down of insidious, strange killers, perhaps as normal to the dear reader as the cop's first suspicious glance, but underneath . . . underneath.

Here are mainstream miscreants such as the self-styled witch-healer Eunice Yvonne Kleinfelder, sadistically gruesome, bubbling with religious zeal and mystical gobbledygook and her all-too-willing victim John Comer, who was literally boiled to death at her hands. You will enter the Chicago apartment of this oddball couple, subtly nudged inside by the authors—you can almost smell the cat litter—and stand with the investigating officers so expertly profiled by Baumann and O'Brien, and you will follow with fascination these astounded cops through one horrific revelation after another.

And then there is the bizarre slaying of Carol Hoffman by her close-to-God husband who reported her missing, frantically searched with others for her while all the while he had cut her to pieces; Hoffman would later lamely tell officers he did it to "get rid of the evil in my house."

They come with many stripes here. Consider Charles Albanese, aptly selected by the authors as a real-life counterpart to Adrian Messenger, a mass poisoner (the old reliable, arsenic) whose get-rich-quick scheme earned him a 1982 death sentence. Reflect upon the calculating plans of ex-Bunny, ex-cop Laurie "Bambi" Bembenek, a blonde bombshell in Milwaukee who, stupidly disguised, entered the home of her husband's ex-wife to bring an end to alimony payments with murder. And Nola Jean Weaver who shot and incinerated a sleeping spouse in her lavish Long Grove, Illinois home for insurance money, and who trapped herself with a story no cop would buy.

These were money killers but not all the slayers herein were motivated by greed. One of them, the authors insist, is the mass killer of thirteen women, maybe more, a man the authors believe to be an Illinois prison inmate serving time for another offense, a demonic, bestial creature who committed mutilation murders in Ohio, Illinois and Michigan, a model prisoner.

O'Brien and Baumann tell other stories, lots of them, including the macabre tale of Belle Gunness, who planted as many as forty husbands and lovers in her garden; and the story of Rudy Bladel, a true night stalker, who made working on the railroad a matter of life and death.

This is a rogue's gallery not basically stemming from the ranks of the super criminal but the average citizenry, and, as such, will provide the reader with more insight into the character of crime than perusing the tarnished exploits of the professional criminal. For it is from our own midst, the heart of our society, not its outcasts, that most true life monsters spring. Average citizens? Yes, on the surface of public communication, but extraordinarily different behind their closed doors.

The authors have unlocked these doors or banged them down with the brute force of a beatcop's sturdy shoulder, as the case may be, and revealed in an exciting style, the secrets beyond. Here, in such books, the style is everything and O'Brien and Baumann have researched and written a consistently gripping narrative in the best tradition of true fact crime reporting. There are no dull characters, phony dialog, loose ends, or sloppy conclusions. The book is a police alarm, fresh, full of terror, obsessively appealing. And there is justice, a bit frayed, moving behind the badge and bench, offering its grim delight through these pages where no one escapes.

Jay Robert Nash
Chicago 1991

CHAPTER 1

BUNNY GIRL IN BEERTOWN

Lawrencia Bembenek was the stuff that dream girls are made of, and more. A statuesque beauty, self-confident and sassy, she exuded poise and charm from a body that could turn strong men into jelly. A modern-day Aphrodite, at the age of twenty-two.

She'd been a Playboy Bunny and calendar girl, and most certainly could have gone on to Hollywood—except that her one consuming ambition was to become a cop, a goal she achieved until her law enforcement career ended abruptly in a nightmare called murder.

Lawrencia, whose friends called her Bambi, was born and reared in an environment of law enforcement. Her father, Joe, had been a Milwaukee patrolman, and no less than ten other police officers lived within two blocks of the family home on South Taylor Avenue.

"She was no dumb blonde," a close friend said of the tall, willowy beauty. "She was a girl who knew what she wanted. She idolized her father, and wanted to follow in his footsteps."

As a teen-ager, Bambi Bembenek was one of the most popular girls in Bay View High, where she played in the band and was a member of the girls' track team. After earning her diploma in 1976 she held a variety of jobs, each a little better than the last, as she moved slowly and self-assuredly toward her all-important goal.

After graduating from Milwaukee's Stratton College with a diploma in fashion merchandising, she landed a job in a fashion shop in one of the large shopping centers. She also worked as an instructor at the Vic Tanny Health Club, and did some modeling for a casting agency in suburban Wauwatosa. From there it was only a short hop to the swank Playboy Club in Lake Geneva, where Bambi became a Bunny.

All the while the five-foot ten-inch wholesome looking all-American girl worked out with weights and ran four miles a day, getting into condition for a tryout with Milwaukee's finest. That day came in March of 1980. She easily passed the entrance exam, breezed through the twenty-one-week training course, and graduated from the Police Academy. Bembenek became a cop like her father, and began patrolling the streets in uniform with a gun and nightstick.

"I finally have the job I've always wanted," she elatedly told friends. "I'm absolutely overjoyed."

Officer Bembenek soon discovered that the thin blue line of police work was not all glamour. She was a member of the National Organization for Women (NOW), and had been a financial contributor and worker for a group known as Women Against Rape (WAR). Her equal rights attitude and determination to prove she was the peer of any man caused problems among the more chauvinist members of the force.

On one occasion a tire on her patrol car went flat at a busy intersection. As she and her macho-male partner got out to survey the damage he gloated loudly for the benefit of passersby, "You want equal rights, you're going to have to change that flat."

Which she did, while her senior partner stood slack-jawed on the corner. Another time, when she had trouble sliding a bullet into the cylinder of her revolver, a male officer hooted, "Want me to put it in for you, honey? Haw! Haw!"

"I just grit my teeth and bear it," she laughed later with friends. "I can take it. I'm what I always wanted to be."

One fellow officer who did not laugh at Bambi or taunt her was thirty-two-year-old Detective Elfred O. Schultz, Jr., strikingly handsome, well tanned and very athletic. The two of them started jogging together, and while they ran they discussed their mutual interests in outdoor sports and physical fitness.

It would appear that Aphrodite had found her Adonis. He liked to call her "Laurie."

Schultz was considered a first-rate cop, though there was one unpleasant blemish on his record. Five years earlier he had shot and killed a fellow police officer in a case of mistaken identity.

The victim was Officer G. Robert Sassan. Every bit as handsome as Schultz, he worked part time as a male fashion model. On a summer day in 1975 Sassan was off-duty in the Northway Tavern on Port Washington Road in the Milwaukee suburb of Glendale, when an unsuspecting pimp offered him a woman for prostitution.

"You just propositioned the wrong guy, buddy," Sassan smiled. "You're under arrest." He slapped the cuffs on the surprised procurer and ordered him to lie spread-eagle on the floor. Turning to another customer he said, "Go to the phone and call the police. Tell them an officer needs assistance."

The customer, an out-of-towner who was just passing through, didn't even know exactly where he was, so he dialed the operator and asked her to notify authorities.

He was unaware that the operator was in Milwaukee, and she unthinkingly directed Milwaukee lawmen instead of Glendale police to the roadhouse. Schultz and two other uniformed officers responded, not knowing what they were getting into. One of them entered the front door while Schultz and his partner went around to the back and positioned themselves behind a partition.

As they poked their heads cautiously above the partition Sassan, who was wearing civilian clothes, whirled and instinctively pointed his service revolver in their direction as he stood over the suspect. Schultz, who had his gun drawn, let loose four shots and the off-duty officer fell dead on top of the terror-stricken pimp.

A highly-publicized investigation followed, after which the Milwaukee district attorney's office ruled the killing was accidental. Schultz had no way of knowing that the gun pointed at him was in the hand of a fellow patrolman. The incident took its toll, however, and for the next year and a half Schultz worked quietly as a bailiff for Municipal Judge John Siefert, letting the shock of killing a brother lawman clear from his mind before returning to the street.

Schultz, married and the father of two young sons, was already embroiled in a complicated divorce proceeding when he and Lawrencia hit it off. It was not long before they became an "item" on the force—the handsome, suntanned detective jogging alongside the lithe patrol officer ten years his junior.

"I'm in better condition than most men," she huffed as they loped along, she in her jogging suit and he wearing tight-fitting, pale yellow shorts and an aloof look on his face. "And I'm just as good as any male on the firing range. I can hack it."

At the time Bembenek was living with a fellow policewoman, Judy Zess. It was an off-duty arrangement that eventually proved her undoing.

Judy was busted for possession of marijuana while the two of them were attending a rock concert and Bambi, in a misplaced show of loyalty, tried to cover for her. Judy was unceremoniously dumped from the force, and after an internal investigation Bambi, too, was fired for filing a false report.

The same determination that led to her becoming a police officer now drove her to fight the charge in an effort to get her shield back. She filed a sex discrimination charge against the department, seeking relief from the Equal Employment Opportunities Commission. "My dismissal is unjustified," she argued. "It is on my record, and any future employer will look at it and think I killed someone or something. They just won't understand."

The spectacle of the stunning ex-Playboy Bunny taking on the entire Milwaukee Police Department was the stuff headlines are made of, and the Milwaukee press ran features about the sex discrimination suit—complete with photos of the plucky Bambi in her jogging outfit.

While the legal action was pending she continued to carry the proud photograph of herself in her police uniform in her wallet. "I want to return to police work more than anything else," she told loyal friends. "Maybe, when this is over, I can get a job as a deputy sheriff." Meanwhile she did the next best thing. She hired on as an officer with Marquette University's Public Safety Department.

Through all her tribulations, Fred Schultz stuck to Bambi like a Band-Aid. On November 17, 1980, after eleven years of marriage, he divorced his thirty-year-old wife, Christine, the mother of his two boys. Two short months later he and Bambi eloped across the state line to Waukegan, where they were married by an Illinois justice of the peace. They honeymooned in Jamaica, and as a gesture of friendship toward her husband's ex-wife, Bambi brought back some rare butterflies for Christine's collection.

High interest rates and a tight housing market made it next to impossible for the newlyweds to find a place of their own, so Schultz moved into the $475-a-month apartment that Bambi shared with Judy Zess on Bay View Terrace.

Later, in another cost-cutting move, the trio took a $433-a-month apartment on South Twentieth Street, splitting the rent three ways. This arrangement of three people under one roof did not sit well at all with Judy's boyfriend, Tom Gaertner—especially considering who the third tenant was.

Gaertner, a forty-one-year-old body building champ, was on parole from a narcotics rap—hardly a person one would expect a police detective to take up with in the first place. The most ironic thing of all was that Gaertner had been a friend of Bob Sassan, the Glendale police officer Schultz had shot to death.

"Your husband is nothing more than a lousy scared

punk! He killed my best friend," he warned Bembenek. "I'm going to get even with the son-of-a-bitch." The situation grew in intensity until May 19, when Judy wisely packed up and left the apartment to the newlyweds.

By a strange coincidence, on the very day that Judy went packing Gaertner was busted by federal narcotics agents on a charge of possession of four ounces of cocaine with intent to distribute it. The natural question was: Did Schultz blow the whistle on Gaertner to get him out of his hair? Nobody was saying anything, but authorities could not help but notice the rather unorthodox lifestyle of a police detective and his wife sharing an apartment with the girlfriend of an ex-convict drug dealer.

Once Judy was off on her own things only got tougher for Fred and Lawrencia, since the rent was no longer a three way split. The only way out was to find cheaper quarters. Fred was already paying $700 a month to his former wife, Christine, and it was slowly draining him.

The money was going for mortgage payments to keep up the house where Chris lived with the two boys. It was a home that Schultz had "built like a fort" with his own hands on West Ramsey Avenue. But now the payments, support money, and his own $433-a-month rent, plus just keeping up with the bare necessities of life, were more than he could handle on a detective's $23,000 salary—even with his new wife's paycheck.

Schultz let it all hang out one night to his partner, Detective Michael Durfee.

"I still hold my ex-wife in high regard—don't get me wrong—and I accept the blame for the marriage not working out. But these damned payments are killing me, Mike. I'm going to have to go back into court and see if I can get them reduced," he beefed to Durfee. "Chris just got herself a job as a shipping clerk in Pewaukee. Now that she has some income of her own I'm hoping I can get my payments reduced by maybe a hundred bucks a month."

The two men gabbed while investigating a burglary on the North Side. Durfee was just letting his partner get his problems off his chest, when they were called in to the station at 2:40 A.M. It was the 28th of May, 1981.

"The captain wants to talk to you," a fellow detective told Schultz, eyeing him strangely. "He's waiting on the line."

Schultz shrugged his shoulders and curiously picked up the phone. "Yes, captain. This is Schultz."

"Fritz, I've got something unpleasant to tell you. Your wife is dead."

"What? My wife? Laurie . . . ?"

"No, Fritz, Christine," the voice came coldly through the phone. "It's Christine that's dead. Your kids are OK."

The detective's handsome face drained of its color as he momentarily dropped the phone. Then, regaining his composure, he picked it up, vaguely thanked the captain, and hung up.

Schultz slouched into a chair for a moment to organize his thoughts. He started to tell his partner what the captain had told him, but Durfee had already heard it from the other cops. Then Schultz telephoned Laurie to make sure she was all right, and to tell her the awful news.

Durfee drove Schultz over to the slain woman's home on Ramsey, about a mile and a half from the apartment where he lived with Laurie. The muscular detective hugged his two sons, eleven-year-old Sean and seven-year-old Shannon. "Everything's going to be all right, guys. Dad's here now."

Christine's body had already been removed. Schultz called one of the detectives aside and asked, "Would you mind filling me in on what happened?"

"She was tied and gagged on the bed, in the bedroom, and shot once in the back at point-blank range," he was told bluntly. "One of the boys struggled with the intruder, who apparently tried to put a rope around the lad's neck while he was asleep. As near as we can determine, Fritz, whoever did it tied your wife up first and forced her to lie face down on the bed in there. Then he went to the boys' room. I understand your older son was sleeping with the little guy because he was afraid of the dark."

Calling Sean over, the detective gently suggested, "Why don't you tell your dad what you told us, son?"

The bewildered youngster, relieved now that his father was at his side, sat on the side of the bed in his pajamas and related: "I felt something pulling on my neck, Dad. It felt like a rope or something. A hand came down on my face. I started screaming and I saw a glove. It was over my eyes."

His screams awakened Shannon, he said, and the stranger retreated from the room. The intruder backtracked across the hallway to the other bedroom, where the boys' mother was struggling to free herself.

"I heard a bang! Then I heard, 'Oh, God. Oh, God' coming from Mom's room," the wide-eyed boy continued. "I got out of bed and started to go to Mom's room, when someone brushed past me and ran down the stairs."

The two frightened boys went into their mother's room, where Christine was lying facedown on the bed, blood oozing from a wound in her back. Her gutsy young sons braced a chair against the inside of the door, fearing the intruder might still be in the house. Then they ripped open their mother's T-shirt and got some gauze to try to stem the bleeding. While little Shannon tried to comfort his mother, who was probably already dead, Sean telephoned a neighbor who was a police officer. The two boys remained huddled behind the barricaded door until authorities arrived.

In talking to the two boys, investigators were able to put together a tentative description of the killer:

It was a white male, nearly six feet tall, wearing a green jogging suit with white and yellow stripes running down the sleeves. He had light colored hair, tied in a ponytail. The boys were unable to see his face however, because of a scarf wrapped around his head covering his mouth and nose. The alert Sean did note that the intruder wore what the boy called "black police shoes, cut low top."

The boys were put in the care of neighbors, as Schultz faced the unpleasant obligation of going to the morgue to officially identify the body of his former wife. It was a task he did not care to face alone, so Durfee drove by the Twentieth Street apartment where they picked up Lawrencia at 6:30 A.M.

Before leaving the apartment Durfee asked Schultz for his off-duty gun. "It's the lieutenant's orders, Fritz," he apologized. "He told me he wants me to check it out. I've got to ask you for it." Schultz went to the back bedroom and dug the .38 caliber Smith & Wesson snub-nosed revolver out of a duffle bag where it was stashed for safe keeping. He sniffed the two-inch barrel, examined it, and turned it over to his partner. Durfee took a whiff, looked the gun over, and passed it back to Schultz.

"Doesn't seem to have been fired recently," he commented.

Schultz slipped the Smith & Wesson into his briefcase to take with him to the medical examiner's office in case his superiors wanted him to turn it in for further examination.

On the way down to the morgue the trio made small talk, trying to keep their minds off the horrible happening of the night. "How've things been going with you since you left the force, Laurie?" Durfee inquired.

"I'm going to take my test for the sheriff's department just as soon as they let me," Bambi responded. "I'm really looking forward to getting back into law enforcement, Mike, even though I think some of their rules are a little petty."

When they arrived at the morgue downtown Schultz sadly made the formal identification. A medical examiner explained to the two detectives that Christine had been shot once with the muzzle of the gun held tightly against her back. It was a deliberate execution. "The bullet tore through her heart and she died of internal hemorrhaging," he said.

Durfee drove the couple back to their apartment and, since no one asked him to turn in his off-duty revolver, Schultz took it back with him.

After Christine's funeral the newlyweds—married less than five months—found themselves confronted with yet another problem: What to do about Sean and Shannon?

Bambi beefed to her girlfriend, Josephine Osuchowski, "All of a sudden we're going to have two kids. I'm still adjusting to marriage, and now I'll have to adjust to two kids. We can't afford two kids. We just signed a lease for an efficiency apartment, and now we're going to have to move again."

It wasn't that Lawrencia didn't like the boys. She told one friend, "They're both cute, but I just hadn't figured on instant motherhood, you know? I knew when I married Fred that he had a vasectomy. I thought it was good that a man finally did something about birth control."

The problem of how to cope with a family of four in an efficiency apartment was temporarily solved when Joseph and Virginia Bembenek announced they were leaving for an extended vacation to Oregon. "Why don't you and Fred and the boys stay in our house for the time being?" Lawrencia's parents suggested. "It's always good to have a house lived in when you're away. It will give you some breathing room, and we won't have to worry about burglars or anything like that."

While the elder Bembeneks did not say so at the time, they had extended the offer after hearing "a terrible argument" between Bambi and Fred about moving into the home on Ramsey Avenue that Schultz had built—and where Christine had died.

"I don't want to move into *that* house!" Lawrencia declared.

"Look, I already own the place. I'm making payments on it," he retorted. "You're going to have to move in there with me and the boys or I'll go there by myself."

"Oh, Fred. You know how I feel about it. My God! You slept there with your first wife. You built it for her. There are baby pictures. Wedding pictures on the walls. Why can't we work out something else?"

"Okay, you win," he finally relented. "We'll sell the damn place. We'll sell it and get a place of our own, somehow."

The generous offer by the Bembeneks would now give them a place to live while they shopped around. They took over the old house on Taylor Avenue, as Schultz' fellow detectives pressed their investigation into his ex-wife's murder. It became one of the most sensitive criminal investigations ever undertaken by the Milwaukee Police Department because of the intimate involvement of one of their own.

Detective Inspector Kenneth Hagopian and Deputy Inspector Rudolph Will, who headed the investigation, warned their men to proceed with deliberate caution. "The public will be watching every move we make, and some people are going to say it's going to be a whitewash," detectives were warned. "You cannot let personal feelings enter into this case in any way. Act like the professionals you are."

Schultz, meanwhile, requested a furlough. He had not returned to work since Christine's murder. It was a time for him and his new wife, and the two boys, to adjust to their new circumstances and it wasn't going to be easy. For one thing, the boys both insisted on sleeping with the lights on. They couldn't get the night of terror out of their minds.

Gradually life drifted back to normal. Neighbors saw the family at the Brady Street Festival, where it appeared that Bambi and the boys had taken a liking to one-another. The youngsters became active in softball and gymnastics in their neighborhood, and their stepmother put up an activities board for the summer months to help keep track of their outside interests. One thing Bambi felt uncomfortable about, though, was the boys' laundry. "You're going to have to wash your own kids' clothes, Fred," she told him.

As part of their investigation into Christine's murder detectives were discreetly checking Fred Schultz' background and present lifestyle. They learned that he'd made $29,628 in the past year, putting his carpentry skills to use doing remodeling work to augment his police salary.

Christine had been earning $205 a month as a part-time shipping clerk. Lawrencia was making about $10,000 a year at Marquette University.

The house Schultz built on Ramsey Avenue had a market value of $80,000, but carried a $27,000 mortgage on which Fred was paying $363 a month. He was also under a court order to pay $330 a month in child support—$165 on the first and another $165 on the fifteenth.

Tom Gaertner, who had threatened to get even with Schultz over the shooting of his policeman friend, was not overlooked as a possible suspect in the slaying—but he had the best possible alibi. Investigators determined he was still in jail awaiting trial on the drug charges.

Meanwhile a seemingly insignificant event was unfolding in the Twentieth Street apartment building where Fred and Laurie lived before moving into her parents' home. Tenants complained to the building superintendent that their toilets were overflowing and he called in Dan McGinnis, a plumber. McGinnis ran a flexible metal "snake" down through the pipes and, to his surprise and amusement, retrieved a reddish-brown ponytailed wig. It had been lodged in a common drain serving the former Schultz apartment and an adjoining unit.

"Here's your trouble," McGinnis laughed, triumphantly turning the dripping trophy over to the astonished apartment manager.

"Jeez, what some people don't flush down their toilets," the manager carped. "Here, toss it in the garbage," he told the janitor.

Police learned of the incident three days later, on June 15, while routinely questioning the Schultz' former neighbors. Curious, they tracked down the dumpster, which had already been hauled away, and after tedious hours of rooting through a mountain of garbage, recovered the wig.

On June 18 Detective James Gauger paid a belated call to the Schultz home. "Come on in and have a cool beer," Fred invited, ushering Gauger into the kitchen. "We don't have very much company these days, as you can imagine."

After taking a long draw on the brew as he sat with the couple at their table the detective got down to business. "This isn't exactly a social call," he said. "I've been sent over to pick up your .38, Fred. They want to make some ballistics tests."

"My God, do they think one of us did it?" Lawrencia laughed incredulously. "Why would I do it? Then I'd be stuck with two kids, and that would be a bitch. I hate those damned rug rats."

"Rug rats?" Gauger asked.

"Oh, Jim, I've just had an exasperating day," she apologized. "The boys have been misbehaving . . . grinding crayons into my folks' carpet. And we've had to take Shannon to a psychiatrist. He's been regressing since his mother's death."

"Well, this has been pretty rough on all of you," Gauger said, finishing his beer. He put the off-duty gun Schultz turned over to him into his briefcase and took it to the Wisconsin Regional Crime Laboratory in New Berlin for testing.

The next Wednesday afternoon, June 24, Lawrencia was on the job at Marquette University when two plainclothes investigators called at the public safety office to talk to her.

"Hi, fellas," she said cheerfully. "What brings you guys out here?"

"Lawrencia, we'd like you to come with us," Detective Thomas Repishak told her.

"Come with you? What do you mean? What's this all about?"

"You have the right to remain silent, Lawrencia. Hold out your arms."

"You're going to cuff me?"

"Sorry. You know the rules. Come on, let's go."

The finale of the month-long investigation was a bombshell. Schultz was utterly devastated when he learned that his bride of less than half a year had been arrested for Christine's murder.

Shaken, he called an eighteen-year-old neighbor girl who had known Bambi all her life and asked her to come and sit with the boys while he drove down to police headquarters to find out what the hell was going on.

"Is it okay if I take the boys to a movie?" she asked innocently.

"No, it's not a good night. Just tell them their daddy had to go to work," he said as he headed for his car.

The next morning the Milwaukee press splashed the sensational arrest all over page one in the biggest type they could find. It was Elfred Schultz' thirty-third birthday, but he suddenly felt like a very old man.

Weeping as he picked up the phone, he dialed his former mother-in-law, Alice Pennings, in Appleton, to break the news to her before she heard it from anyone else. Just four weeks earlier he had to call and tell her that her daughter, Christine, was dead. Now he had to report that the woman who replaced her in his bed had been charged with her murder. "My new life has gone down the drain," he sobbed.

How could the cops possibly arrest Lawrencia, the policeman's daughter; the policeman's wife; and an ex-police officer herself? Before the end of the day it would all come out. After conferring for eight hours with Rudolph Will, deputy inspector of detectives, District Attorney E. Michael McCann filed a formal complaint against Lawrencia Bembenek Schultz listing the state's case against her.

The most damning evidence of all was the fact that ballistics tests showed that the .200-grain round-nose bullet removed from Christine's body had been fired from her husband's .38 caliber off-duty revolver.

It had already been established that only two people—Bambi and Fred Schultz—had access to the murder weapon. And Fred's partner, Durfee, could attest to the fact that Schultz was on duty with him at 2:20 A.M. on May 28 when his former wife was shot in the back.

But a lot of other things had also fallen into place along the way from Christine's deathbed to the Milwaukee courtroom.

Authorities disclosed for the first time that Schultz had taken and passed a lie test which indicated he knew nothing about Christine's untimely death; but Lawrencia had politely declined to go on the polygraph.

Then there was the financial evidence, showing that Schultz was paying about $700 a month to his ex-wife, and he and his new bride were strapped for funds.

And the prosecutor produced a statement from Bambi's former roommate, Judy Lee Zess, who told police that at a dinner party several weeks prior to the killing Bambi had broached the idea of "having Chris rubbed out." Judy said Bambi had asked her boyfriend, Gaertner, "Do you know anybody who could have Chris blown away?"

Judy's mother, Frances, who was at the party, corroborated the statement. "Lawrencia was complaining about all their debts, and her husband's child support and mortgage payments," she related. "She said she'd pay to have her [Christine] blown away. I thought she was joking, and I laughed it off at the time."

Detective Repishak, one of the arresting officers, said Lawrencia's supervisor at Marquette University, Thomas Conway, had searched the suspect's locker at the request of police, and turned over to them a white plastic hairbrush. The detective said samples of hair taken from the brush matched hairs on the bandana that had been used to gag the murder victim.

The ponytail wig fished out of the toilet drain in the apartment where Lawrencia and Fred Schultz had lived was also tied to Bambi. Marilyn Gehrt, a South Side shop owner, recalled having sold such a wig to the suspect. "She came in and requested a long wig. Something that could be pulled back in a ponytail. She said it was for a man, not for her, for a joke," Mrs. Gehrt told detectives. "I remember the name because I had a friend named Bembenek, and I asked the customer whether they could have been related."

A police lab report showed that fibers found on the dead woman's body were identical in character to those from the toilet-flushed wig.

The two Schultz boys had said their mother's killer wore a "green jogging suit" with white or yellow stripes down the sleeves. Police had turned up at least four witnesses who had seen Bambi wearing such attire. One was a security guard at the Southridge Boston Store where Lawrencia once worked. "I remember seeing her leave the store wearing a very pretty, forest/kelly green velour jogging suit," the guard, Annette Wilson, related.

Another witness was equally credible—Milwaukee Police Officer Gary Shaw. The nineteen-year police veteran said he and his wife, Darlene, had seen Lawrencia wearing a green jogging outfit while attending a movie with her new husband, Fred. Shaw specifically remembered the green jogging suit with a white stripe along the side of the arm because he commented to his wife at the time, "It's rather odd that a person would be wearing such light clothing on such a cold evening."

It was the night of February 16, when *Fort Apache, the Bronx* was playing at the Spring Mall Theater, Shaw said. A record of a meal he had charged to his credit card before the movie verified the date.

And then there was the photo of Lawrencia published in the *Milwaukee Journal* on December 19, in connection with the story about her discrimination suit against the police department. Robert Goessner, a forty-six-year-old studio photographer and lab technician for the paper, remembered taking her photo in the green jogging suit with white stripes. He produced a copy of the shot for investigators.

In yet another facet of the painstaking probe, detectives determined that Christine's home showed no sign of forced entry on the night she was murdered in her bed. They also established that Schultz had kept a spare key to the house in a jewelry box in his and Bambi's bedroom.

The evidence was all circumstantial, but there was more than enough to justify holding the ex-policewoman and one-time Playboy Bunny to face trial for first-degree murder. Lawrencia was arraigned before Judge Thomas Doherty, still wearing the white shirt, black trousers, and shiny black shoes that constituted her Marquette University public safety uniform.

Doherty set bail at $10,000—a seemingly impossible sum for anyone as deeply in debt as Fred and Lawrencia—but Bambi didn't spend a night in jail. The money was produced immediately, and she was permitted to return to her parents' home to await trial. Robert Reilly, an attorney engaged by Schultz to represent his wife, refused to comment as to the source of the money.

Schultz, meanwhile, hired a second lawyer, Joseph P. Balistrieri, to represent his own interests in the case. The son of Frank Balistrieri, described by the FBI as "the Organized Crime chieftain in Milwaukee," Joseph Balistrieri was, himself, the target of a federal grand jury investigation. His selection to represent a police detective caused considerable eyebrow-raising.

At a preliminary hearing for Bambi, Schultz took the Fifth Amendment and refused to answer any questions on the advice of his lawyer. If his position caused his superiors any uneasiness he quickly relieved them of it. He abruptly resigned from the force, ending a thirteen-year career as a lawman. Life for the one-time detective had gone from the fast track to a downhill roller-coaster. It seemed that if anything else could go wrong, it surely would.

It wasn't enough that the mother of his children was dead and his wife was charged with her murder—Schultz suddenly found Bambi wasn't even his wife. Under Wisconsin law, a divorced person cannot remarry for six months, so the couple's romantic elopement across the state line had been illegal. The courts did not recognize them as man and wife. They quickly took out a Wisconsin license and drove over to Madison where a Dane County judge legally tied the knot over the Thanksgiving holiday.

Another marriage also took place at about the same time. Tom Gaertner had been sentenced to twelve years for possession of cocaine, and Judy Zess went down to Chicago where she married the former body builder in his cell at the Metropolitan Correctional Center. The unhappy groom was then shipped off to the federal pen in Oxford, Wisconsin.

Meanwhile, a federal grand jury in Milwaukee indicted Fred's lawyer, Balistrieri, for mail fraud, and he was sentenced to five years in prison.

Then Schultz lost custody of his two sons. A judge awarded the boys to one of their mother's relatives, and after learning that Schultz had received $13,219 in pension benefits on resigning from the police force, ordered him to cough up $6,000 in support money.

But the worst was yet to come. Bambi's murder trial

began before Judge Michael J. Skwierawski on February 22, 1982—George Washington's birthday.

The defense was pretty much a family affair, with father and one son both testifying on Lawrencia's behalf. Schultz took the stand to declare, "I am 100 per cent behind my wife." He told the jury that he had personally inspected his off-duty revolver after Christine's murder and, "In my opinion, it had not been fired."

Little Sean related how he'd been awakened by the intruder who tied a rope around his neck and put a gloved hand over his face. He said he did not think it was his stepmother. Asked by Bambi's new defense lawyer Donald Eisenberg if he loved his new mother, the eleven-year-old responded, "Yes."

Every eye in the crowded courtroom was on Bambi when the former Playboy Bunny, wearing a stunning see-through dress, took the stand on her own behalf to swear, under oath, that she had not killed her husband's previous wife.

But the jurors didn't take her at her word. On Tuesday night, March 9, after hearing testimony from 49 witnesses and sifting through 134 pieces of evidence, they found her guilty as charged.

The twenty-three-year-old defendant, every blonde hair precisely in place and exhibiting the poise and self-control she had shown all her life, displayed no emotion when the verdict was read, or when Judge Skwierawski sentenced her to life in prison.

Justice is swift in "America's Dairyland." Within minutes Lawrencia was on her way to the women's prison at Taycheedah, where she would be required to serve a minimum of eleven years and three months before becoming eligible for parole. It happened so fast that she left her purse and coat behind in the courtroom—along with her thoroughly devastated husband.

Elfred Schultz, the ex-detective whose gun had been declared the murder weapon, sat hunched in a front row pew, his head in his hands, and tears streaming down his cheeks.

Bambi's parents, who had returned from Oregon for the trial, stood for a moment beside their sobbing son-in-law. Then they left to take their own grief back home. Schultz' father, Elfred O. Schultz, Sr., sat next to his boy, put his hand on his shoulder, and asked, "Do you want to come home with me, son?" The handsome, ex-policeman wept, "Stay with me awhile, Pa."

Schultz' undying belief in his wife's innocence lasted all of three months. In June 1982 he wrote Laurie a "Dear Jane" letter in prison telling her, "Good luck, and good-bye." He then packed his suitcase and moved to Bokeelia, Florida.

"I came to my senses," he said. "She murdered a person I loved and still loved a little bit and probably always will love a little bit, and attempted to strangle one of my sons. I don't think there is any doubt about it. I think she's exactly where she belongs."

As the Fourth of July weekend approached the following year Lawrencia decided to give Fred an Independence Day present. She sued him for divorce and asked for alimony. Her new lawyer, Robert Weidenbaum, explained, "For somebody who is getting sixteen cents an hour [for prison work], it's hard to even buy toothpaste and shampoo."

For eight years Lawrencia Bembenek was a model prisoner, all the while proclaiming her innocence. Then, on Sunday night, July 15, 1990, she went over the wall. Taycheedah authorities, searching the prison grounds after discovering her missing at a 9:25 P.M. bedcheck, found her belt draped over a seven-foot high chainlink fence, topped by five ugly strands of barbed wire.

At the same time Bembenek disappeared, relatives of thirty-four-year-old Dominic Gugliatto, a Milwaukee factory worker, reported him missing as well. Gugliatto, divorced and the father of three children, had met Lawrencia while he was visiting a relative at Taycheedah, and had become enamored with her.

In the ensuing weeks sightings of the fugitive felon and her paramour were reported everywhere, from Florida to

London. But an international search for Bembenek and her boyfriend failed to turn up the slightest trace of the elusive couple. While fears were expressed in some quarters that Bambi Bembenek would never be heard from again, Fond du Lac County Sheriff James Gilmore wryly suggested that it would be only a matter of time before the glamorous fugitive would be back in the hands of the law. "Where can you hide with a face like that?" he asked.

The sheriff was right. On October 17, 1990, a customer in a bar and grill in Thunder Bay, Ontario, thought the waitress, who called herself Jennifer Gazzana, looked familiar. He tipped off the Royal Canadian Mounted Police.

The Mounties and Constable Andrew Rozdolsky went to the basement apartment where the waitress lived, just in time to find Bembenek and Gugliatto hastily packing their bags.

"You got us," Gugliatto muttered.

Lawrencia looked up from her suitcase and sighed, "Ten more minutes and we'd have gotten away."

EPILOGUE

Dominic Gugliatto was returned to the States in December, and ordered to stand trial for helping Lawrencia escape from prison.

Bembenek sought refugee status in Canada, claiming she faced persecution back home. Her Canadian lawyer, Frank Marrocco, an expert on immigration law, filed a ninety-five-page brief in which he questioned five major pieces of circumstantial evidence used to convict Lawrencia:

1. A hair matching Bembenek's, found on the bandana used to gag Christine Schultz, might have been planted in the police evidence room.

2. Sloppy police work, in not originally recording the serial number of her husband's off-duty revolver, to which Bembenek had access, meant there was no way to prove it was the same weapon as the murder gun, recovered later.

3. Bembenek may not have owned a green jogging suit, such as the killer wore, but witnesses who could have verified this were not called to testify at her trial.

4. The wig found in the drain pipe could have been flushed down the toilet by anyone. In fact Bembenek's former roommate, Judy Zess, had been visiting the adjoining apartment shortly before the toilet overflowed.

5. There were only two keys to Christine's home, and both were in possession of her ex-husband, Elfred Schultz, on the night of the murder.

It was a good try, but the Canadian government rejected the argument and declared the escaped murderess a public danger, barring her from making a refugee claim to stay in the country.

She appealed the ruling, and a government spokesman said the case could "ultimately take years" to decide. Bambi, meanwhile, remains in a Toronto jail at a cost to Canadian taxpayers of $106 a day.

CHAPTER 2

THE "WHISTLER" SOLVES A MURDER— HIS OWN

Only Everett Clarke's dearest friends knew that the kindly old Chicago drama coach was "The Whistler." He'd been a shining star in the Golden Days of radio—back in the thirties and forties before the glowing tube changed the American way of life. Every night after supper a nation of mystery fans, hungry for something to take their minds off the dreary Depression, huddled around their Majestics and Philcos and turned the dials in search of a good thriller to give them the bedtime shudders.

"The Whistler" was one of those shows. It featured a private investigator who, in the course of his thirty minutes of air time, would bring all manner of criminals—from jewel thieves, to blackmailers and murderers—to justice through his own deductive reasoning. No one knew the true identity of "The Whistler," to be sure. But there was no mistaking his eerie approach through the fog or night shadows—the hollow echo of his footsteps on the pavement and the low, mournful whistle that gave his show its name.

The ghastly death Everett Clarke met in real life two generations later had all the macabre ingredients of his old radio melodramas. There was the chilling scream behind a locked door, a name called out, and the victim's mutilated body lying in the center of the stage. A bloody scissors, an open appointment book. And the mysterious killer disappearing through a window ten dizzying stories above Michigan Avenue.

From the very beginning, to Everett Clarke's last dying gasp, there was nothing routine about this Chicago homicide.

Almost from the day he was born in 1912, Everett Clarke's goal in life had been to be an actor and a damned good one. He worked at it. He worked hard, and by the time he was in his twenties, and radio came of age, he was a star. He was "The Whistler." An envious friend told him, "Ev, you've got a God-given voice. It's so rich. Only you could play The Whistler."

In radio's heyday Clarke was also a cast member of "The Shadow," another classic—"Who knows what evil lurks in the hearts of men? The Shadow knows . . ." And throughout the 1930s he appeared as a regular on the "Betty and Bob" soap opera. Except for his starring role in "The Whistler" he usually played the villain.

He did children's shows as well, but was most widely known publicly as the announcer-narrator of WGN Radio's "Chicago Theatre of the Air," broadcast throughout the United States and Canada in the 1940s and early 1950s.

With the coming of television and the demise of radio mystery dramas, Clarke turned his attention to voice and drama coaching. His next twenty-five years were dedicated to coaching many television and radio personalities, including some who followed his advice all the way to the top. One was Robert Urich, the star of ABC-TV's "Vega$," whose autographed picture was proudly displayed on the master's office wall. Urich would go on to star in "Spenser: For Hire," and play the bad guy in "Lonesome Dove."

In the late 1960s Clarke organized the non-professional Chicago Community Theater, a group of actors who performed under his direction in the Auditorium of the Fine Arts Building, where he rented office space.

There was one piece of advice he always gave his actors: "No one is paid for performing, except for the pleasure of participation. The important thing is the good the theater can do for the individual. A person finds himself in it. It becomes social therapy."

The last thirty years—nearly half his life—Clarke shared an apartment with a fellow bachelor, Arnold Thomas, on Chicago's Near North Side within walking distance of the Loop. Extremely popular in his circle of friends, he was known as a warm person, with a vibrant voice and ready wit that made the handsome sixty-eight-year-old easy to like. He still carried the well-formed physique he had developed in college sports, followed by four years of rigorous dance training to round out his education on the stage.

Shirley Spencer, a graphologist who years before had analyzed Clarke's handwriting, picked out his traits immediately. "The stimulation of an audience is very necessary for him to be at his best and keep him from getting stale. His handwriting indicates humor, and reveals a combative quality," she said. "This young man can be devastatingly sarcastic if opposed, and he can be stubborn, too. But for the most part he is cheerful and optimistic, but if his energies are depleted, he can have a very depressed reaction. He gives out a great deal of warmth and emotion. He is vivacious and loves to talk."

But now the old man's energies were depleting. He had been ill of late and his many friends were concerned. They would telephone regularly to cheer him up, or just chat to make sure everything was all right.

Clarke continued to visit his downtown office daily, where he was taking on an increasing number of young students. Practicing what he preached about "social therapy," he often gave "scholarships" to his acting school out of his own pocket—free lessons to young people who could not otherwise afford them—in order to do what he could to help them become somebody.

"One of my great thrills was watching the wonderful change in two leather-jacketed kids who carried knives," he told one theater critic. "They were interested in drama. They had talent. Their activity in the community nipped juvenile delinquency in the bud."

It was this blind faith in others that eventually cost Everett Clarke his life.

On Tuesday, September 9, 1980, he made his usual visit to the drama studio and office he occupied on the top floor of the Fine Arts Building overlooking Grant Park on the Lake Michigan shoreline. "Morning, George," he said cheerfully as he stepped into the ornamental wrought iron cage of one of the few manually operated elevators left in creation.

"Best of the day to you, Mr. Clarke," smiled the operator, as he rammed the old throttle home and the antique car creaked and shook its way to the summit. "Busy day ahead?"

"Oh, not too bad," smiled Clarke. "I've got several students coming in for appointments. I'm sort of looking forward to it. You know, you can do so much with these young people if they're interested. You just have to be able to stimulate them."

When he emerged from the elevator on the tenth floor Clarke found two of his students already waiting on the wooden bench in the corridor outside his office. He unlocked the door and motioned them inside.

As they exchanged small talk he went over to the appointment book on his desk, opened it to September 9, and checked off their names.

"Promptness is a virtue, gentlemen," he said. "Remember that, no matter what you do in life. It is especially important in the theater, you know. You can't keep your audience waiting."

Clarke ushered the two students over to the "stage" which was, in fact, his own private theater. It was a small platform, raised about six inches off the floor in the center of the studio, designed to give the feel of actually being on stage. It was here that the master tutored the would-be Thespians. First he would make his grand entry onto the stage and act out the role himself. Then the student would take the spotlight, before a make-believe audience, and apply himself to the lines the teacher had just recited.

At noon the lesson ended, and the students left, enthusiastic over their morning accomplishments, after scheduling their next visit in Clarke's log. His young proteges gone, Clarke made a few notes of the morning's activities. Then he locked his office and went down the hall to where his friend, Annie Lane, had an art studio, to keep a date for lunch.

The two dined together often, as old friends do. George, the elevator operator, would later recall that the couple returned just after two o'clock, chatting animatedly, as the metal cage rattled its course to the top.

"Perhaps we can do this again tomorrow," the old actor suggested in his resonant voice as Annie turned to enter her studio. "Please give me a call, Ev. I don't think I have anything going," she smiled.

Clarke, feeling somewhat bloated from having stayed too long at the boards, let the door swing shut behind him as he walked into his small loft-like studio.

The walls were lined with books, nearly 3,000 of them, in leather bindings with gold leaf trim. For the most part they were about the world of drama, the theater, and the arts. Other shelves were stacked with scripts, including those from Clarke's old radio shows, some going back half a century. Against one wall stood an old organ and a piano, side by side, both littered with music sheets. Clarke was proficient at both, and occasionally sat at the keyboard to provide background music for his acting students.

"Smells musty in here," the venerable actor announced to himself as he walked around the small stage and raised a window to let in some air. The Fine Arts Building faced the lakefront park, but Clarke's studio was around the corner from the front, with his window looking across an areaway to an adjoining building.

He walked over to his desk and flipped open the appointment book as there was a knock at the door. "Enter!" he commanded, without looking up. Then he remembered that the door automatically locked when it was closed, and he walked over to turn the knob to admit his visitor.

At 2:30 P.M. Annie Lane, who had been painting in her neighboring studio, walked down the hall to the ladies room. As she passed Clarke's door she heard muffled shouts of "No, Paul! No!" And the clattering of books falling to the floor.

"That Ev," she smiled, as she continued down the hall. "He puts everything he's got into it. No wonder he was so good. You'd think he was performing at the Civic Auditorium."

That evening Clarke did not arrive home at his usual time, and his roommate became worried. He called the studio but got no answer. Then he telephoned mutual friends, to see whether Clarke had stopped off to visit any of them. They had not heard from him, either.

Finally Thomas called the maintenance office at the Fine Arts Building and asked the night janitor if he would mind checking Clarke's studio. People didn't usually check up on the old actor, but since his illness his friends were concerned about him.

The janitor, shaking his head in amusement, obediently clambered aboard the old wrought iron lift and waited patiently as it creaked and rattled its way to the top floor.

By eight o'clock at night the building was mostly deserted, and the janitor's rubber-soled shoes played a muted thump, thump, thump as he plodded across the marble floor. He rapped sharply several times on the frosted glass door to Clarke's studio with his passkey, but got no response. Then he inserted the key into the lock and let himself into the shadowy office.

At first he could see nothing unusual. The last rays of the setting sun were deflected off the neighboring building and through the open window. The janitor moved toward the window, to shut it in case of rain, when he noticed the macabre scene on the center stage. He drew a deep breath and stopped short. "What in the name of . . . ?"

Lying on his back in the center of the tiny stage was the lifeless body of Everett Clarke. He was fully clothed, in a sports shirt, open at the neck to display a gold chain, a light sweater, and slacks. His mouth was agape. His sightless eyes bored unflinchingly at the ceiling, and he was surrounded by a sea of bright, red blood.

The horrified janitor backed slowly out of the room. This scene was not for him. His heart pounding, he retreated to the waiting elevator. He drove it down to the main floor, went directly to the maintenance office, and telephoned police headquarters a half mile away.

Within minutes the tiny studio, no bigger than a two-car garage, was crawling with uniformed and plainclothed cops.

Everett Clarke had been stabbed nine times—once in the left side of the neck through the jugular vein, and eight times in the chest. A bloody scissors lay alongside his body. Death had been almost instantaneous.

In falling to the stage, on which he had acted so many roles in life, Clarke had pulled down a stack of books on his desk. They lay scattered on the floor beside the body, soaking up their owner's blood.

Aside from the jumble of books on the floor nothing in the office appeared to have been disturbed. Investigators ruled out robbery as a motive in the slaying when they noted the expensive gold chain around the dead actor's neck, and found $107 in cash in his wallet.

"Aw, who the hell would want to do something like this to such a nice old guy? And why?" mused one homicide detective, looking puzzled at the grotesque scene laid out before him.

"Beats the hell out of me," grunted Lieutenant John Hensley, Area One Homicide Commander, who arrived on the scene to take personal charge of the investigation. "Some killers don't need a motive."

Hensley, a stocky, street-wise cop with a thick, black head of hair, who liked to sip his coffee from a beer mug, had been on the force for nineteen years. His wife was also a police officer, serving as a bodyguard for Mayor Jane Byrne.

Hensley's command was the busiest in Chicago. It took in all of downtown, from the site of old Fort Dearborn on the Chicago River to the north, to the city's South Side. As homicide commander he worked out of a second floor office near White Sox Park, overlooking the world's busiest freeway—the Dan Ryan.

His office was one of those small, functional cubicles that could easily put a person to sleep. It contained his desk and beer mug, a swivel chair, a couple of metal file cabinets, two visitors chairs, and a bulletin board decorated with the police slogan: "We, the willing, led by the unknowing, are doing the impossible for the ungrateful."

The Fine Arts Building was in the very heart of Hensley's beat. Killings in Chicago are far from unique, but when a well-known person is found dead under circumstances such as this, in the cultural center of the community, tracking down the murderer assumes top priority.

The veteran lawman blanched when he was told the identity of the victim. "Jeez, you know, I was just a kid when The Whistler was on the air, but I remember him well. It was a kind of spooky show. Now this! Gives you goose bumps, doesn't it?"

"Makes me want to puke," said the detective, turning away.

As the crime lab technicians went over the body and checked out the bloody scissors, Hensley wasted no time in getting his dicks moving. "I want you guys to fan out through this entire building before anybody else goes home for the night. Talk to everybody—the janitor, the elevator guy, office workers, switchboard operators—anybody who might have seen anything. Find out who else works in the building, and get hold of 'em at home if you have to."

"Here, look at this, lieutenant," offered one of the detectives, handing Hensley a note he'd found stuffed into the mail slot in the office door. It was a hastily scribbled message, undoubtedly to the dead man. "We hope you didn't forget us. Whatever kept you from us must have been really important," it said. It bore two signatures.

"Find out who the hell wrote this note," Hensley directed. "Find out exactly when these people were here, and what time it was they were expected. And, you know, did they see or hear anything . . ."

Hensley went over to the dead man's desk and the open appointment book. He found a pair of names matching those on the note. They had been scheduled for three o'clock.

"Students. They're a couple of students," he noted. "This pretty much rules them out. You don't go around leaving a note with your name on it at the murder scene if you're the gaffer who did it. Check 'em out, though. They could have heard or seen something.

"In fact, check out this whole friggin' appointment book. Every name in it, from A to Z. Start out with today— whoever's name is down for today, and work backward. There's no sign of a forced entry. It looks like whoever did this was let in by the old guy. It had to be someone he knew."

When the news of Clarke's slaying hit the newscasts and the morning papers the acting crowd was aghast. The murder was the second to rock the Windy City's theatrical community in as many weeks. On Thursday night, August 21, Carl Stohn, Jr., a fifty-eight-year-old producer at Drury Lane and Pheasant Run theaters for the past twenty-five years, was found shot to death on a North Side street across from Henrotin Hospital.

He had just left the movie production of *Thief* starring James Caan, in which he had an acting role himself. Stohn's murder, still unsolved when police were called in on the Clarke homicide, was believed to have been at the hands of a thief.

Clarke's body was removed to the Cook County Morgue where an autopsy indicated the time of death had been somewhere between two and three o'clock that afternoon.

This finding was bolstered by the elevator operator, who recalled that Clarke was alive and well when he brought the actor and his artist friend up to their studios at 2:00 P.M. when they returned from lunch. And the note from the two students who had a three o'clock lesson scheduled indicated the drama coach was in no condition to answer the door when they called at their appointed time.

George, the elevator operator, was an old-timer who knew everyone who worked in the building. "I brought Mr. Clarke and Miss Lane up to the top at two o'clock, sure enough, but he never came back down," he told police.

"How about other people? Did you bring anyone else up there around two o'clock or so, and bring them back down?"

"No, not that I can recollect. I didn't bring anybody up or down that time of day that I didn't know. No one at all."

"Did you notice anyone acting nervous or suspicious? Whoever it was that did this to Mr. Clarke must have been covered with blood."

"Nope. Nobody like that got into my elevator," he said, shrugging his shoulders. "I sure wouldn't have missed that. No way. Covered with blood, I'd have seen him."

"Great," snapped Hensley. "Now we've got a mystery killer who disappears into thin air. This guy didn't sneak in and out in the dead of night, you know. He goes into the damned building when it's full of people, does his act, and slips out without anyone seeing him."

The mystery of how the killer apparently made his escape was cleared up the following day, Wednesday, when Detectives James Hickey and John Jandra talked to an occupant of a nearby office building who had been turned up by police canvassing the neighborhood.

"I know this sounds crazy, but I swear to you that I saw some guy walking the tenth floor ledge outside the Fine Arts Building yesterday afternoon," he said. "I just glanced out my window, and there this son-of-a-bitch was. I though it was a stunt of some kind. You know, this is Chicago . . ."

The skeptical detectives questioned the office worker at length but he stuck to his story. "I tell you, I really saw this guy out on the ledge. Why the hell would I make up a story like that? It's too nutty."

"This 'human fly'—just what did he look like?"

"Young guy. Big. You know, not fat, but well built, like one of those ballet dancers. And he had long hair. Not real long like a hippy, I'd say, but hanging straight down to his shoulders in back."

"Could you identify this man if you saw him again?"

"Yeah, I think I could. You don't see something like that every day, right?"

"Right. We'll be in touch."

Hickey and Jandra went back to Clarke's office and raised the window. There was, indeed, a decorative marble ledge, no more than ten inches wide, circling the building at the tenth floor level. There was a fire escape on the adjoining building, but in order to reach it from the ledge the suspect would have to have leaped five feet, more than ten dizzying stories up from the litter-strewn alley below.

"We don't have no human fly. We've got a cat-man on our hands," Jandra said. "If our witness wasn't seeing things."

"Nobody saw the killer leave. That's the way he had to go," Hickey agreed. "Like you say, we've got a cat-man out there somewhere."

The two investigators were then referred to Annie Lane, Clarke's artist friend. She had told other detectives of hearing cries coming from the actor's studio, and it was with some hesitation that she repeated her story to Jandra and Hickey.

"I heard, 'No, Paul! No!' and I think he screamed 'God!' I didn't attach any importance to it at all," she related. "Then I heard books falling, almost as if they were being thrown. I assumed it was just another acting lesson. You know, another improvisation with a student. It seemed realistic, but I just figured it was play acting."

Another tenant of the building, Merrill Rose, a violin restorer who worked in a studio next door to Clarke's, told the detectives, "I can't imagine that Mr. Clarke had any enemies. He was like a father to his students. They confided in him, and he had very fine ideals. He was here sometimes in the early morning, and often late at night. His pupils came from all over the United States. He had contacts in New York and Hollywood. He was a real old-timer on the stage. It was his life."

"Yeah, and it was his death," commented Lieutenant Hensley, when the two detectives repeated the statement to him as he surveyed the now quiet studio, looking for something that would tell him where to move next.

In the clutter atop the teacher's desk Hensley found a color snapshot of Clarke, white haired and smiling, seated at the piano near where his body was found. The lieutenant slipped the photo into his jacket pocket.

"This goes up on my bulletin board," he explained. "I want to keep this case in my mind every minute of the day, even when I'm sipping my morning coffee. 'Cause we're gonna get the guy who did it."

Meanwhile homicide Sergeant Joseph Stuparitz ran down the two students who had shoved the cryptic note through Clarke's mail slot. As indicated in the appointment book, they had been scheduled for drama lessons the afternoon of the murder. When they got there they found Clarke's door locked, and thought he might have gone on an errand, so they waited. They sat for more than an hour on the bench in the corridor. Then they left Clarke the note and headed home disappointed. During the hour they sat outside the studio neither saw nor heard anything unusual.

"We didn't hear any sounds at all. We didn't think anyone was in there," they told Stuparitz.

While the two youths' stories checked out, Hensley was mindful of the fact that it was Clarke's appointment book that led police to them. The book, lying on the victim's desk, open to the day of the murder, contained their names—and others.

"This damned book here could be the key we're looking for," he told Jandra and Hickey. "You get into some cases, and you don't have one lousy name to go on. Here—right here in this little book—we've got a ton of 'em. And one of them could be our elusive cat-man."

Hensley knew it would take weeks, perhaps months, to check out every name in the book, and the trail of the killer was growing colder by the minute. With this in mind he enlisted the aid of Annie Lane and Clarke's apartment mate,

Arnold Thomas, the two people who seemed to be most familiar with his professional and personal life.

They agreed to sit down with detectives and go over the list of names, one by one. With their help priorities could be formed. They would be able to provide information about some of the people listed in the book, tell how well Clarke might have known them, and whether any had any unusual quirks.

On Wednesday night, nearly twenty-four hours after The Whistler's body was found, the detectives came upon the name of Paul DeWit in the dead man's ledger. The name didn't ring a bell with either Lane or Thomas, but the appointment book indicated he'd been scheduled for an acting lesson on Monday afternoon—the day before the murder. A notation after DeWit's name said he had failed to show up.

"The book lists a pretty swanky address," Jandra pointed out. "Look at this—3550 North Lake Shore Drive. That ain't the low rent district."

"Well, the name's Paul," Hickey noted. "Paul's the only thing we've got to go on so far. Let's ask records to run a make on him and we'll talk to him in the ayem."

Thursday morning, the second day after the slaying, found Hickey and Jandra crowded into Hensley's tiny office, parked none too comfortably on his two "visitor" chairs. The burly lieutenant had just finished his breakfast roll, and was scraping the crumbs off his desk into the cellophane wrapper it had come in. On his bulletin board, the detectives observed, was tacked the snapshot of Everett Clarke seated at the piano.

"Lieutenant, take a peep at this," Jandra said, handing Hensley an arrest sheet. "The guy's name is Paul DeWit, with one 't'—and he's listed in the maestro's appointment book."

The experienced policeman's eyes raced over the photocopy in his beefy hands. DeWit, Paul. Age, 21. Address, 3550 N. Lake Shore Drive. Height, 6 feet 3 inches. Weight, 180. Charge, battery.

"Big fellow, well built—maybe like the human fly on the

building ledge," Hickey interjected as Hensley looked up from the sheet.

"He was supposed to keep an appointment with Everett Clarke on Monday, but he couldn't make it because he was in the slammer up on the North Side on a battery charge," Jandra added.

"But it gets more interesting, lieutenant," Hickey added.

"Hmmm. I see it does. Yes, indeed," murmured Hensley.

"On 8 April he's busted for prostitution. On 6 May he fails to show up in court. Then, on 1 July, he gets one year court supervision. What's that one about? You guys checked it out, or you wouldn't be here."

"Okay, listen to this, lieutenant," Jandra began. "A vice dick up in Area Six reads an ad in a gay men's newspaper on the North Side. It lists a phone number, so the undercover copper calls it up out of curiosity."

"The report said he suspected the newspaper advertisement might lead to illicit activities," Hickey added sarcastically.

"So he calls the number and the guy offers to cop his joint for fifty bucks," Jandra said, almost shouting with enthusiasm.

"Just what, exactly, does the report say?" Hensley asked wryly.

"Okay," continued Jandra. "According to the report, the vice dick telephoned the number in the ad. The male who answered offered to perform a sex act on him for $50. He gave the copper the address—Apartment 8K—and said to ask for Paul. The cop made an appointment for 1:30 P.M. He went to this Paul DeWit's address and DeWit invited him in. They confirmed the deal. The dick gave him $50 in marked bills and arrested him on a charge of prostitution."

"And?"

"Well, he was supposed to appear in court May 6, but he didn't show so they issued a warrant for his arrest. Then, when he came up on July 1 he pleaded guilty and the judge gave him a year supervision, because he comes from a good family."

"What does this kid do?" Hensley asked.

"He cops joints," Hickey guffawed.

"All right, let's get serious," Hensley growled. "We've got a homicide to clear up."

"No visible means of support. He lives alone. He used to share the apartment with some guy the vice dicks suspect of running a call-boy operation, but his boyfriend moved out a couple of weeks ago."

"All right. Bring him in," said Hensley, walking over to the bulletin board and examining the smiling photo of the late Everett Clarke. "Let's see what he's got to say."

Jandra and Hickey checked out an unmarked car and headed east toward Lake Michigan, then north on Lake Shore Drive, battling the morning rush-hour traffic. They pulled into a no-parking zone outside the high-rise listed as DeWit's address, and walked toward the double glass doors. The detectives flashed their badges to a custodian, who let them in, so they would not have to ring the upstairs apartment from the lobby and tip off their presence. Then they rode the elevator to the eighth floor and rang the buzzer alongside the door marked 8K.

A tall, strapping muscular youth answered their ring. He was firm-jawed, and had sandy hair that hung down over his eyes in front, and almost to his shoulders in back. He brushed the hair aside, wiped the sleep from his eyes, and looked inquisitively at the two callers.

"Paul DeWit?"

"Yes."

"We're police officers. We'd like to talk to you for a minute. Mind if we come in?"

DeWit stepped nimbly aside, butler-like, to permit his unexpected visitors to enter. They looked quickly around the furnished apartment, noting it was not cheap by any means. From the windows overlooking Lake Shore Drive they could look down on Belmont Harbor with its flotilla of expensive yachts.

The handsome, broad-shouldered youth showed no emotion when Hickey and Jandra explained the purpose of their visit, and asked if he'd mind coming downtown where it would be more convenient to talk. Mission accomplished, the detectives radioed ahead that they were on the way in with "the individual in question."

Hensley, meanwhile, wasted no time in dispatching other investigators to talk to DeWit's friends and acquaintances, to determine what more could be developed regarding the suspect.

From various sources investigators learned that the Adonis-like youth, who had no steady job, was an aspiring actor. Frustrated at his inability to find theatrical work, he had gone to Clarke a year earlier for drama lessons. Because he was unemployed, Clarke took him on as one of his "Scholarship" students, coaching him free for the satisfaction of watching him develop his talents.

People who knew DeWit described him as high-strung and extremely paranoid. He was also characterized as a "health nut" who enjoyed weight lifting. A native-born Chicagoan, he came from a well-to-do family. His father was a successful engineer.

Neighbors in the Lake Shore Drive high-rise described him as a nice, quiet young man who hosted numerous parties. He was known to have "a lot of male visitors" to the apartment he shared, until quite recently, with another youth.

The building's custodian, Jack Trout, said DeWit's roommate moved out of the leased, four-room condominium after the two youths engaged in a heated argument during which a rear window was smashed.

"Mr. DeWit said he was sorry and told me he'd repair the damage himself if I'd show him how to remove the glass from the window frame," he explained. "He was quiet, but weird, if you know what I mean. But, whenever I asked him to hold the noise down, during those parties, he'd apologize and promise to be quiet."

While those who knew DeWit were helping police put together a picture of the suspect's lifestyle, DeWit, clad in tight-fitting jeans and a white T-shirt was doing little, himself, to cooperate with the investigation.

For one thing, he denied ever having been one of Clarke's students, despite the fact that his name was in the actor's appointment book, and friends said he'd been seeing the drama coach since the summer of 1979.

From his opening denial, Jandra and Hickey realized DeWit was trying to cover up more than just his homosexual lifestyle. So, while Hickey kept the suspect in conversation, Jandra sent for the witness who had insisted he'd seen someone cat-walking the narrow ledge near the summit of the Fine Arts Building on the afternoon of Everett Clarke's murder.

Several other young men about DeWit's age were brought into the interrogation room, and while they lounged around self-consciously the witness was asked to view them through a two-way mirror.

"That guy over there, sitting at the table. No question about it," the witness declared, pointing to DeWit. "That's the same guy I saw walking the friggin' ledge Tuesday afternoon. Honest to God! He's the one. I'm sure of it. Where in the hell did you come up with him? Now do you guys believe me, or what?"

Hickey and Jandra advised Hensley of the positive I.D., and he put in a call to the state's attorney's office. The lieutenant then issued a brief statement to the inquiring press that a "suspect is being questioned in connection with the slaying of Everett Clarke."

Word was flashed from the detective bureau press room to the various newspapers, and the City News Bureau wire passed the information on to subscribing radio and television stations.

News deadlines were fast approaching, and the press began to gather in force outside Hensley's office, clamoring for details. Shortly before noon he advised anxious newsmen that Paul DeWit, age twenty-one, had been charged with Clarke's murder, and added that the suspect had offered a statement.

"What did he say in his confession?" badgered one reporter.

"I did not say anything about any confession," Hensley replied firmly. "I said we have a 'statement,' and certain evidence. I don't want to say anything more at this time because the state's attorney is still preparing the case."

"Well, without going into particulars, can you tell us what happened, lieutenant, as far as how the murder was committed?"

"Yeah, fill us in, lieutenant," another reporter chimed in. "Cracking this son-of-a-bitch in only two days makes your guys look pretty good, you know."

Hensley offered the TV newsman who made the remark an irritated glance, and then proceeded to divulge what information he was ready for the media to have.

"Based on information we have been able to assemble, the homicide took place around 2:15 or 2:30 P.M. When Mr. Clarke returned from lunch, someone was waiting for him in the darkened hallway outside his office. After Mr. Clarke let himself in, this individual was also admitted, and the incident took place within seconds."

"By 'incident' you mean murder," one reporter asserted.

"Correct."

"How about the books strewn about? Was there a struggle of some kind?"

"We believe the individual first struck Mr. Clarke with his hand, causing him to cry out, before he plunged the scissors into him," Hensley continued. "In collapsing to the practice stage, the victim knocked over a stack of books on his desk. Otherwise, no, there was no appreciable struggle. The suspect then went out one of three windows in Mr. Clarke's studio. He climbed out and made his way along a narrow ledge—about ten inches wide—and in doing so he passed another office window where he was observed by a witness. He then jumped across an open space to the fire escape of an adjoining building and made good his escape."

"Does the suspect admit being there, lieutenant?" hammered one reporter, taking penciled notes on folded scratch paper.

"We are not saying that the suspect admits anything at this time. We are only advising you that one Paul DeWit has been charged with the murder."

"Has your witness fingered him as the guy he saw walking the ledge?"

"You can draw your own conclusions," Hensley responded, attempting to draw the news conference to a graceful conclusion.

"Is there any evidence of a homosexual relationship?" one reporter persisted.

"The only evidence we have is that of a student-teacher relationship," Hensley said patiently. "That's how we see it."

"Well, then. How about a motive, lieutenant?"

"At this point we have no motive," Hensley admitted. "We simply do not know. Now, if you birds don't mind, I have to get back to work before the taxpayers start complaining."

"Can we get pictures?" bellowed several photographers, holding their cameras aloft as if they needed identification.

"The suspect will be arraigned tomorrow. If you are there to take your pictures when he's being taken to court, there's no way we can stop you. I'm not dragging him out here to pose for you unwillingly, however."

The following morning, Friday—the third morning after the famed actor's body was found in his own blood—Paul DeWit was indicted by the Cook County Grand Jury for Everett Clarke's murder. He was arraigned before Associate Judge Joseph J. Urso of Criminal Court on charges of murder and armed violence. The suspect's distraught father, his mother, his brother, and his brother's wife stood at his side as Brian Collins, assistant prosecutor, read the charges as outlined in the indictment. The two women wept.

Judge Urso set bond at $500,000 and ordered DeWit remanded to the county jail pending formal arraignment before Chief Judge Richard J. Fitzgerald, who would assign the case to another courtroom for trial. Based on the current backlog in the Cook County court system, the defendant could expect to wait at least a year before going to trial.

Back at Area One homicide headquarters Hensley, Hickey and Jandra sat in the lieutenant's cramped quarters, sipping coffee while they put the finishing touches on the Clarke file so it could be passed on to the state's attorney's office in an orderly fashion. The file had started three days earlier, with the discovery of the corpse. It contained the names, addresses, and statements of various witnesses whom the prosecution might want to call.

And it ended with several copies of police mug shots of the accused, Paul DeWit. Hensley pulled one of the photos out of the file, walked over to his bulletin board, and tacked DeWit's sullen likeness alongside the smiling photo of Everett Clarke at the piano.

"From all we've been able to find out, he was a very compassionate man," Hensley mused. "He gave scholarships out of his own pocket—free acting lessons—to punks like this."

"Well, it's over now, lieutenant. We got our man," Jandra said.

"We?" Hensley asked, looking up from his beer-mug coffee cup. "Think about this one for a minute: Who was it who gave us the killer's name by shouting, 'No, Paul! No!' as the scissors was about to be plunged into his throat?"

The two detectives stared across the desk at their chief.

"And who was it who left his appointment book open on his desk, so we could find the name of the suspect, so meticulously recorded?"

Hickey and Jandra nodded. They knew what Hensley was getting to. It was one of the quickest homicides they had ever wrapped up, because the victim had made the case easy for them.

"I know this sounds corny as all hell," Hensley said, draining his coffee cup. "But, you could say that The Whistler solved his own murder."

EPILOGUE

On October 1, 1981, a Criminal Court jury found Paul DeWit "guilty but mentally ill" in the murder of Everett Clarke. Psychiatrists testified during his trial that DeWit was paranoid and schizophrenic, and had delusions that Clarke was a Mafia figure bent on destroying his acting career. DeWit became the first person convicted by a jury in Cook County under the new law, which went into effect only two weeks earlier. On Wednesday, November 18, Judge Arthur J. Cieslik sentenced the youthful slayer to twenty-two years in prison. He spent the next decade in a minimum security facility at East Moline, Illinois, until his release in the spring of 1991.

CHAPTER 3

THE NIGHT MOMMY WENT DOWN THE DRAIN

Police in Corcoran, Minnesota, a resort community northwest of Minneapolis, had a first-rate mystery on their hands with the unusual disappearance of Carol Lynn Hoffman, an attractive twenty-six-year-old housewife and mother of two small children.

It was on Monday morning, August 11, 1980, that her red-eyed husband, Dave, after an all but sleepless night, walked into the Corcoran police station to report that his wife of nearly ten years was nowhere to be found.

"Gosh, I'm worried sick. She's never done anything like this before," he said. "We had words last night. I guess you might say a serious quarrel, and she stormed out of the house. I thought she'd come back after she cooled off, but she didn't. Now I'm afraid something might have happened to her."

"What kind of car was she driving?"

"That's just it. She wasn't. She was walking. She wanted to take the keys to the car but I wouldn't give 'em to her. She was so damned agitated, I was afraid she'd have a smash-up and hurt herself, or someone else. She just took off into the night."

"Who've you got watching the kids, Dave?"

"My mom's taking care of Heidi and Bridgette. She lives with us now, you know. Matter of fact, that's what the darn argument was about."

"Okay, Dave. You trot back home and stay by the phone. We know what your wife looks like. We'll take it from here."

Corcoran police notified Sheriff Don Omodt of Hennepin County. He told his chief deputy, Ray Gamman, to get together a search party and see if they could find the pixie-faced brunette.

The Hoffmans were well-known in the Corcoran area, where they had lived for the past year. They'd been married a little over nine years earlier, when Carol was seventeen and Dave was twenty-five. Heidi was two, and Carol was pregnant with Bridgette when they moved into their split-level dream house on Hillside Drive. The bright yellow home, bordered by neat rows of flowers and a vegetable garden that Carol lovingly tended was a model for the community.

The Hoffmans made friends easily, and both were well-liked. Dave was always available to help other men around the neighborhood with their chores, and Carol loved kaffee klatsching with their wives. "The thing I like best about my kitchen is the garbage disposal," she liked to tell the girls. "No more carrying soggy bags out to the garbage can. Just pour the chicken bones down the sink, turn on the faucet, and away they go."

The attraction that brought Dave and Carol to the area was nearby Weaver Lake, just minutes from their back door. Crystal clear and well-stocked with fish, they liked to think of it as their own private playground.

The first thing the Hoffmans did when they moved into their new home was put a trailer hitch on the family car. Then they got themselves a small boat. Dave would often head out to the lake in the early morning hours to fish. Later he'd return for Carol, and they'd spend hours scuba diving together, like tadpoles in a pond.

Carol was the product of an unhappy childhood, and Dave was doing his best to make it up to her. "Tell me that you love me, Dave. I want to hear you say it." He always complied, whether it was while splashing around in Weaver Lake or in the comfort of their bed at night. "I sure do love you, Carol."

His other love was little Heidi. He liked to take her on motorcycle rides around the neighborhood, with the wind whipping her silky hair against his chest. And whenever Dave did the lawn, she was his partner, riding along with dad on the power mower.

Throughout their marriage Dave worked as a machine operator for Graco, Inc., in Minneapolis. Like most young couples, the Hoffmans had trouble making ends meet, and shortly after Bridgette was born Carol went back to her old job as a factory worker for Honeywell, in nearby Golden Valley.

Going back to work created new problems, however— finding reliable baby-sitters, and the expense of paying them. Furthermore, the added responsibility of holding down a full-time job, trying to take care of two little girls, and keeping the house in order was becoming more than Carol could cope with. It left her little time for her craft parties and social life, and when she did get out with her neighborhood friends they noticed she was always edgy.

Dave came up with a solution that summer that he hoped would make everybody happy. Heidi was now three, and Bridgette was nine months old, and his sixty-five-year-old mother, Helen Catherine Ulvinen, loved them both dearly. So Dave told Grandma Ulvinen, "Why don't you close up your home in Minneapolis, Mom, and come to live with me and Carol?" The prospect of being with her grandchildren full time delighted her, and she could also help Carol keep up the house. She accepted with pleasure, and moved into a room Dave had prepared as guest quarters in the basement of the split-level dream home.

But Carol was a private person who valued her personal life. The prospect of having an extra somebody at the dinner table night after night did not sit well with her, and she felt herself having to share her precious evening moments with her children with the ever-present mother-in-law.

Less than two weeks after Grandma Ulvinen moved in tensions developed, and Carol confided to neighbors, "I am not the least bit happy with this arrangement. I wish Dave's mother would leave." She broached the subject to Dave that Sunday night—which was what led to the spat and her storming out, he told police.

Several hours after Hoffman reported his wife missing, her purse, still containing her rings and a small amount of cash, was found lying alongside Minnesota Highway 101 north of Corcoran, on the outskirts of Maple Grove. With that discovery, police took the wife's disappearance seriously. A runaway mother does not leave her purse lying by the side of the road. There appeared little doubt, now, that Carol Hoffman had been abducted, probably while walking along the highway working off her "mad."

Efforts to find the missing woman intensified. In the days that followed her thirty-three-year-old husband organized several search parties among his fellow workers, but nary a trace of her could be found. Frantic, Dave drove into Minneapolis, where he appeared tearfully on television, pleading for Carol's return, for the sake of himself and their children.

On the Sunday following his wife's disappearance, Hoffman, not a deeply religious man, went to church with a group of friends to offer prayers for her safe return. But his prayers were not to be answered.

By Monday, August 18, a week after Carol's disappearance, hope that she was still alive began to dwindle.

A massive search party composed of sheriff's deputies, Maple Grove police, volunteers, Boy Scouts, and seventy-five of Carol's co-workers combed the area where the purse was found, but found nothing more.

Meanwhile sheriff's detectives Jessie Huckaby, Archie Sonenstaht, and Robert Salitros, under the direction of Lieutenant Brent Running, were questioning anyone who might have known the missing woman in an effort to come up with anything that might help in tracing her movements.

"They were very normal people," neighbors told the detectives. "They were good parents, who seemed genuinely happy. Dave is terrific. Real nice with his kids."

One neighbor suggested, however, that all had not been well of late under the Hoffman roof. "Carol was having problems," she told Huckaby. "She confided in me that she was not too happy about having her mother-in-law living with them. There was a lot of tension there. She was unhappy about that arrangement from the start."

This jibed with what Hoffman had told police, about the quarrel the night his wife left home. But the fact that neighbors were in on it meant that it might have gone a little deeper. Lieutenant Running's investigators questioned Hoffman's co-workers at the Minneapolis plant, and slowly began to piece together a picture of a man who was not quite the paragon of virtue his neighbors had made him out to be.

"Dave was afraid Carol might divorce him and take the kids with her," one worker recalled.

Another offered an even more damning recollection. A woman with whom Dave worked told the detectives, "He told me he was thinking about cutting off her oxygen supply one day while they were scuba diving. He was going to make it look like an accident.

"When I said I was shocked that he would even suggest such a thing, Dave offered me $5,000 to help pay my bills if I promised to keep my mouth shut about what he said."

"I take it you never got the money," Huckaby interjected. "Why didn't you come forward with this before?"

"I couldn't believe Dave would do a thing like that," she answered. "I still can't believe it. I think he was just talking. You know, just talking."

"Maybe we should do some more talking to Dave ourselves," Huckaby said, in discussing his findings with Lieutenant Running. "Hell, everybody has some domestic strife, we all do. But you don't go around talking about pinching the hose when you're scuba diving. There are a couple of things here that aren't following the old 'domestic' pattern."

"Well, the lady didn't throw her own purse away, that's for sure," Running said. "A woman on the run isn't going to dump her cash and rings. She might need them later."

"And if she was picked up by somebody, how come that person didn't take the dough and the rings before he tossed the purse out of the car?" Huckaby continued. "It's a strange one. I've got vibrations about this. The husband might know a little more than he's letting on."

"Okay, we've got these neighbors who say they weren't getting along so well lately," Running said. "One woman says she saw Mrs. Hoffman crying, and said she told her, 'Dave and his mom are against me.' What do you think?"

"Like I said, I think we ought to have the boy in for another talk," said Huckaby. "I talked to him twice and he seemed okay to me, but that was before we picked up this earloft about scuba diving, and the old lady and her son plotting against her."

"Where's Dave Hoffman now?"

"Out in the fields organizing search parties. He acts frantic as hell, but it could be part of a masquerade."

"Bring the guy in. See what he has to say about the latest," Running ordered.

Hoffman, a lean, handsome man with dark brown hair and a craggy jaw, was out with the search parties when the sheriff's men located him that Tuesday morning, eight days after he'd reported the mysterious disappearance of his wife. He was wearing faded blue jeans and a navy blue T-shirt inscribed "Underwater School of America."

He wiped the beads of perspiration from his forehead as the August sun beat down, smiled, and readily agreed to the detectives' request to come in for a little talk. He accompanied them to the downtown Minneapolis office, and was ushered into an interrogation room where Huckaby and several other detectives were waiting.

"Hi, fellows, what can I do for you?" Hoffman beamed, offering his hand to Huckaby. "How's it going? The investigation, I mean. You got anything yet?"

"Dave, there are a couple of things we'd like to kick around with you," answered Huckaby, ignoring the out-stretched hand. Then, to Hoffman's surprise, the detective pulled a white card from his pocket and began reading him his Miranda rights. "You have the right to remain silent . . ." When he had finished Huckaby asked Hoffman, "Do you want a lawyer?"

The missing woman's husband fidgeted uneasily in his chair, then looked directly at his interrogators and declared, "God will be my lawyer!"

"Is there something you'd like to get off your chest, Dave?" Huckaby asked gently.

"What do you want to know?"

"We want to know what happened to Carol. What happened to her that night you and she had the fight?"

"She wouldn't do anything."

"What do you mean, 'She wouldn't do anything,' Dave?"

"Just what I said," Hoffman continued, leaning forward slightly. "I'll explain it to you."

Carol seemed to be drifting away from him for some time, he related. She had abstained from having sex with him for several weeks, and his masculinity was building up inside to the boiling point. On that Saturday night—the night before Carol disappeared, Hoffman said he made amorous advances but she spurned him and taunted, "Why don't you go down-stairs and sleep with your mom?"

"I loved my wife, but she told me, 'Why don't you go downstairs and sleep with your mom?' Can you believe that? I decided then and there that I would have to get rid of the evil in my house. The next day I told my mom I was going to have to put her to sleep. Tonight's got to be the night. My mom said it would be for the best. It would be best for the kids," he continued.

"On Sunday night Carol tantalized me by coming to bed naked. I tried to make sexual advances, but she turned her back on me." As she tried to brush him away, he said he kissed her and caressed her, and shifted his body on top of hers. Then he put his hands around her throat and began to squeeze.

"She said my name, 'Dave!' I kept squeezing tighter and tighter and tighter . . . until she went limp. When my arms got tired I placed my knees around her neck and squeezed again."

"Until she was dead?"

"I was removing the evil from my house. You do believe in God, don't you?"

The detectives' eyes bored into the intense young man as he recounted the night of horror, step by step, as though he were reviewing a movie. They were hearing it, yet they could hardly believe it. They had not expected anything like this—and what was coming was even worse.

"Dave, tell us what happened next," Huckaby said softly. "What happened to Carol? We can't seem to find her. What did you do with her?"

"I took her into the bathroom. Then I put on some clothes and went down to the basement and awakened my mother. I told her I needed her to stand guard outside the bathroom door so Heidi wouldn't come in, in case she woke up during the night."

"Your mother stood guard outside the bathroom?"

"Uh huh. She put on her robe and came upstairs. Then she laid on the couch, where she could see the bathroom door, while I had Carol inside."

"Tell us about it, Dave."

"Well, I shut the door, and . . ." And young David Hoffman proceeded to tell the astonished deputies in detail how he exorcised the evil from his house. First, he explained, he took a scissors and clipped off his wife's beautiful hair. Then he got a ten-inch serrated scuba knife and a twelve-inch butcher knife from the kitchen and dismembered her in the bathtub of her dream home.

First, he said, he amputated her legs at the thighs. Next he laboriously sliced her torso in two, just below the rib cage. Then, as Carol's blood swirled down the bathtub drain he cut open her abdomen and scooped out her internal organs. He deposited the bloody viscera into a bucket and, with his mother still standing by, he carried the pail into the kitchen, where he dumped its grisly contents down the garbage disposal in the sink.

Hoffman turned on the cold water and flipped the switch with his bloody hands. The disposal unit groaned into action, rumbled, and shook. It did not whir cleanly the way it did with regular garbage, however. It had not been built for this kind of work, and grumbled slowly to a stop.

The case-hardened lawmen stared in disbelief as the clean-cut young father seated before them calmly related how, when the garbage disposal failed to grind up his wife and swish her remains down the sewer system, he realized he would have to make other arrangements for the rest of her.

The interrogation room was quiet now, save for the scratching of pencils across yellow legal pads, as Huckaby nodded for Hoffman to continue his macabre tale of horror.

Returning to the bathroom he scooped up his wife's hair and burned it in a wood-burning stove. Then he went downstairs for a duffle bag and a gunny sack. Taking them into the bathroom, he divided his wife's dismembered body between the two. Then he went out to the garden Carol had so lovingly tended, picked up a few decorative rocks, and put them into the bags to weight them down.

"My mom went back downstairs to bed, and I cleaned up the mess," he continued, matter-of-factly. "Then I took a shower and went to bed for a short nap." It was 3:30 or 4:00 A.M. by the time he'd finished the housecleaning, Hoffman recalled, and he was sweating profusely from his night's work. "I felt like a big burden was off myself and my mother," he added.

Hoffman slept until about 6:30 Monday morning and awoke refreshed. He still had work to do. But first he went to the kitchen and popped two slices of bread into the toaster for breakfast. Then the new widower went out into the yard and hefted the two bags containing his late wife's remains into the rowboat. He hooked the boat trailer to the back of the car and towed the boat the six miles to Weaver Lake, where he and Carol had spent so many happy hours scuba diving together.

He backed down the ramp, launched the boat, and rowed it out to where the water was deep.

He carefully dropped anchor. Then he slipped the two sacks over the side and watched them disappear beneath the surface, leaving a pale crimson trail as they sank to the bottom. Finally, to make it look good in case anyone had seen him out on the lake, Hoffman cast his line into the water and enjoyed a bit of fishing. At long last, he could relax.

"We understand you and your wife liked to go scuba diving, Dave. Did you ever consider doing anything to her when you were out on the lake together?"

"Oh, yeah. In fact, I had taken Carol scuba diving on two occasions with that specific thought in mind, but I didn't carry it out because we were having too much fun."

"You didn't kill your wife those other times because you were having too much fun?" Huckaby asked incredulously.

"That's right," Hoffman smiled, seeming to recall those moments with pleasure. "We had a lot of fun together."

The mystery of what happened to Carol Lynn Hoffman had been solved. Hoffman was ushered to a cell while formal charges against him were being prepared. Chief Deputy Gammon, meanwhile, ordered a three-square-mile area around the Hoffman house combed inch by inch, and dispatched the sheriff's water patrol and rescue units to explore the depths of Weaver Lake.

A squad was also sent to the victim's home, where Dave's sixty-five-year-old mother was taken into custody. The two children, Heidi and Bridgette, were turned over to county authorities and temporarily placed in a foster home.

On Wednesday, August 20, scuba divers brought up the duffle bag containing Carol's torso. The next day the gunny sack with its ghastly contents was recovered and brought to the surface.

Lieutenant Running obtained a search warrant for the Hoffman home. As curious neighbors gathered out in front his men laboriously dismantled the garbage disposal unit under the sink, the kitchen drain, and the drain in the bathtub. Some tissue was found, along with minute blood stains. After his night's work, however, the tidy Hoffman had thoroughly cleaned and scoured the sink and tub, and poured Drano down the pipes.

Dave's bloody clothing was found in a laundry hamper, waiting for Grandma Ulvinan to wash them. The two serrated knives were recovered in the house. Deputies also impounded the boat and trailer.

On Friday, August 22, just eleven days after Dave Hoffman walked into the Corcoran police station and reported his young wife missing, he and his mother, Helen Catherine Ulvinen, were formally charged with first-degree murder.

Two months later, on October 23, from his cell in the Hennepin County Jail in Minneapolis, Hoffman wrote a letter to his mother's lawyer, Stephen Doyle, absolving her of all blame in Carol's death. The letter said in part:

Dear Steve,

I am writing in regard to my mother's charge involving her with the death of my wife Carol on August 10th.

I am not trying to protect her because she is guilty but because she is innocent. I would try to help anyone who I believed to be innocent and I want you to believe she is.

For many months I had been asking my mother to move in with me and Carol to babysit while we worked. Carol and I had pretty high financial depts [sic] and she became irritable when I would stop at my mother's house to mow the lawn or fix things at her house.

I was hoping that with Mom there taking care of my girls and us not having to get them up in the morning to go to the babysitters it would make it easier on our financial output as well as making it easier getting up and getting ready for work.

My Mom loved taking care of my girls and it would be giving her some purpose in life, rather than living all by herself in her lonely world.

Carol had my mind in torment before my mother moved in. I was so frustrated with her that I actually planned on drowning her while scuba diving. On two occasions this summer we went diving and I had intentions of drowning her. But when the time came we were enjoying our dives and my mind wasn't in the same state as when I was thinking of drowning her. We were having fun.

On August 19th when I made my statement to detectives I wasn't in my right mind. I had no idea I would be put in jail for killing Carol. I thought the detectives understood what strain Carol had put me through. And it never hit my mind once I would go to prison. My mother never realized I was going to hurt Carol and I didn't believe I could either. My mother was sleeping downstairs—when I chocked [sic] Carol. She said something to me that set me in a rage and I lost control of myself.

Afterwords [sic] I went downstairs and asked Mom to come up stairs and lay on the couch to prevent Heidi from waking up and going to the bathroom. I had to go downstairs and ask her a second time. I don't think she believed me the first time that I had killed Carol. My mother seemed to be in a state of shock.

In almost ten years of marriage I had never hurt Carol or even argued back with her when she would violently lose her temper which was quite often.

My mother had no control over my actions, earlier that morning she was looking in the newspaper for another house, she said she couldn't live with Carol when Carol was being so nasty to her and not welcoming her there.

I can remember telling her to give it a little more time—and maybe Carol would change her attitude. I told Mom that Carol was driving me crazy but maybe she would straighten out . . .

When I was dismembering my wife . . . I felt I was driving the devil out of her and what I did was best for my girls.

Sincerely,

David Hoffman

That was the first letter—an insight into the mind of the man who placed himself in the role of the exorcist—and who could not understand why police arrested him for it. Six weeks later, on December 5, shortly before their mother was scheduled to go to trial, he wrote to his sister, Delores:

Dear Delores,
Sorry I haven't written sooner. I've been answering other mail. You are right about me being scared in court but I guess if I weren't worried I wouldn't be human . . . I'm going to testify

for her and there is no way she could have stopped what happened unless she would have been standing in our bedroom with us and maybe pulled me off her . . .

Sure I talked about killing Carol but I never really planned it. I just said them things as a mental release and Mom never believed any harm could ever come to Carol.

I didn't realize I was going to take her life that night or any night. All I wanted was for things to work out for us all. But Carol came to bed naked that night after about three weeks of no lovemaking. I thought she wanted to make love to me, but she was just teasing me and in the state of frustration I was already in, I lost control of myself . . .

I think while I was choking her I started to think I was doing the right thing, in getting the devil out of her I had to dismember her, Delores. I know I went out of my mind.

I'm not the kind of person who could have done this in my right mind. I have repented over and over for taking her life. I wish I could just get up in front of the jury and explain what happened that night so I can clear Mom. I do worry about myself also but I think God is with me now at last I feel he is taking care of me. I accepted God into my life when I went to the Evangelical Church on Aug 17th and I was so hurt inside that Carol would never be back to go to the church with me and Heidi. I was so lost at that point I thought I would die. I was missing the good side of Carol and had forgotten about the bad side of her . . .

. . . That night I thought the end of the world was coming after the big storm we had and I opened the window and knealt on the bed with the window open waiting for God to appear in front of me. I waited about 20 min but he never came but I knew he was out there in the yard somewhere and that the storm was a warning of the End of the World. This might sound pretty crazy to you. But to me it was all very real.

I'll never forget the love I had for her for so long. Since her death that night I've released all the frustration that I had on my mind . . .

Love,

David

When Grandma Ulvinen went on trial for murder in Hennepin District Court on Friday, December 12, David, himself, read both letters to the jury. His mother's only defense was, "I didn't know what was going on." She wasn't the only one.

Carol Lynn Hoffman was deliriously happy when she and Dave moved into their split-level dream house with the built-in garbage disposal. Little did she realize that, within a year's time, she would be going down her own drain.

EPILOGUE

Dave's letter-writing project didn't help his mother one iota. On December 17, 1980, after sixteen hours of deliberation, a jury found Grandma Ulvinen guilty of first-degree murder. On December 22, Judge Patrick Fitzgerald sentenced her to life in prison, and she became the oldest inmate at the Minnesota State Prison for Women at Shakopee.

David Hoffman's trial was moved to Rochester where, on February 11, 1981, a jury found him guilty of murdering his wife. On February 19, Judge Fitzgerald sentenced him to the mandatory life term under Minnesota law, to be served in the State Reformatory at St. Cloud.

CHAPTER 4

ARSENIC AND OLD RELATIVES

In spite of their ages Mary Lambert, eighty-nine, and Marion Mueller, sixty-nine, were known as a pair of get-up-and-go women who could outwalk anyone else in the village. Old Mary, a widow, and her divorcee daughter, who were as close as any mother and daughter could be, were two of the more familiar residents of the Leisure Village retirement community near Fox Lake, Illinois.

"They are the pictures of health," friends would say as the ladies waved to them on their way to ceramics classes. The two of them attended every outing sponsored by the local community association, sightseeing trips and dinner party forays to the variety of restaurants abounding in the Chain-O-Lakes resort area some forty-five miles northwest of Chicago.

And they were more fortunate than many of their fellow residents in the community of rolling hills adjoining the Fox Lake Country Club, with their own par-three golf course, lake, and swimming pool. They had family. In addition to her daughter, Marion, with whom she lived, Mary Lambert had another daughter and son in the nearby Chicago suburbs. Marion Mueller's daughter, Virginia, and devoted son-in-law, Charles Albanese, also lived close by and visited the two women regularly.

The last happy occasion they had together was a family-style Sunday dinner at the Albanese home in Spring Grove on August 3, 1980. Virginia Albanese remembered the event vividly—because three days later her elderly grandmother was dead. Mary Lambert came down with a fierce diarrhea and vomiting attack while attending a local outing. She was taken to McHenry Hospital just over the county line, where she died on August 6.

The cause of death was listed as "cardiac arrest"—natural causes, and Mrs. Lambert was laid to rest in the family plot in River Grove. Then—only twelve days after her mother's death—Marion Mueller died in St. Therese Hospital in Waukegan. Again, because of the woman's advanced age, death was listed as due to natural causes, and she was buried in the small cemetery in nearby Fremont Center.

The deaths of her mother and grandmother in less than two-weeks time weighed heavily on Virginia Albanese and her forty-four-year-old husband, a wealthy manufacturer of trophies and loving cups. Because of their closeness to the women, they were saddled with the responsibility of disposing of much of their estates.

The deaths of two such active members of the community in so short a time caused considerable consternation among their neighbors in Leisure Village, and near panic among some of the elderly residents. Some suspected the mother and daughter might have contracted a form of botulism while dining in a local restaurant, or feared that the village water supply might have become contaminated.

They took their problem to W.J. "Bingo Bill" Murphy, a sixty-five-year-old former legislator and leader of the community. Murphy, a prominent area Republican, earned his nickname thirty years earlier while campaigning in the Illinois House of Representatives for legalized bingo and other games in churches and private clubs. Though now retired, Murphy still had a host of friends in high places, and took his neighborhood problem to a long-time crony, Lake County Coroner Robert H. "Mickey" Babcox.

"Mick, something's fishy as all hell here, and the folks in the village are mighty upset," he told the coroner. They want to know how two healthy women can suddenly die twelve days apart, and—to tell the truth—it's got me wondering, too."

"You might have something there, Murph," responded Babcox, a veteran coroner who would later become sheriff. "I'll have somebody look into it right away. If there's something out there, we'll find it."

"Folks are especially concerned about the drinking water, or maybe it's some form of sewer gas," Murphy speculated. "All I can tell you, Mick, is that they're disturbed and something's got to be done to set their minds at ease."

Babcox put in a call to Dr. Thomas Nedved of the Lake County Health Department, who ordered a thorough investigation. An analysis was made of the Leisure Village drinking water, and the community's sewage disposal system was thoroughly checked out. Dr. Nedved also checked the food supply and examined kitchens in area restaurants, but the results of all the tests came back negative.

"We can't find a damn thing, Murph," Babcox reported to his friend. "We've checked out everything we can think of. It looks like these deaths could just have been a fluke. They were up in years, and it happened."

Things gradually returned to normal in the resort community and talk turned to other things. Nine months later, however, Babcox found himself talking to McHenry County Coroner Alvin Querhammer at a convention in Rockford.

"I've got a funny one for you, Mick," Querhammer said. "I just got a call from a doctor at McHenry Hospital. He advised me there's some evidence of arsenic poisoning, just found in the blood serum of one of his patients."

"Well, what do you think it is, Al—industrial poisoning of some kind?"

"Yeah, it could be. They're still trying to check it out. But that's not what I'm getting at. The strange thing is, this guy's father, Mike Albanese, just died in the very same hospital."

"Albanese? Do I know him?" asked Babcox, who was

born and reared in the area. "The name rings a bell from somewhere."

"The guy who died was Michael Senior, sixty-nine years old, and the one in the hospital with arsenic poisoning is Michael Junior. He's thirty-four," Querhammer replied. "The old man founded the Allied Die Casting Company in McHenry. They make trophies and stuff like that. Maybe you even won one when you were playing football. His kids more or less run the place now. Michael Junior is the treasurer. Then there's another son, Chuck . . ."

"That's where I heard the name," Babcox interjected, snapping his fingers. "Mueller! We had a Mueller woman die in my county last year and there was some question about it at the time. She was somehow related to an Albanese family."

"You think there could be some kind of connection?"

"Who knows, Al? There was another one, too," Babcox recalled. "Yeah, Mrs. Mueller and her elderly mother. The two old broads died less than two weeks apart, and nobody could figure it out because they seemed so damned healthy. Now you've got a father and son from the same family—one dead and the other full of arsenic."

"The old man hasn't been buried yet," Querhammer noted. "I think I'll have the doc take some fingernail scrapings and hair samples, what the hell. Routine procedure. What do you think?"

"I'd do it, Al."

The two coroners looked at one another with raised eyebrows. "I'm thinking the same thing you are, Mickey," Querhammer said, the smile gone from his face. "I'll have 'em analyzed."

"How 'bout the hospital. Did they take blood samples from the old man?"

"Yeah, they always do. I'll have that checked, too."

"Let me know, Al."

"I sure as hell will."

The test results showed traces of arsenic in the dead man's hair and fingernails. "There was some evidence of arsenic found in blood serum that was sent to the laboratory," McHenry Hospital officials further advised Querhammer.

A coroner is not a detective, although Querhammer and Babcox were doing a pretty good imitation. After going over the results of the hospital and pathological tests Querhammer took the information he had uncovered to McHenry County State's Attorney Theodore Floro and McHenry Police Chief George Pasenelli. After conferring, they concluded that the death of Michael Albanese, Sr., and the crippling illness of his son could both be due to some type of industrial poisoning.

Pasenelli proceeded to investigate this possibility, in hopes of determining the source before anyone else could be stricken. His probe of manufacturing procedures in the Albanese family plant turned up no evidence of arsenic, however, or anything else that could have caused the poisoning of the father and son. Furthermore, his investigators established that no one else connected with the firm had become ill.

In neighboring Lake County, meanwhile, Babcox was becoming more than a little bit disturbed about the unexpected and unexplained deaths of the mother and daughter, both related to the Albanese clan through marriage. He kicked the matter around with Lake County State's Attorney Fred Foreman and with his own medical investigator, Glen MacIntyre. Foreman then put in a call to Ted Floro in McHenry, and the two agreed that a thorough investigation was in order. Because of jurisdictional questions, they decided to form a bi-county "Arsenic Task Force" consisting of the two coroners, two prosecutors, and Chief Pasenelli, who would provide additional manpower as needed.

Early in August Querhammer and Babcox met with Virginia Albanese and her husband, Charles, who had taken over operation of the trophy firm on the death of his father and illness of his brother, Michael. After a brief discussion they obtained permission from Mrs. Albanese to exhume the bodies of her mother and grandmother.

And, just to make sure everything was legal, the coroners obtained a court order from Circuit Judge Jack Hoogasian in

Waukegan to disinter the remains of the two women, along with that of Michael Albanese, Sr., who was buried in nearby Libertyville. After Hoogasian, a former prosecutor, signed the order, all three bodies were dug up on August 31 and brought to the Lake County Morgue in Waukegan.

There autopsies were performed by Dr. John Spikes, chief toxicologist for the Illinois Department of Public Health. After concluding the postmortems he advised Babcox, "All three of your victims suffered from the Borres syndrome."

"What does that mean in English, Doc?"

"Their bodies were heavily laced with arsenic!"

"All three of 'em?"

"Absolutely, Mick. All three. Enough arsenic to kill several people. We found 370 times the normal level in Mrs. Mueller's body, and as much as 80 times the normal levels in the other two."

Dr. Helen Young, chief medical officer for the county, and Jorge Pirl, assistant chief toxicologist for the public health department, who conducted tests on the cadavers, said Mrs. Lambert appeared to have succumbed to a single massive dose of poison, while Albanese possibly ingested small amounts over a period of as long as four months. Babcox relayed the information to Querhammer who, after digesting what he'd been told, remarked, "I hate to say it, Mick, but I think we've stumbled onto something big."

"I know what you mean, Al. I feel like Quincy on TV."

The two coroners turned the autopsy reports over to Foreman and Floro at a hastily-called meeting of the Arsenic Task Force, and Pasenelli agreed to quietly step up his investigation.

Detectives questioned nurses at the two hospitals where Mrs. Lambert and Mrs. Mueller died, but they could shed little light on the case. Attendants at both institutions remembered, however, the loyal visits paid the dying women by Charles Albanese and his wife. In fact, they often brought the women little snacks, such as cookies, not available on the hospital bill of fare.

Pasenelli ordered a background check on every person known to have had contact with the Albanese, Lambert, and Mueller families, including Charles Albanese. His investigators learned that the clean-cut young man about town was a somber, industrious person who seemed to derive his main pleasures through quiet evenings with his wife and children, and going on luxurious vacations. Townspeople knew Chuck as a "loner" who did not readily mix with fellow businessmen or hook up with the usual clubs or fraternal organizations around which small town community life centers. In fact, Mayor Eugene May of Spring Grove, where Albanese lived with his wife and two daughters in a $200,000 home, told Pasenelli, "I've never heard of the guy."

The family had moved into the sprawling Tudor-style home in August of 1978. They added a swimming pool in the summer of 1981—a year after the deaths of Mary Lambert and Marion Mueller—and were planning to enclose it with a dome for year-around use. Chuck Albanese had several cars, including two Cadillacs, one of which had belonged to his late father.

Employees at Allied Die Casting told investigators the stocky, intense-looking president was not renowned for keeping long hours, but the time he did spend at the plant was spent productively.

If Charles Albanese was an introvert around Spring Grove he was an entirely different person when it came to vacation time. There were annual trips to Jamaica or Marco Island, with a babysitter usually going along to play nanny for his daughters, ages five and seven.

And as they dug deeper, investigators learned that Albanese had not always been the Mister Good Citizen he appeared to be. He was an ex-convict, and had been a bigamist.

Records showed that in 1965, while working as an automobile salesman in the Chicago suburb of Morton Grove, the twenty-seven-year-old Albanese was arrested for home invasion and robbery. He and another man, posing as detectives, had invaded the home of a Chicago bus driver and made off with $160. They were quickly nabbed, however, after a suspicious neighbor gave police the license number of their getaway car.

Albanese was convicted of armed robbery and placed on five years probation. At about that same time his first wife, the former Frances Annongisto, divorced him after six years of marriage and took their three daughters to live in Wisconsin.

Little is known about Albanese's second wife, Julie. However, court records show he married Virginia, his third wife, in Las Vegas over the 1972 Labor Day weekend—even though his divorce from Julie did not become final until the following year.

Wife trouble continued to plague him during his rise to becoming a successful businessman. His first wife, Frances, filed a complaint against him in McHenry County in 1977 saying he was $1,475 behind in child support payments. Then, on the day of Mary Lambert's funeral in 1980, he was arrested for nonsupport on a petition filed in Cook County Circuit in Chicago by his second wife, Julie.

Yet there was nothing in Albanese's past to suggest he was a man of violence, and investigators did not consider him a suspect in the deaths of his father, mother-in-law, and his wife's grandmother, or the poisoning of his brother. What they seemed to have was a classic example of the "man who led two lives." In view of what they had learned, however, the two coroners, prosecutors, and Chief Pasenelli agreed to concentrate their investigation on him, for the time being, to see what else they could learn about his character.

As president of the family-owned trophy company, Charles Albanese drew an annual salary of $60,000, and shared a three-way split of the profits with his mother, Clara, and brother, Michael, Jr. He enjoyed demonstrating his affluence, and was the envy of some neighbors, who told detectives, "It must be nice to have his money. He always has everything done for him. We mow our lawns; he hires somebody to do his."

Other associates of Albanese referred to him as "a spoiled brat who always wanted to be a big shot." One family friend told investigators, "Charles was very ambitious. He wanted money right away. He didn't want to have to work for it." Yet another told Pasenelli's men, "Charles was a lot of headaches to his father. The old man used to say, 'I don't know what to do with Charles.'"

There was no question that Albanese was in a position to gain from the deaths of the two women; although he would profit most from the demise of his father, and possible death of his brother. Investigators learned that he began making regular visits to Mrs. Lambert and Mrs. Mueller in mid-1980. He brought little gifts of jewelry and trinkets to their home, and dined with the ladies whenever he had an opportunity. They reveled in his dotings, and told friends what a marvelous son-in-law and grandson he was. They were both, they said, "truly fortunate."

It was during these periods of congeniality that Albanese prevailed on the eighty-nine-year-old woman to change her will, leaving all of her property to her daughter, Marion— bypassing her son, Francis Lambert, who lived in the same area, and her other daughter, Elizabeth Voges, in Park Ridge, Illinois. Once the legal machinations were complete, Albanese became an almost daily visitor to the women's home. It did not last long, however. Mrs. Lambert fell ill and died, leaving her estate to her daughter, Marion Mueller. And twelve short days later Mrs. Mueller, too, was gone, and everything went to her daughter, Virginia—who was Chuck's wife.

Police estimated the combined Lambert and Mueller estates totaled around $150,000. The women also left their home, one of 365 such dwelling units in the retirement community, which were valued at between $45,000 and $95,000. Investigators learned that Albanese sold his in-laws' house for less than market value in exchange for quick cash.

"That's when Bill Murphy came to me with suspicions that everything wasn't right," Babcox told fellow members of the Arsenic Task Force. He explained how the water, sewage, and food had been tested—but since arsenic poisoning resembles heart failure, and because of the ages of the two women, sophisticated toxicological tests were not considered at the time. "Nobody, not even their nearest relative, ever suspected the women had been poisoned," he said. Not long after the deaths of the two women, Charles and his father had a serious falling-out at the plant. Allied attorney Donald Fishbein told investigators he was present at a meeting on September 4, 1980, in which the elder Albanese told his son, "Chuck, I want you out! I don't want you to be in the plant anymore. I don't want you under the same roof. I don't even want you to be a director of the company."

A few days later the old man softened his stand, however. He demoted Charles from president to treasurer, thus allowing him to retain his $60,000 salary as an executive officer. And the repentant son—in an apparent gesture of friendship—began bringing cookies to his dad at work. He also brought snacks for his brother, Michael, Jr., who was comptroller of the firm.

On September 8, four days after the family blow-up, Michael, Jr., came down with severe vomiting and nausea and had to be hospitalized. He became violently ill again after eating lunch in his office one January day in 1981, and again the following month. In late February and early March he was hospitalized twice more, with severe nausea and deteriorating nerve problems.

Meanwhile, during March and April, his father was hospitalized with similar problems. The sixty-nine-year-old owner of the family company finally died on May 16.

By that time Michael, Jr., who was a patient in the same hospital, was unable to dress and feed himself, and could not walk unattended. His wife, Gayle, told investigators that just hours before their father died she had to hold a pen for her husband to sign legal papers making Charles vice president of the company.

It was then that physicians, attempting to pinpoint young Michael's ailment, sent blood samples to a laboratory in

California. The lab analysis showed traces of arsenic in his blood, and his doctors suspected some type of industrial poisoning. That was when the two curious coroners came into the picture. According to court records the elder Albanese's will left an estate valued at $267,373, including $150,000 in stock holdings in the family business. His entire estate, along with a $200,000 life insurance benefit, went to his widow, Clara—making Charles Albanese's mother a wealthy woman.

There was also a $200,000 policy on Michael, Jr.'s, life. He survived the poisoning because of his youth and vigor, but remained critically ill, confined to a wheelchair. He was unable to perform the simplest task, such as picking up a coin, due to the effect of the arsenic on his nervous system.

Had Michael died, along with the others, Charles would have gained full control of the firm. Michael's $60,000 salary would have been eliminated, and Charles would only have had to share profits with his elderly mother.

No question about it. Members of the task force were in 100 per cent agreement that if anyone had a motive to do away with the rest of the family it was Charles Albanese. Yet there was no evidence to link him to the lethal arsenic.

Up to this point Pasenelli's team had conducted the investigation with the utmost tact and secrecy, and Charles was totally unaware that he was considered a suspect. Because known cases of arsenic poisoning are rare, Babcox asked the *Chicago Tribune* to dig out information on arsenic poisoning in other parts of the country. He then contacted authorities in those communities to determine how they had proceeded with their investigations.

"This is one we aren't going to blow," he told Querhammer. "We're going to sit on this one until George and his guys have got everything nailed down." Pasenelli now directed his investigators to probe every facet of Charles Albanese's business life, and ordered the suspect placed under surveillance. In checking Albanese's business activities, detectives learned that he had sold scrap zinc from Allied Die Casting to a metal plating firm in Elkhorn, Wisconsin. Curiously, he charged only thirty-five cents a pound for the scrap, although industry sources indicated the zinc was worth fifty cents a pound. And instead of placing the $25,000 to $35,000 the zinc had brought him on company ledgers, Chuck apparently pocketed the cash.

In mid-November task force investigators drove up to Wisconsin to talk to Joseph Reichel, Jr., operator of the Elkhorn firm. "Chuck Albanese is what you might call a business acquaintance," he related. "We've been purchasing scrap zinc from him since July." As a routine part of their investigation the detectives also questioned Reichel about his own business operation, and discovered he occasionally used arsenic in metal plating.

"Did you ever have any occasion to provide Charles Albanese with arsenic?" he was asked.

"Yes, I did. I gave him about two pounds of it. He asked me if I had anything he could use to get rid of some pests around his house. I suggested arsenic. Then he asked me how to use it. I told him, 'Maybe you could mix it with oatmeal, but if you have a dog, be careful.'"

It was now seven months since the chance conversation between the two small-town coroners had touched off the bizarre murder investigation—and the Arsenic Task Force had suddenly placed what could be the murder weapon in the suspect's hands.

Prosecutors Foreman in Waukegan and Floro in McHenry were in daily contact, working out who would have jurisdiction over what, when the time came to bring charges against the suspect. They had the motive, and had positively linked him to an arsenic supply. It was now just a matter of ironing out legal technicalities between the two counties before they could move in on the unsuspecting Albanese. Then, without warning, the case took yet another unpredictable turn. Investigators learned through a travel agent that Albanese was planning a hurry-up Thanksgiving holiday in Jamaica with his wife and mother. This struck them as peculiar since the suspect and his mother, Clara, were not known to be on friendly terms.

"Suddenly he's cozying up to the old dame," Babcox commented as task force members pondered their next move. "It doesn't look right," Querhammer agreed. "We've got to watch him."

From the travel bureau, investigators learned that Albanese was leaving the kids home and had booked passage for three on a November 20 flight, leaving Chicago's O'Hare International Airport at 9:15 A.M. As a precaution, Pasenelli and Querhammer booked McHenry Police Detective Patrick Joyce and Chief Deputy Coroner Marlene Lantz on the same Air Jamaica liner with orders not to let Albanese out of their sight.

Jamaican authorities were also notified, as was the office of U.S. Attorney Dan K. Webb in Chicago, since the investigation was about to become an international affair.

With Clara Albanese's profit sharing from the trophy firm, her $60,000 salary, and her husband's estate and life insurance payment amounting to more than half a million dollars, the arsenic task force team feared she could well be the next victim.

Authorities were now fighting the clock as Foreman met with Webb's staff to arrange for an exhaustive search by customs agents of Albanese's baggage, in an effort to determine whether he was carrying arsenic on the trip. They also considered warning both his wife and mother to be wary of their eating habits while on vacation. The women would be under the watchful eyes of the two undercover task force members on the flight, and would be observed by Jamaican authorities once they met their destination, but Lake and McHenry County authorities were still apprehensive. "Dammit, I still say it's too risky," Querhammer asserted as the five task force leaders pondered their next move. "One or both of these women could be in peril. We just shouldn't take this chance."

"I certainly agree with Al," Babcox said. "If anything happens to either one of those women down in the islands, we're gonna be sitting here ass-deep in egg on our face."

"What's their exact schedule?" Foreman asked.

"We understand that the two ladies are going in to Chicago on Thursday night, the nineteenth. They're going to spend the night at the Conrad Hilton. Chuck is supposed to pick them up Friday morning, and they all go out to the airport," Pasenelli said.

"What do you think, George?" Foreman inquired.

"It's my gut feeling that we should stop them," Pasenelli replied. "There's no way we can protect those women outside the community."

The five agreed: "Okay, let's do it!"

That Wednesday night, just thirty hours before he was scheduled to take off for Jamaica—and as his wife and mother were packing their bags to go to Chicago to await him— Albanese was arrested in his McHenry office.

Specifically he was charged with two counts of murder in Lake County—those of Mrs. Mary Lambert and her daughter, Marion Mueller. McHenry County authorities charged him with two counts of murder for the deaths of his father, and of Mrs. Lambert, who died in McHenry Hospital after being stricken in her Lake County home. He was also charged in McHenry County with attempted murder in the arsenic poisoning of his younger brother, and with theft for stealing more than $30,000 worth of scrap zinc from the trophy company.

The arrest was announced Thursday morning at a joint press conference with Babcox, Querhammer, and Pasenelli, surrounded by jubilant members of the arsenic task force investigative team.

"The motive was greed," Babcox announced. "In my twenty years as coroner I have never encountered, nor been involved, in such a cold-blooded, calculated, sordid destruction of two families." He commended the exceptional cooperation between various agencies, and the professionalism of Pasenelli's investigators, and told reporters: "It was Al Querhammer's alertness that triggered the whole thing. The symptoms of arsenic look much like those of congestive heart failure. They include vomiting, nausea, blacking out, dizzy spells, gastric problems, including ulcers. We were starting from zero with three dead people and nothing more to go on. There was a tremendous amount of investigative work involving many agencies, including the FBI."

Pasenelli had nothing but praise for the detectives who worked on the case. "I can't tell you the hours these people put in," he said. "They'd hit brick walls, back up, and start hitting them again. This investigation was one of intense dedication and perseverance, and we had 110 per cent cooperation from everyone we talked to."

"This can't be called a crime of passion," Prosecutor Floro added. "It's not a case where somebody gets mad and shoots or hits someone on the spur of the moment."

As the investigators finally marked the case of the curious coroners "closed," one final irony did not go unnoticed. A sign outside the McHenry bank flashed the news that the high school class in neighboring Marengo was putting on the play, "Arsenic and Old Lace."

EPILOGUE

On May 5, 1982, Charles Albanese went on trial for the murder of his father and his wife's grandmother; for attempted murder of his brother; and for stealing $38,000 from the family's lucrative business. Because of extensive publicity at home, the trial was moved to Bloomington, 150 miles southwest of Chicago. He was convicted on all charges and on June 23, Judge Henry L. Cowlin of McHenry Circuit Court sentenced him to death in the electric chair.

In October 1982, after being divorced by his third wife, Virginia, Albanese went on trial in Waukegan for the arsenic murder of her mother, Marion Mueller. Once again a jury found him guilty. On Friday, October 29, Circuit Judge Lawrence Inglis—calling the defendant "a cold and calculating killer"—again sentenced Albanese to death by electrocution.

His get-rich-quick scheme a bust, he was transferred to death row at the Menard Correctional Center in downstate Chester to await his executioner.

On November 3 the people of Lake County showed their appreciation for Coroner Babcox by electing him sheriff. He subsequently died in office. Floro, who was reelected state's attorney of McHenry County in 1984, died two years later in an auto accident. In the fall of 1990, President George Bush elevated Prosecutor Foreman to the position of U.S. Attorney for Northern Illinois.

The legal machinery for Albanese continued to grind as he put on fifteen pounds around the waistline during the seemingly endless appeals process. The Illinois Supreme Court affirmed both of Albanese's convictions in 1984, and again in 1988. In May 1989, the U.S. Supreme Court refused to hear his latest appeal, letting stand previous rulings that he was properly convicted and that the death sentence was valid.

Meanwhile the electric chair went the way of the gallows as the ultimate punishment in Illinois, and Albanese today faces death by lethal injection or—as his fifty-seven fellow inmates on Menard's Death Row irreverently call it—"the Green Needle."

CHAPTER 5

THE WITCH WHO BOILED HER LOVER

John Comer was a strapping six-foot 175-pounder who had no trouble single-handedly hefting around 200-pound pinball machines at the Bally Manufacturing plant where he worked in Chicago.

Yvonne Kleinfelder, on the other hand, was a petite 125-pounder, only five-foot-two, who worked as a volunteer dial-a-prayer telephone counselor for a religious television station.

Question: How was the tiny brunette able to exercise such uncompromising control over the burly, well-educated Comer that would cause him to meet an agonizing death? The only answer that made sense to police was that she completely dominated his mind.

Kleinfelder, who also liked to be known as "Satan's Voodoo Dancer," was a self-described devil worshipper who claimed to have headed two covens of witches. The mild-mannered Comer died with her name on his lips. The last words ever to come out of his mouth were: "Yvonne boiled me."

Their paths first crossed in 1975 when Yvonne was thirty-nine years old and John was forty-two. Not long thereafter she moved into his tiny second-floor apartment on the city's North Side.

Police first got wind of the arrangement on Thursday, May 1, 1980, when they were called to 745 West Gordon Terrace shortly after 11:00 A.M. Patrolman Joseph Andruzzi, the first man on the scene, was met outside by a friend of the couple who identified herself as Shemia Brewer. "It's apartment 201 at the top of the stairs," she said. "Hurry."

Andruzzi was hardly prepared for what greeted him next. Stepping into the acrid smelling three-room apartment he found himself in a combination living room-kitchenette, dominated by a large, cluttered table in the center.

Lying on his back on the floor under the table, with his wrists fastened to the table legs by adhesive tape and sash cord and his ankles bound tightly together was a completely naked man. Andruzzi bent over the moaning, semiconscious figure and observed that the man's back, chest, abdomen, legs, and groin were nothing but a mass of festering blisters.

The officer all but gagged as he turned to the woman who brought him there and asked, "Where's the phone? This man's got to get to the hospital."

"They don't have one. I had to call you from the restaurant down the street," she replied. "The ambulance is coming."

They could hear the siren wailing as they spoke. Andruzzi called headquarters on his hand-held radio and outlined the situation. He was told to stand by until detectives arrived. Brewer, meanwhile, rushed downstairs to await the ambulance.

The paramedics quickly examined the writhing form on the carpet, cut the bonds from his wrists, and hefted him gently onto the stretcher with his ankles still tied together.

As they were carrying him from the room the man, haggard and unshaven, tugged weakly at Andruzzi's sleeve and mumbled, "Yvonne did it. Yvonne boiled me!"

Belmont Area Homicide Investigators Richard P. Zuley and Joseph Stachula pulled up in front of the yellow-brick apartment building just as the ambulance was leaving. Andruzzi was relieved when they walked into the room. The two were considered among the best in the business.

The thirty-four-year-old Zuley had earned sixty-five honorable mentions in a decade on the force, along with a Jaycee Award for Bravery and commendations from the U.S. Treasury Department. He was the department's Outstanding Police Officer of 1974, and in 1979 had been nominated for the Superintendent's Award for Valor.

Stachula, a forty-two-year-old ex-Marine sergeant, was a policeman's policeman with an incredible eighty-five honorable mentions in his personnel file. He'd made nationwide headlines three years earlier in tracking down the killer of a young Filipina, Teresita Basa, and getting a confession in the so-called "Voice from the Grave" murder case. His efforts also earned him a good deal of ribbing from fellow officers for his dealings with the supernatural.

He expertly surveyed the surroundings, noting the unkempt apartment that reeked with cat odors, and the severed bonds still attached to the table legs. Then, with a look of resignation, he turned to Zuley and said, "I'm afraid to ask."

"It's another weird one, Joe," Andruzzi announced as he filled the dicks in on the details. "The guy's name is John Comer. He's forty-seven, but I wouldn't bet on him making forty-eight. You should have seen the poor son-of-a-bitch. That's the lady who called us, on the couch. Name's Shemia Brewer. She's twenty-four; lives over on West Buena."

Zuley took out his note pad as the seasoned detectives routinely asked the distraught woman if she could tell them what had happened there.

"I'm a friend of the woman who lives here, Yvonne Kleinfelder," she related. "At around 9:30 this morning she came over to my place and told me that something had happened. She said her roommate had been hurt and there was some trouble. She asked me to come over here and help her. I came back with her, and when I got here John was lying on the floor over there, under a blanket."

She said Yvonne walked over to the man, who appeared to be delirious, dramatically pulled off the blanket, and announced, "Look what happened to John!" When Brewer asked about Comer's sickening wounds she said Kleinfelder told her, "He got burned while trying to put out a fire."

"We've got to get help. He looks like he's going to die," the shocked friend responded.

She said the two of them went to a neighborhood restaurant and telephoned Yvonne's pastor, the Reverend Alexander Szicko of the Good Shepherd Pentecostal Church on Belmont Avenue. His advice to them was, "Call the police at once."

"Then, while we were sitting in the restaurant trying to figure out what to do next, Yvonne told me John didn't get burned in a fire like she said. She said that she threw boiling water on him. She said John misbehaved at a prayer meeting last Friday, and when they got home she decided to punish him."

"You mean that poor devil was lying there like that for six days?" Stachula asked incredulously.

"That's what Yvonne said. She told me she beat John with a cat leash, and then kicked him with the pointy-toe boots he just bought her on her forty-fifth birthday. She said, 'I'm sick and tired of his antisocial behavior toward me and my cats.' Then she told me, 'And do you know what else he did? He spoiled my Bible school homework.'"

"How did she explain about John getting burned?"

"Well, she said when she punished John he tried to attack her, and she threw boiling water on him. I told her, 'If you throw water on somebody, it's either at their front or their back, not all over them.' Then she said, 'Yeah, I know. I planned it. I boiled the water.' That's when I called the police."

"Where's Yvonne now, at the restaurant?"

"No. She left while I was on the phone."

"Do you have any idea where she might have gone?"

"To the church, maybe. I don't know where else she'd go."

After taking a statement from Brewer, the two detectives checked out the rest of the apartment. It soon became apparent that although John Comer and Yvonne Kleinfelder lived under the same roof, they did not share the same bed on a regular basis.

Just off the living room-kitchen was a small sun room, piled high with men's clothing and containing a cramped sleeping area. This was Comer's quarters. On the other side of the bathroom was Yvonne's bedroom, messy and unkempt and reeking with the ammonia-like aroma of cat urine. There was cat litter everywhere.

"Phew! Let's get the hell out of here," Stachula urged, wrinkling his nose.

Stachula drove over and checked out the church, but was told by Reverend Szicko that Yvonne was not there. "She came by for a little while, but she left," he said. Zuley headed for Cook County Hospital to try to talk to Comer, but with no luck. "Yvonne boiled me" were the last words he would ever utter.

"He's still alive, but I don't know why," a physician in the burn unit told the detective. "He's got second- and third-degree burns over 40 per cent of his body. They're so massive, so infected and dehydrated, that one of our nurses went home sick to her stomach after she looked at him.

"His heart stopped beating four times since he was brought in, and we've brought him back . . ."

An emergency signal sounded, and the doctor took leave of Zuley, saying, "There he goes again." "I'll check with you tomorrow, doc," Zuley called after him.

Daylight was still hanging on as Zuley headed back to his North Side detective headquarters to compare notes with his partner. Yvonne Kleinfelder, meanwhile, was about to be arrested. Brother Edward Bartus of the Church of the Good Shepherd telephoned police at 7:00 P.M. to report that she had returned. Homicide Investigators Thomas Keane and Daniel Sampila drove over to the church on Belmont Avenue and took her into custody without incident. She was booked on a charge of aggravated battery—which hardly spelled out what had happened to Comer.

Stachula and Zuley went out digging to find everything they could about the suspect. What they were able to put together was a confused and curious picture of a woman who was baptized a Presbyterian, became a witch and Satan worshipper and "high priestess of a double coven" while still in her 30s, and a born-again Christian by the time she had hit forty.

In recent years she had gone by the name of Reseda Lavita Vaniah, which she said meant "God's healing, God's gracious gift." Before that, in the early 1970s, she was known as Colindas Mendes Media—"Satan's Voodoo Dancer." At other times in her life she told people her name was Linda Margarita, or Linda Carroll.

The strange woman who had as many names as there are seasons, was actually born Eunice Yvonne Kleinfelder on April 10, 1935. A high school dropout, she grew up in the same Uptown neighborhood of Chicago where she was eventually arrested for her soon-to-be fatal relationship with the unfortunate Comer. It was not her first time behind bars, however.

Friends and relatives described her as a domineering person with a sharp eye for weaknesses in others. She was rebellious, secretive, and evasive, always hinting of some dark acquaintance with a mysterious life, exotic cults, witchcraft, Satan, drug trafficking, and the seamier Rush Street honky-tonks.

An older sister, who was married to a Presbyterian minister, told investigators, "We were nonpersons to her. We've never really known where she was. We were always waiting for the other shoe to drop. I always knew something would happen."

Yvonne became a drifter in her twenties and early thirties, working in sleazy bars along Rush Street or nearby State Street as a B-girl and stripper. It was there, under the name of Linda Carroll, that she was arrested three times by vice detectives in the early 1960s on charges of being an inmate of a house of ill repute.

She plunged deeply into witchcraft in the 1970s, traveling to New York, Florida, Toronto, and taking in the voodoo cultism of New Orleans as Colindas Mendes Media, Satan's Voodoo Dancer.

All four areas harbored chapters of a far-out British religious sect known as the Process—Church of the Final Judgment. Its clergy wore long black capes adorned with figures of goat heads—an ancient Satanic symbol—and serpents.

As it was explained to Zuley and Stachula, members of the sect gave almost equal weight to God and Satan. They worshipped God but believed that Satan, the god of ultimate destruction, was in control. But their belief told them they could conquer Satan through love, and certainly the Devil was an enemy of God.

Yvonne became an acolyte in a Christian offshoot of the sect known as the Foundation Faith of God. With her change in religion she also changed her name, and became Reseda Lavita Vaniah as she sold the sect's magazines on street corners. She worked in their kitchens, did odd jobs, and helped care for members' children, cats, and dogs in Chicago, New York, New Orleans, and Toronto in exchange for food, and sometimes clothing and shelter.

"A lot of people who were attracted to us, like Reseda, had no love, no acceptance, no understanding in their lives. She was a very bombed-out person who was trying to straighten out," the Reverend Hope White of the Foundation's New Orleans congregation explained.

"I knew her in New York. She was a hard worker, good with children, and she wanted to heal. She felt she had something special because of having survived ovarian cancer."

That was one side of the woman who called herself Reseda. Reverend White also remembered a darker side, and stories the woman had divulged of her other, secret life.

"In 1975 she said she was working in a disco nightclub as a stripper and was heavily into heroin. She said her boyfriend, who had some sort of shady ties with the Mafia, was beating her up a lot. Somehow she managed to escape. She said she did it by tying him up and leaving him in a motel room."

How she was able to tie up a man who was brutal enough to beat her was never explained, any more than one could explain how she was able to cow the husky John Comer, the next male to enter her turbulent life.

He was a big man and he had a mind of his own, at least until he cast his lot with Yvonne. Comer had studied economics at the University of Alabama, but never graduated. He took a job, instead, as troubleshooter for Bally, the Chicago pinball maker, when he came to town in 1952 at the age of twenty.

He eventually became an inspector, and was well-thought of by his coworkers. "He inspected the machines to make sure they worked right. You have to know what you're doing around those machines," explained his foreman, Charles Volpe. "John was also in a bowling league with the guys. He was an avid sports fan, you know, and he could tell you who won the World Series ten years ago."

Comer's mother in Alabama disapproved of her son's relationship with Yvonne and told him so. "I remember when John came home to visit in 1979, and I saw him with his shirt off," she said. "He had bruises, and his back was all covered with welts that looked like lash marks."

Hospital records showed that he was admitted for treatment for lacerations and injuries to his face and back three times in 1978, after he took up with Yvonne.

Comer's friends at work noticed a change come over him in the last six months. The once-robust athlete lost nearly thirty pounds, appeared haggard, and would fall asleep on the job. He no longer had money to buy lunch, or even cigarettes, and became increasingly unkempt.

"One day I saw John over at the Kentucky Fried Chicken place on Belmont and California, digging through the trash bins," his foreman told Zuley. "He was picking out the bones and eating them, poor guy."

His coworkers also noticed signs of physical abuse, scratches, burns, and black-and-blue marks. One of them told Zuley, "A few weeks ago he told me she lit cigarettes and burned him on the arms and neck. He showed me the burns."

Another fellow employee said, "One time he came in with what looked to be a rope burn around his neck. Jeez, you should have seen it. And another time his ears were cut real bad in the back, like they were just about torn off. His arms were all scratched up and there was what definitely looked like a cigarette burn on his cheek. We told him he should get the hell out of that house."

On Monday, April 28, Comer's foreman received a phone call from a man who did not give his name. "I'm a friend of John Comer. He's very sick in bed. Probably has a touch of the flu. He won't be in for work," the caller said.

At the time the call was made Comer had already been lying scalded on the floor, tied to the table, for two days and three nights while Yvonne inflicted her own brand of "punishment" on him.

On Friday morning, May 2—the day after her arrest—Zuley brought Yvonne into an interrogation room at headquarters to discuss her relationship with Comer. After advising her of her rights, he asked her to start from the beginning.

"I've been taking care of John for the last five years because I did not feel he could care for himself," she related. "During the last eight months he started doing antisocial things. He would twist my cats' paws, or gouge at their eyes, and I had to discipline him."

"Tell me, just how did you 'discipline' him?"

"I beat him with a belt."

"Did John ever strike back at you?"

"No, he was like a child. He never fought back. He never hit me or beat me at all."

She said that about seven o'clock Friday night, April 25, while she was boiling a "lobster pot" full of water on the stove to make stew, Comer entered the kitchen wearing only swim trunks and carrying a small steak knife.

She said she picked up the pot of boiling water and threw it on him, splashing it across his back. As he collapsed on the floor, screaming in agony, she poured the rest of the scalding water over his genitals.

"Did he make any threatening gesture toward you with the knife?" Zuley asked.

"No. When I saw him, I just freaked."

"Now, when we found Mr. Comer he was tied to the table. Why was that, Yvonne?"

"Well, I had been treating his wounds with burn ointment and bandages, and I was forced to tie his arms to the table legs so he wouldn't scratch the sores."

As the two conversed, seated across from one another at a small table in the green-painted interrogation room, Yvonne abruptly rose to her feet, walked around, and sat on the edge of the table facing Zuley. Reaching out, she took the detective's hand in hers, bowed her head, and whispered, "Please, pray with me for John."

The astonished detective said nothing, but stared at the woman's bowed head for several minutes. Then she opened her eyes and softly said, "Thank you."

Zuley realized the self-professed witch was trying to dominate him now, by positioning herself so that she was looking down at him as he sat in the chair. As he pondered his next move, there was a short rap on the door and a fellow detective poked his head into the room.

"Can I see you a minute, Rich?"

The other shoe was about to drop. Zuley excused himself and followed the other detective out into the large squad room.

"What's up?"

"Your guy, Comer? The hospital just called. He died at 10:10 A.M. Thought you'd like to know."

Now it was a homicide. Zuley decided it would be prudent to postpone further questioning until after an autopsy, just to make sure. Yvonne was escorted back to the women's lockup and he hopped into an unmarked car and headed out to the West Side morgue, now known as the Fishbein Institute.

Dr. Tae L. An, a pathologist, was performing the post-mortem examination. "As you can see, this man has suffered extensive scalding on the left side of the neck and face, the forehead, the right side of the face, and the tip of the nose," he explained. "Also on both buttocks, the entire lower abdomen, the penis and scrotum. His entire back was also boiled, and there were scalding burns on his upper and lower right and left arms."

"What a terrible sight," Zuley remarked as he looked for the first time on the remains of the man who had named his killer before he died. "The poor guy must have suffered something awful."

"Yes, I would think so," Dr. An commented. "His scalp is a mess, but the worst burns are in his crotch."

As Zuley turned his eyes away from the victim's pubic area, he noticed something else. A clear white strip of unburned skin encircled each of the dead man's wrists and ankles.

"I see you spotted that," the pathologist said as their eyes met. "Does it tell you anything?"

"It tells me that he was tied up *before* he was scalded," the detective responded. Yvonne's story about splashing the pot of boiling water on Comer as he walked into the kitchen could not have happened.

Zuley drove back to detective headquarters, and had the prisoner brought back into the interview room where he brusquely informed her of her boyfriend's death. Then, before she could again try to gain the upper hand, he rose and looked down at the petite brunette. "You lied to me!" he said. "Yvonne, if you lie to me you will lie to God."

He waited for an answer but there was only silence. Yvonne stared at him, trying to bore into his body with her witch's eyes, for more than sixty seconds. Zuley could hear his own watch tick. But he met her gaze and held it. Suddenly she turned her head away and said, "He misbehaved in church."

"All right. You are now charged with murder. Do you understand that?" Zuley continued softly. She nodded. "Now, there are a number of things you told me earlier, Yvonne, that the evidence does not support. So, suppose we start over, and you tell me the truth this time about what happened on Friday night, April 25."

Yvonne looked at the table top, fixed her eyes on the coffee-can ashtray, and took a deep breath. "I told John I was going to punish him. Our friend, Robert Tooke, was there. He heard me make the statement. When John and I got home I ordered him to get undressed, which he did. Then I punished him with my cat leash over and over again on the buttocks."

As Comer cowered on the floor, whipped, she said she tied him to the table legs. And when he tried to raise himself she kicked him sharply in the face "with my boots."

"How many times would you say you kicked him?"

"Three times. He didn't fight back. He was just like a child, and he just took it."

"And after you kicked him with your boots, then what happened?"

"Uh, I remember standing over him, pouring out the hot, steamy water right into his crotch. He screamed, but nobody came to help him. The walls in that building are thick."

Zuley then asked Yvonne, "Is it true what I've been hearing about you? Your friends say you claim to be a witch."

"I have worshipped the devil," she replied. "I have attended black masses for the devil, and have practiced the black arts."

"Did you praise the devil?"

"Yes."

"Did you ever pray to Satan?"

"Yes."

It was now mid-afternoon. Zuley contacted Assistant State's Attorney Elaine Geer and briefed her on the case. The prosecutor then brought in a court reporter, advised Yvonne again of her rights, and took a formal statement.

After it was over Zuley asked Yvonne for written permission to search her apartment. She gave it to him, and he went out to Gordon Terrace the next morning. As Yvonne's cats eyed him suspiciously the detective pawed his way through the mess. The only things he found that might be of interest were several tape cassettes and a hand-written power of attorney.

The document was executed by Comer on March 30, just three weeks before he was scalded. It gave Yvonne the right to sign his name to his income tax refund check. The document was witnessed by Robert Tooke, whose address was in nearby Evanston. Zuley looked up the seventy-six-year-old retiree and asked him what he knew about the unusual couple.

"Oh, I used to accompany them from time to time, and I often visited them in their apartment," he related. "Once, while the three of us were in a restaurant, Yvonne told John to go outside and stand with his arms in the air, and he did just as he was told, by God.

"Oh, she punished John a lot. She would only let him watch religious programs on Channel 38, where she worked as a volunteer. He couldn't watch any other television."

"She was pretty much into religion, would you say?" Zuley asked.

"Oh, yes. Religion seemed to consume her life. She went to daily prayer meetings at Good Shepherd, and to Sunday services. And in addition to her telephone counseling at the TV station she was taking classes at Moody Bible Institute."

"Well, what was her relationship with Mr. Comer?"

"John seemed to do things to deliberately make her mad," Tooke answered. "He wouldn't wash. He'd pick up her school papers with his greasy hands after feeding the cats. He burned out her electric typewriter. He'd leave cigarettes burning on the bathroom sink. He'd hurt her cats, but always when no one was around to see."

Tooke said Yvonne once "punished" Comer by hitting him in the face with a belt buckle. Afterward she boasted, "Look at his face. It looks like a roadmap."

"How about you, Mr. Tooke? Didn't she ever bother you?"

"Yeah, as a matter of fact she did. Last New Year's day she became intoxicated and kicked me in the face. On the day in March when I witnessed the power of attorney, Yvonne said she was going to kill John, and she threatened me, too, if I wouldn't sign the paper."

Tooke disclosed that it was he who had telephoned Comer's boss at Bally Manufacturing Company after Comer had been scalded, and reported him sick with the flu.

Zuley thanked the old man and headed back to Chicago. He still had the tape cassettes he'd found in the apartment, and figured they, too, might contain useful evidence in the case.

The detective spent the next several days listening to the cassettes on his car radio as he drove to and from work, but all he could pick up was Yvonne's eerie voice reading passages from the Book of Revelations in a raspy monotone.

Zuley also had a chat with Brother Bartus at Good Shepherd Pentecostal Church, where Yvonne worshipped.

"Some of her friends told us that she could not wear a cross because she possessed demons inside herself. Did she even mention anything like that to you?"

"We were counseling and praying," Brother Bartus responded. "She was struggling to develop a new lifestyle. She was a sincere seeker, and there was a struggle going on inside her. She did represent her problems as demons inside her, and we did help her exorcise them. Demons were troublemakers in her life, interfering with her spiritual development."

The detective made one last stop, at the pinball machine factory, to see whether Comer's friends could recall anything else about the odd couple.

"On the last day that John worked, I told him, 'Don't go home,'" Comer's foreman recalled. "I said, 'John, you have enough money in your paycheck there to start all over again, even if you don't get your clothes. Stay away from that woman. What's the matter with you? She's going to kill you some day.'"

"And what did Mr. Comer say when you told him that?"
"She'll have to live with it."

EPILOGUE

On December 10, 1980, Yvonne Kleinfelder—alias Reseda Lavita Vaniah, aka Colindas Mendes Media—was found guilty in Cook County Criminal Court of the torture murder of John Comer by boiling him alive. On Tuesday December 30, as she stood before Judge Frank Machala for sentencing, he told her, "Any method of killing someone is cruel. But this method of killing is incredibly cruel and, I believe, indicative of wanton cruelty and heinous behavior." With that he sentenced Satan's Voodoo Dancer to twenty-five years in prison.

She is presently incarcerated in the state's newest co-educational prison in Dixon, Illinois. And, unless she tries to put a hex on somebody, she is scheduled to come up for parole early in 1992.

CHAPTER 6

A LATIN LOVER'S LAST RIDE

Major V. T. Birchfield, chief deputy to Raleigh County Sheriff Claude England, turned to Corporal R. G. Sullivan, who shared the front seat of the squad car, wrinkled his weather-beaten snout and huffed, "Phew! Ol' Emmit was right, R. G. Something's sure as hell rotten as a dead possum 'round here."

The two West Virginia lawmen slid casually out of the car, pulled partway off Secondary Route 29 in the roadside community known as Pemberton, and sniffed the sickening atmosphere.

The deep-down hill country is decorated with drowsy little crossroad towns like this—Slab Fork, Odd, Pipestem, Cool Ridge, and insignificant Pemberton. Why, just about the biggest thing that ever happened hereabouts was the godaw-ful smell that fouled the lush countryside that muggy June afternoon in 1981.

It had been worsening with each passing sunrise, and by the tenth of the month Emmit S. Hungate, Jr., got on the line to the sheriff's office over in Beckley and told Sergeant J. H. Canterberry, "Somebody ought to do something. This old burned-out car's been parked by the side of the road for some time now, and there's really a heck of a stink comin' from it."

"Okay, Emmit. We'll send someone out to take a look-see," Canterberry drawled, noting the time of the call, 2:41 P.M., on his log.

Birchfield and Sullivan spotted Hungate as they climbed out of their vehicle and he motioned them to the burned-out, rusted hulk of a 1973 Chevrolet on the side of the road. All four tires were melted flat, the windows had burst out from the intense heat, and the interior had been gutted by a furious blaze, no doubt fed by the Chevy's own fuel supply.

"I thought for sure there was a dead animal or somethin' around here," Hungate related as the trio ambled over to the abandoned four-door on the grassy strip between the country road and a little used railway spur line. "But it's comin' from that old car right enough."

"Sure smells that way, Emmit," Sullivan agreed.

The deputies checked to see if the car was local, but it had no license plates. And there was nothing inside except the rusted springs where the seats had been. They got a crowbar and, with considerable difficulty, popped the lid of the trunk.

"Good lord!" coughed Sullivan, as the aroma burst out at them like a hot oven blast. There wasn't much left to see, but the toothy skull told them it wasn't a dead animal they were gaping at. It was just a mishmash of bones, with traces of putrid flesh clinging here and there, crawling with millions of wiggly white maggots. Decomposition had reached a stage that made it impossible to tell whether it had been a man or a woman—but it had once been somebody, that's for sure.

The deputies radioed the news of their grisly discovery to headquarters on Beckley's Main Street, and Sheriff England and Detective J. R. Lilly joined them at the scene. While Sullivan and Birchfield secured the area, England and Lilly photographed the death car and the skeleton in the luggage compartment.

The sheriff put out calls to Dr. M. Jamil Ahmed, the county medical examiner, and F. Winston Polly, assistant prosecuting attorney. He also radioed the volunteer fire department in Sofia, the nearest town, to send over its ambulance.

After inspecting the remains in the trunk, Dr. Ahmed authorized the Sofia volunteers to place the bones in a plastic bag for removal to the Raleigh General Hospital. There, at 4:35 P.M., he officially pronounced the victim dead as required by law. After preliminary examination he directed the Beckley Funeral Service to deliver the skeleton to the state medical examiner's office in Charleston.

Lilly had remained behind at the scene, where he questioned residents of the area. Reverend James Ford, Reverend Bill Dalton, and Kim and Larry Dalton all recollected that the vehicle had been brought up there and dumped by a tow truck eleven days earlier. They said it was a commercial wrecker, not known to them locally, that dropped off the disabled auto on Saturday night, May 30.

"That old car was intact at the time when he left it there," Ford said. "Then, about four o'clock in the morning—WHOOOOF!—she exploded and woke up darn near everybody."

He explained that no one had bothered calling authorities at the time because it appeared that the car had been deliberately abandoned by its owner, and the fire did not endanger nearby property.

After taking statements from the witnesses, Lilly called the D & A Wrecker Service from nearby Coal City to haul the charred hulk to the county garage in Beckley where it could be gone over more thoroughly. One way or another, detectives would have to establish the identity of the incinerated occupant of the trunk before they could proceed any further in their investigation.

Although the burned-out Chevrolet appeared to have been stripped, and its license plates removed, England's men were able to recover its VIN (Vehicle Identification Number) plate from under the hood. The number, 1L29H31124160, was sent out over the police teletype network.

As computers whirred across the country in an effort to trace the vehicle's ancestry through its VIN number, starting with the point of manufacture, Dr. Irving M. Sopher, on the morning of June 11, was beginning a nauseous postmortem examination of the trunk's victim at the state morgue in Charleston.

Dr. Sopher, a noted West Virginia pathologist, was the expert who would be called on four months later to perform an autopsy on the exhumed body of Lee Harvey Oswald to confirm once and for all the identity of the man accused of assassinating President John F. Kennedy. On this morning, however, he was concerned only with the skeletal remains of what he determined to have been a "totally charred male."

The body, itself, was in several sections due to burning and the process of decomposition. The forearms and wrists, which had become separated, were found to have been bound with a two-inch wide leather belt, size forty. Whoever the man was, he had not entered the trunk voluntarily.

Both of his fists were clenched in a "pugilist attitude," causing Dr. Sopher to exclaim, "This is a piece of luck! Although the body was almost totally burned, the clenched fists protected the fingertips from the flames to the extent that we should be able to obtain some identifiable fingerprints."

The pathologist also discovered several short dark hairs beneath the nasal cavity of the skull, indicating the color of the victim's hair, and that he apparently wore a mustache. Furthermore, the teeth were intact, enabling him to prepare a dental chart. If the detectives were unable to learn anything from the car, Dr. Sopher could at least provide them with the dead man's fingerprints and a record of his dental work.

A broken right posterior second rib among the bones also told the pathologist that the man probably died of a gunshot wound to the right lung, just below the throat.

In performing other tests he was able to establish that the fire victim had been a man with "non-Negroid" features, about five feet nine inches tall, and thirty-five to forty-five years of age. He estimated he had been dead two to three weeks.

A small necklace containing multicolored beads was found mixed in with the bones, along with a small broken metallic chain necklace which dangled about the neck; a man's Elgin wristwatch stopped at 2:15; a gold wedding band; and a gold design ring containing a shiny, gray oval stone. There were also remains of a tan sweater.

Now police had something to go on. The trunk victim was a male, about forty, with black hair, but not Negro. He liked masculine jewelry, was apparently a married man, and he had been shot to death.

Next the VIN number check came through. Raleigh County was notified that the Chevrolet was most recently registered in Illinois to Jose "Joe" Vidal Ramos, age forty-two, who had a Chicago address.

"Get on it, quick," England told his investigators. "Mr. Ramos is either the guy in the trunk, or he knows something about it." Sullivan got on the horn to Chicago, and before the day ended he heard back. At 10:00 P.M., June 11—just over thirty hours since the skeleton had been found—Sullivan got a call from Chicago Detectives John Smith and Gene Daly.

"Well, we didn't find your Joe Ramos but we talked to his wife," Sullivan was told. "Her name's Juanita. She says Jose left home around 6:30 P.M. on May 25—that was Memorial Day up here—and she hasn't seen him since. He was driving a 1973 Chevrolet. By the way, she says his birthday was June 3. He would have been forty-three."

"Then there's every possibility that he's the dead one we have down here," Sullivan suggested. "We all appreciate the fast work you fellas have done for us."

"We've got something else that might help," Daley added. "Mrs. Ramos gave us the name and phone number of her husband's dentist. Got your pencil out?"

Sullivan took down the information to be relayed to Dr. Sopher first thing in the morning. Meanwhile he asked the Chicago detectives if they could run a background check on Ramos, and to see whether there might be a photograph or fingerprints of the missing man on file.

Chicago detectives were able to locate both, and put them in the weekend mail. The prints arrived at the Raleigh County sheriff's office first thing Monday, June 15, and Trooper Marc Roberts of the West Virginia State Police delivered them to Charleston and turned them over to the pathologist.

By five o'clock that afternoon Dr. Sopher was able to telephone Sullivan with the information that he had positively identified the skeleton with the clenched fists as Jose Vidal Ramos.

Next came an unhappy task that the Southern police did not ask Chicago to assist with. Sullivan personally telephoned Mrs. Ramos and broke the news to her as gently as possible. Then, acting quickly before the shock of her husband's death could set in, he asked enough pertinent questions to determine that the couple had been married six years, Ramos had never disappeared from home before for any extended period, and—to the best of his wife's knowledge—did not know a living soul in West Virginia.

If Ramos had never been to West Virginia and did not know anyone there, how, then, did he manage to end up entombed in the trunk of his own car so far off the beaten path in Pemberton?

The widow provided the deputy with the names of the victim's brother and sister-in-law, Antonio and Herminia Ramos. Sullivan notified them of the death in the family and asked them the same questions. But they, like Mrs. Ramos, could offer no explanation for the dead man's presence in the blazing auto in the backwoods country 500 miles from home.

"Now that we know who he is, the next thing we have to do is find out how the hell he got here," Sullivan told fellow investigators. A concerted effort was made to locate the tow truck that had hauled the disabled Chevrolet into Pemberton, but no commercial wrecker in the area had ever handled such an assignment.

Investigators had hit a dead end on the West Virginia leg of the trail. Sullivan then decided to try to start at square one—in Chicago—and July 12 found him huddled with Detectives John Smith and Thomas Brankin in Area Three Violent Crimes Headquarters on the city's Southwest Side. First he brought the Chicago dicks up-to-date on the investigation in West Virginia. "The key to what this guy was doing down in our neck of the woods could lie in his past," he suggested. "What I'd like to do while I'm up here is talk to members of family, and any other folks who might have been close to him."

The Chicago detectives agreed that somebody might know something that would appear insignificant to them, but coupled with what authorities already knew, could provide an important clue in the investigation. For the next twelve days Smith and Brankin escorted the West Virginian around the Windy City and assisted him in extensive interrogations of the murdered man's family and friends.

Their first stop was the modest home on South Claremont Avenue, where they talked to Ramos' widow. Next they interviewed his brother, Antonio, on West Division Street. Relatives told the officers that Ramos had worked as a butcher, operating a small meat market on Milwaukee Avenue. He leased the shop from a man named Jose Aroca. The detectives went to see him next.

"I knew something must have happened," Aroca told them. "Some people who live near the shop called me to say that something must be wrong. They told me they hadn't seen Joe Ramos for several days, and that the business was locked but a terrible odor was coming from the building."

The landlord said he went to the shop at 1566 North Milwaukee and found that the meat coolers had been turned off, and their contents had become rancid. How ironic! While the meat in the butcher shop was decomposing, the butcher himself was festering in the trunk of his car 500 miles away.

In compiling a list of acquaintances from friends and relatives the detectives learned that Ramos had carried on a long-time relationship with one Patricia Gil. His brother, Antonio, said Ramos was supposed to have met Mrs. Gil on the evening of May 25 in a bar run by Felepe Vallejo on West Division Street. That was the night he disappeared, according to his wife.

Sullivan, Smith, and Brankin paid Vallejo a visit. It was now July 18, but Vallejo remembered the night Ramos had been in his joint because of a loud telephone conversation. He told the detectives both he and an employee, Maria Rivera, overheard Ramos arguing bitterly with the person on the other end of the line.

Finally, around 9:30 or 10:00 P.M., he left in a huff and they never saw him again.

On the following day Sullivan went to the meat market, and discovered it had reopened, minus its owner. Pablo Ortega and his wife had taken over the business when Ramos failed to return. He and his wife both remembered a curious incident that occurred several days after they reopened the shop.

"Joe's wife came into the store and asked us if he had left any of his belongings here," Ortega related. "We showed her some clothes, but she said she didn't want any of it. She didn't take anything. She just left."

The scenario didn't make sense to Sullivan. "This Mrs. Ramos, what did she look like?" he asked Ortega.

"Oh, a big woman. Over 200 pounds, I'd say. About thirty, a little over five feet tall, and she had on those large horn-rimmed glasses."

"She was Hispanic?"

"Oh, no. She wasn't," Ortega said, shaking his head from side to side. "She was a white woman, but not a Latino, I'm sure of that."

The detectives looked at one another. The woman described as the victim's wife definitely was not Juanita Ramos. But whoever it was who inquired about the missing man's belongings did match the description relatives of the dead man had given of Patricia Gil. "Well, fellas, I think we oughta try to find this Gil lady, don't you?" Sullivan suggested.

"If she's around, we'll find her for you," Smith promised.

On the following day, Sunday, Sullivan and Smith located her at the home of relatives on the city's South Side. She was all she had been described to be—a hefty brunette, twenty-eight years old, five-feet-three-inches tall, and weighing some 220 pounds. The mother of three small children, she lived with her husband, William, in suburban Midlothian and worked at the *Daily Racing Form*.

Mrs. Gil was quite open about her relationship with the married Ramos. She had enjoyed a lengthy affair with him, almost from the time he came up from Puerto Rico. "I've known Joe for about seven years," she said. "We lived together until July 19 of last year. Joe is the daddy of two of my young ones, and he's been giving me support money for 'em."

"When was the last time you saw Joe Ramos, Mrs. Gil?"

"Hmmm. I met him at Vallejo's on Sunday—that would have been May 24," she said, after first going over it in her mind. "And we were supposed to meet there again the next night, but we didn't. I drove over there on Division Street around a quarter to five, but I didn't see Joe's car so I didn't stop. I just drove by."

"Did Mr. Ramos have relatives, or know anybody that you can think of, in West Virginia? Can you think of any earthly reason why he might have been down there?"

"No, none at all," she replied. But by a strange coincidence, as the detectives drew Mrs. Gil out, they learned that she had kinfolk in West Virginia—two uncles, Herbert and Millard Dancy. They lived in Coal City, about five miles from where the body was found in the burned-out car. She had other relatives in Charleston and Bluefield. "I talk to them every now and again by phone, but I've never been down that way myself," she volunteered.

The investigators were now more than a little interested in Patricia Gil, since the dead man had fathered two of her children, and she had established a West Virginia connection. At their request she underwent a lie-detector examination conducted by Officer Robert M. Bartik in Chicago police headquarters. The results, unfortunately, were not conclusive.

After the polygraph exam Mrs. Gil confided to Sullivan that she had dreamed she had seen a woman shoot her former lover on the very day Ramos disappeared. The dream was so vivid, in fact, that she telephoned a friend, Tina Rzepka, and told her about it.

Silly as it seemed, the cops were now chasing a dream, but Sullivan wasn't about to leave any base uncovered. On Monday, July 21, with Smith's help, he located Tina Rzepka in her home in suburban Orland Park. Her real name turned out to be Christine, and she was the wife of Cook County Forest Ranger Ronald Rzepka, a former Chicago policeman.

"I remember Pat's call," she said. "She phoned around 12:30 in the morning and told me she was in trouble. She said she wanted to speak to Ron. I handed my husband the phone and he asked her, 'What's going on?'"

"I'm in Chicago and I shot Joe," she said Pat told her husband. "He called me and said he was going to kill me. I had Billy take the kids to Chicago. Joe came into the house with a baseball bat and swung the bat, hitting the wall. When he hit the wall I shot him in the neck. He fell on the kitchen floor, and I grabbed the car keys and left."

"Where are you now, Pat?"

"In Chicago."

"Where are the kids?"

"At my Mom's house."

"All right, Pat. Here's what I want you to do. You call the Midlothian police, or go to them, and tell them exactly what happened."

"I can't do that, Ron. I'm too scared."

"What did you do with the gun?" he asked her.

"I threw the gun and the bat into the Calumet River."

"Here, talk to Tina, and try to get hold of yourself," Rzepka said, handing the phone back to his wife. While she chatted with Mrs. Gil he pulled on his clothes. As soon as his wife finished talking with the distraught woman, Rzepka telephoned Midlothian police and reported the incident. Then he got in to his car and headed for the station.

Midlothian Detective Neal Cauuwe and Officer Michael Bard were dispatched to the home at 4233 West 147th Street, in the far south suburb. The building had once been St.

Christopher's rectory, but was now occupied by William and Patricia Gil and their children—and possibly one dead body.

The old rectory seemed deserted, and there were no cars in the driveway. Getting no response to their knock, Cauuwe and Bard climbed in through a window. They flashed their lights around the interior, moving from room to room, but there was no body or any sign that there had ever been one. "This joint is spotless," Cauuwe commented. "Everything is in perfect order. Looks like maybe we've been sent on a wild goose chase."

As the officers were about to leave, the back door opened and in walked Mrs. Gil, dragging along two sleepy-eyed boys. "What in the world's going on here?" she demanded. Cauuwe explained the presence of police in the housewife's kitchen.

"I never shot anyone, and I didn't call Ron Rzepka," she said in astonishment. "I have been having trouble with Joe Ramos, but I haven't seen him recently. This has got to be some kind of a hoax, and I don't think it's funny."

She appeared completely relaxed, and fully cooperative with the lawmen. They returned to the Midlothian station and marked the incident "unfounded."

Ex-policeman Rzepka, however, knew full well that he had not not dreamed the phone call. He filed a detailed report of the conversation with the Cook County Forest Preserve District, just for the record.

He was glad he had done so, after talking to Sullivan, who was now having reservations about Mrs. Gil's story— dream or no dream.

No sooner had the Dixie deputy finished talking to the Rzepkas than Sullivan put in a call to his fellow officer, Corporal R.J. Osborne, back in Raleigh County. He briefed Osborne on what he had learned in Chicago, and told him, "R.J., I'd like for you to check out this Gil woman's relatives over in Coal City."

Osborne easily located the Dancy family, down where everybody knows everyone else, and learned in short order that Patricia Gil had not told the truth when she insisted she had never been to West Virginia. He first talked to thirty-year-old Ethel Dancy, who recalled that Mrs. Gil, whom she knew as Patricia Ramos, had first visited her kinfolk in Raleigh County in 1970.

She had been down there since, however, and briefly visited Ethel's in-laws, sixty-eight-year-old Herbert Dancy and his wife, Lucy, who lived in the trailer next to hers in the mobile home park. "It must have been, oh, just five or six weeks ago, I figure," she said.

Herbert Dancy was able to pinpoint the date exactly by producing his telephone bill for the lawman. It was May 30.

He told Osborne that Mrs. Gil first telephoned him early in the morning on May 27, which would have been two days after Ramos disappeared. She asked to speak to Herbert's brother, Millard, who was not there at the moment. Five minutes later, at 7:54 A.M., she called again and succeeded in speaking to her uncle, Millard.

"She told Millard she was in trouble, and she wanted him to drive up to Midlothian right away," Herbert Dancy recalled.

Millard asked, "Well, just what kind of trouble are you in?"

"I can't tell you over the phone," she replied.

"Well, if you can't tell me what kind of trouble you're in, I can't run all the way up to Chicago," he told her.

Both calls were collect, which was how Herbert Dancy was able to be so precise about the date and times. According to his phone bill, neither call came from Chicago, however. Both were placed from a pay phone in Galesburg, Michigan, a small town about halfway between Battle Creek and Kalamazoo.

The next evening she called again, collect, from a number police subsequently traced to the Freezer Cone concession booth in Chicago's Union Station. Lucy Dancy took the call. "She became very upset and cried when I told her that her uncle wasn't here," she recalled.

Two days later, which would have been May 30, Mrs. Gil

again called Herbert and Lucy Dancy. It was 3:30 in the afternoon, and the call came from just ten miles outside of Huntington, on the West Virginia side of the river from Ohio. "She told Lucy that she was broken down," Herbert told the officer. "She said a problem had developed with one of the two cars she was traveling with. She wondered if we could drive up to Huntington and help her out. I told her it would be impossible, but if she could get to Coal City the wife and I would see what we could do.

"Well, at about seven o'clock that night she called again, to report that she had just pulled off the turnpike into Beckley, and she wanted to know how to get to my house," Dancy related. She was only a few miles away, but for some inexplicable reason the Dancys did not hear from her again until four hours later, when she called again.

"We're at the Sureway Supermarket in Coal City," she said. "How do we get to your place from here?"

"Just stay where you are and I'll come and get you," Herbert Dancy advised. He drove to the town grocery where Mrs. Gil and two companions were waiting in a brown Plymouth. His niece introduced the two men as her husband, Billy, and her sister Cora's boyfriend. They got into the Plymouth and followed Uncle Herbert back to his trailer.

"We were in Ohio to see somebody, and just decided to drop down and look in on you, 'cause I knew you'd been sick," Mrs. Gil explained.

Shortly after midnight, after about two hours of small talk and getting up-to-date on relatives, Mrs. Gil, her husband, and their young friend got up to leave. "She said that she was going to see about that car, what they were going to do with it," Dancy said.

"Was that their other car, that was broken down?" Osborne asked.

"Yeah, that's the way I took it."

"Did she say anything about the car, like where she left it?"

"She said she left it at Pemberton."

"Now, let me get this straight, Mr. Dancy," Osborne continued. "You said there were only three people there. Did she explain why there were only three people and two cars?"

"No," Dancy said. "And the man and the boy didn't talk hardly any."

The lawman asked Dancy if he could describe his niece's male companions. "Oh, sure. The man was about five-foot-ten, 170 pounds, kind of slender, probably around thirty to thirty-five years old, light hair, and short. He looked American-like to me. The young lad looked around eighteen years old, weighed 150 or 155 pounds, had sandy colored hair, and was about five-foot-six."

Osborne showed Dancy a snapshot of Jose Ramos and asked whether either of the two looked like him. "No, neither of them don't," Dancy answered.

"You're sure that she told you she had left the other car down at Pemberton?"

"I'm positive."

It had been a good day's work for Osborne, who relayed the information to Sullivan in Chicago. Despite her denial that she had ever been to West Virginia, Mrs. Gill had been there, and she had "left a car" at Pemberton.

On Wednesday, July 22, Sullivan and the Chicago detectives attempted to locate Patricia Gil for further questioning, but without success. They found her husband, William, at the Midlothian residence and took him to the Southwest Side Chicago police headquarters for questioning, but he refused to make a statement. It was hardly the attitude of a man who had nothing to hide.

Sullivan knew he was onto something, but it was still not solid enough to make a case that would stand up in court. He had to tie Mrs. Gil firmly to the burned-out Chevy in Pemberton. The answer to the puzzle, or at least the next piece of it, could lie back home in West Virginia, and that's where he headed on July 24.

After follow-up interviews with the Dancy brothers, he sent teletype messages to every law enforcement agency between Beckley and Huntington, as well as those in the Ashland, Kentucky, and Ironton, Ohio, areas. The messages asked police in those communities to attempt to locate the tow truck that had hauled a green 1973 Chevrolet to Pemberton on May 30.

It was Monday, August 3, when Detective Sergeant Terry Gray of the Kentucky State Police notified Sullivan that he had located the wrecker in the town of Catlettsburg, about eight miles below Ashland. He had also found the driver, Larry Mayo, who worked for Reynolds' Ashland Oil Service on Louisa Road.

Mayo told Gray he remembered the tow job because of the long haul, and something else—a noxious aroma emanating from the disabled car. He told the trooper that a woman driving an auto with Illinois license plates had come into the station around four o'clock in the afternoon and asked him to check another car she was having trouble with.

"She was a stocky lady, about five-feet-five. Dark hair, and wearing glasses," Mayo recalled. He said he followed her brown Plymouth Volare for about a mile, to an area known as England Hill, where a dark green Chevy with Illinois plates was parked on the side of the road.

The Chevrolet had a faulty thermostat, and its engine had burned out. Mayo told the woman, and the two men who were waiting by the stalled car, that he could not repair it. He said she then asked him to tow the disabled vehicle to Beckley, West Virginia.

"I told her I couldn't do that without authorization from Jim Reynolds. He owns the station," Mayo said. "So we went back to the station and Mr. Reynolds okayed the job. But he wanted $150 in advance. The lady paid him with mostly new $20 bills.

"When I went back and hooked the Chevy up to my tow truck I noticed a really bad odor, like something was decaying," he recalled.

"I want you to take the back roads all the way," the woman told him.

"I can't do that, ma'am. Mr. Reynolds says to stick with the major highways," Mayo replied.

So off they went, with Mayo leading the way in his tow truck, followed by the Chevrolet with nobody at the wheel and Ramos in the trunk, and Mrs. Gil and her two companions bringing up the rear in the Plymouth. It was a three-car funeral cortege, but Mayo hadn't been let in on it. The odd caravan wound its way through the West Virginia hills, through Beckley, where Mrs. Gil pulled around in front of the wrecker and took the lead.

"We drove all around Beckley and finally went to a church a ways out of town, where there were several people, and the woman told me to drop the car," Mayo said.

"Do you remember anything else about the trip?" Gray inquired.

"Well, we made two stops driving around Beckley, and the lady made a phone call. I remember that one of the men asked the lady for a cigarette, and he called her Pat."

Sullivan thanked the Kentucky state trooper for his valuable assistance, and the next day he and Osborne drove up to Catlettsburg to take statements from Mayo and Reynolds. Mayo also identified photos of the burned-out death car as the auto he had towed to Pemberton.

After Mayo detailed the route the tow truck funeral procession had taken from Kentucky through West Virginia, the two deputies were able to locate other witnesses who gave corroborating statements. All remembered the incident because of the odor.

It seemed a certainty now that the body of Jose Ramos was already in the trunk of his car, and had been for some time, before the auto ended up in the Raleigh County hills. Pemberton served only as the impromptu cremation site after a homicide that had taken place somewhere else.

It was now up to the northern authorities. After conferring with Sullivan and Osborne, Sheriff England forwarded copies of their reports to Police Chief William Fischer in Midlothian. He thanked Fischer for the assistance his department, particularly Sergeant Harold Kaufman, had given Sullivan while he was in the Chicago area, and advised him, "It now appears that the death of Jose Ramos occurred within the jurisdiction of Cook County, Illinois."

The ball was back in Midlothian's court. The West Virginia deputies and Kentucky State Police had all but wrapped up the case. All that remained was to nail the suspects the southern officers had identified.

Chief Fischer's men took over the investigation, assisted by Sergeant Don Shaw and Investigator David Carter of the Cook County Sheriff's department. But they got nowhere. Patricia Gil had already stonewalled Chicago police by insisting she knew nothing about the murder, and she would continue to stonewall Midlothian police and the sheriff's investigators for nearly six more months.

Carter and Shaw were not the types to give up easily, however. They had no intention of throwing in the towel after their southern counterparts had done so much work on the case. In mid-January, the two sheriff's men paid a call on Mrs. Gil's mother in Chicago on the outside chance they might pick up something new.

While chatting with her, they noticed a "bereavement notice" on a nearby desk. The deceased had been a relative of one of her daughter's friends, the woman explained.

The name of the deceased was Anderson—a name that had not yet surfaced in the investigation. Carter and Shaw, clutching at straws, went to the funeral parlor and questioned the mortician. He gave them a copy of the obituary notice that had appeared in the *Chicago Tribune*, listing survivors.

The detectives began checking out the next of kin, one of whom turned out to be seventeen-year-old Danny Anderson. They found him living with a friend in Chicago. Young Anderson matched the description of the mystery youth who had accompanied Mrs. Gil and her husband on their eerie tow truck odyssey through the South.

It did not take Shaw and Carter long to find out that Danny was Patricia Gil's younger sister's boyfriend. But he became evasive when they asked whether he had been at the Gil home on the night of May 25, and it soon became apparent that he was hiding something.

The nervous youth was taken to headquarters, and left with his thoughts for an hour in an isolation cell. The brief experience behind bars proved a sobering one, and when Anderson was brought back for requestioning he opened up like the gate of Niagara.

He was in the old rectory on 147th Street on the night Ramos was shot. And he was, as suspected, the third person in the macabre funeral procession to West Virginia. He just got into the car, he told officers, without knowing where they were going. He told the detectives he and William Gil were hiding in the bushes outside the Midlothian home when the fatal shot was fired. He said they ran into the house to find Ramos lying in a pool of blood, and pleading for help. He said he left with Mrs. Gil and her children, and when they returned several hours later, the house was clean and Gil and Ramos were gone. He was apparently unaware at the time that Ramos had died and was already laid out in the trunk of his own car.

After being told for the first time exactly what happened on the night Ramos disappeared, Shaw and Carter sought out Mrs. Gil for the last time. They found her Friday night, January 22, and confronted her with the case authorities in three states had built against her—the shooting, the trip down south, the towing incident, and the visit to relatives she had earlier denied.

It was all over, and Patricia Gil knew it. At 2:30 A.M. on Saturday, January 23, Shaw brought her to the Criminal Courts Building on Chicago's West Side where she gave a twenty-three-page statement to Assistant State's Attorney Joseph Locallo.

She told the deputy prosecutor she had lived with Ramos for about nine years before marrying William Gil in May 1980, and moving into old St. Christopher's rectory. Ramos did not discover until a year later that the mother of his two children had married another man.

"I don't quite recall if he called me or if I called him," she told Locallo. "He was very upset, and said he was coming out to the house. I told him not to come, told him I didn't want to see him, and that I wouldn't care to talk nothing over with him that night. But he told me, no, he was coming. He flew out there, that sucker. I don't know how he got out there so fast, but he flew out there."

In the meantime, she said, she had gone out to the car and "asked Billy for his gun." She explained that it was a warm night and her husband, her kid brother, Johnny, seventeen, and Danny were out in the yard listening to the car radio. She said her husband took his .38 caliber pistol from the dashboard and handed it to her.

"He sat there and loaded the gun and handed it to me. I told him to take my kids and leave. I kissed all my kids. He took my kids and I thought he left."

She said she went back into the house, fixed herself a stiff drink, and turned on the stereo. "And then Joe came . . ."

She told Locallo that Ramos chided her about being drunk, and about the way she dressed. "Oh, my God, yes, the way I was dressed. And about why I didn't tell him that I was married, and why did he have to hear it from somebody else?"

She said Ramos picked up a baseball bat by the door and told her, "You know, I could smash the shit out of you." With that he swung the bat at the side of the door.

"Then he started laughing at me, and I picked up the gun. I said, 'Joe, I'm not playing with you,' and he said, 'I'm not playing with you, either.' And then I shot him!"

"Where did you hit him?" Locallo asked.

"In the neck."

As Ramos collapsed to the floor moaning "Oh, my God!" her husband and the two teen-aged boys "came flying into the house." She said Anderson tried to run to the phone, but her husband restrained him. He then took the gun away from her and told her, "Get the hell out of here!"

She said she drove her three children to her mother's home in Chicago, where she told them, "Go with grandma."

Then she drove to the home of another friend and telephoned the Rzepkas. After telling them she had shot Ramos, she said, she followed Rzepka's advice and phoned her husband. She urged him to call the police, but said he told her, "Get hold of yourself."

She returned home to find the blood in the kitchen had been cleaned up, the body was gone, and the two Midlothian officers were on the scene. After denying that anything had happened, she said, "I went upstairs and went to sleep."

She went to work as usual the following morning, and for the next four days the body of her former lover reposed in the trunk of his car parked outside old St. Christopher's. It was a fitting beginning for the long-distance funeral that was about to begin.

On Friday night, May 29, Mrs. Gil left the children again with her mother. Then she and her husband took off for Michigan in Joe's Chevrolet, with Ramos still in the trunk. They drove down around the bottom of Lake Michigan, across the top of Indiana, and all the way across the state of Michigan to the Detroit suburb of Taylor, where they visited relatives.

If the relatives couldn't come to Joe's funeral, the funeral would go to them—only they didn't know it at the time. The Gils then motored back to Midlothian, where they picked up young Anderson and headed south.

"Me and Danny went in my car. I followed Billy, who was driving Joe's car," she continued. She told the prosecutor how the car, with the body decaying in the trunk, broke down outside Ashland, Kentucky, and how they had to engage the wrecker to take it to its final destination.

"It was Billy's idea to take it to the mountains, and nobody would find it."

After abandoning the death car she described the visit with her Uncle Herbert and Aunt Lucy—a house call that positively established that she was on the scene after earlier denying ever having been in West Virginia. It was almost as if she hadn't wanted to waste the trip, being as she was already in the neighborhood to dump off Joe, so she just dropped in to say hello.

The family obligation out of the way, she said she and her companions bought a can of gasoline and drove back to Pemberton. There they doused the disabled Chevrolet with the volatile fluid and torched it. As the auto erupted into a funeral pyre for the trunked butcher of Milwaukee Avenue the trio piled into Mrs. Gil's Plymouth and hightailed it into the night.

Locallo asked, "Why didn't you just leave the car there . . . on the side of the road?"

"Ask Billy!" she snapped. "That was his bright idea."

Patricia and William Gil were convicted of voluntary homicide in the murder of Joe Vidal Ramos in November 1982. On January 7, 1983, Judge Cornelius Houtsma of Cook County Circuit Court sentenced each of them to eighteen years in prison—fourteen years for the actual slaying and four years for concealment of a homicide. Prosecutor Michael Boyle pointed out that going for a "one-way ride" was a term that originated in Chicago back in the Prohibition Era. But nothing in the annals of crime ever compared to the modern-day "long-distance last ride" of Patricia Gil's Latin lover.

EPILOGUE

The Gils were among many convicts to win "early release" due to overcrowded conditions in Illinois prisons. Gil was turned out of a state prison facility at Danville on August 21, 1987 after serving less than five years, and his wife was released from the women's prison at Dwight five days later.

CHAPTER 7

![black bar]

CALLING DR. BRANION! YOU'RE WANTED FOR MURDER

"On 22nd December 1967, a call was received at the office of D.D.A #1 (Detective Division) Homicide Unit, for the detectives to investigate the death of one BRANION, Donna, F/N41 yrs., the socially prominent wife of the equally prominent BRANION, John M., M.D., and eminent gynecologist, who had found his wife dead of multiple gunshot wounds, in the utility room of their spacious apartment located at 5054 S. Woodlawn Avenue, 1st floor.

"Following the 'on the scene' investigation the subject named detectives requested the doctor to proceed to the office of D.D.A. #1 Homicide Unit, at 749 East 56th Place, in an effort to determine the circumstances surrounding the case. The doctor appeared, in company with one BROWN, Nelson, Attorney, also the brother of the decedent.

"The doctor related that he had left the Ida Mae Scott Hospital, where he had been treating patients, then proceeded directly to the Hyde Park Neighborhood Center where he picked up his son, BRANION, John M. III, 4 yrs. old, at 1130 hours then proceeded immediately to his home, where he found the body of his wife."

The foregoing paragraphs are from an official report by Chicago Homicide Commander Francis Flanagan dated 25

June, 1968, recommending the "subject named detectives"—
John Mannion, Michael Boyle, and James McGreal—for department commendations for their untiring efforts in bringing about a solution to the murder of Mrs. Donna Branion,
F (female)/N (Negro)/41 (years of age). It was a truly ugly
international affair.

The victim's husband, Dr. John Marshall Branion, Jr.,
came from a good, solid family that could trace its roots to the
antebellum cotton fields down South. His late father, John
Marshall Branion, Sr., had the power and mind to rise above
the poverty in which he was spawned in Mississippi.

Orphaned at the age of thirteen, he put himself through
school. After World War I he headed north, where he graduated from the University of Chicago Law School in 1923. A
proud, self-made man, the elder Branion could easily have
become a millionaire as one of the few minority attorneys in
Chicago practicing criminal law. He chose public service
instead, spending the next thirty-four years as assistant public
defender of Cook County, helping the indigent who had been
accused of crimes.

Though he never became wealthy, the defender's job
provided enough income to bring his small family through the
Great Depression without being in need. There was only
Branion, his wife, and their son.

As an only child John, Jr., became his father's pride and
joy and, yes, he most certainly was spoiled. It was his parents'
fondest dream that he become a doctor, but his unfortunate
grades in school did not warrant admission to any of the
medical colleges in the United States. That problem was
solved by his folks sending him abroad to study medicine in
Europe.

When he returned to Chicago he did his internship, set
up practice in obstetrics and gynecology, and married well.
His wife was the former Donna Brown, daughter of Chicago
banker Sidney Brown. She was a cousin of the noted jazz
musician, Oscar Brown, Jr. The couple had two children, a
boy and a girl.

As a black physician on Chicago's teeming South Side, Dr. Branion should have had it made, except for three consuming weaknesses: fast money, fast horses, and fancy women. He couldn't seem to get enough of any of them. He was indicted as a member of an abortion ring, but got off the hook by the good fortune that an abortion victim who was about to testify against him died before the trial.

Dr. Branion owned his own horses, which he stabled in neighboring Indiana, and when he wasn't with his steeds he was frequently seen in the company of the other kind of fillies. He also made frequent ski trips to Colorado. The dashing playboy physician hardly followed his father's footsteps when it came to dedicating his life to public service.

His dedication to pleasuredom did not go over well at home, however, and there was nasty talk of divorce. It was something the socially prominent Donna Branion did not want, for her own pride as well as the sake of the children.

Mrs. Branion's sister, Joyce Tyler, was probably the last person who ever spoke to her. Donna telephoned her sister at 8:30 in the morning on Friday, December 22, and again at 10:15 to discuss baby-sitting. Within a little more than an hour the doctor's wife would be dead.

Theresa Kentra, a neighbor whose adjoining apartment shared a back porch with the Branions' posh ten-room apartment on South Woodlawn Avenue came home from shopping that day at a few minutes before eleven o'clock. While putting away the groceries about twenty minutes later she heard a commotion in the Branion apartment, then a sharp report, followed by three more.

Dr. Branion, meanwhile, had been having a busy morning with his patients at the Ida Mae Scott Hospital on South Prairie Avenue, and barely got cleaned up in time to pick up his four-year-old son at nursery school. He signed out on the hospital log at 11:20 A.M.

The doctor picked up his son at the Hyde Park Neighborhood Club on South Kenwood Avenue a short time later, and then drove over to East Fifty-third Street to meet Maxine

Brown, the ex-wife of Oscar Brown, Jr. They had scheduled a luncheon engagement but Mrs. Brown had to break it because of a business commitment. "I'm sorry, John. Maybe we can do it another time," she apologized.

So the doctor trundled his bundled-up offspring back into the car and they headed home. Christmas was just three days away and little John was chattering about Santa Claus as they pulled up in front of the apartment building. It was not yet noon when the father unlocked the apartment door and pushed it open. "You wait out here a minute," he said, motioning the youngster to stay put. Branion then entered the first-floor apartment, walked through the kitchen, and found his wife lying dead in a pool of blood on the utility room floor.

He did not touch the body. After pausing for only a moment he ran out onto the back porch and called upward, "Helen! Helen!" Dr. Helen Payne, a physician who lived on the third floor, heard the cry and hurried downstairs accompanied by her brother, William Payne. Dr. Branion met them at his apartment door and motioned, "In there. It's Donna."

As Dr. Payne and her brother moved curiously into the apartment, Dr. Branion hustled his son upstairs to a relative of his wife's on the second floor. He returned to his own apartment in time to hear William Payne calling the police.

Patrolman William Catizone was on routine patrol in the neighborhood when he received a radio call at 11:58 A.M. to meet Dr. Branion at 5054 South Woodlawn "regarding his wife." When he arrived, he was ushered into the apartment by Branion who directed him to the blood-covered body on the utility room floor.

"I haven't touched her," the handsome physician asserted. "As soon as I observed the lividity (settling of blood) in her legs I knew she was dead."

The patrolman knelt beside the body and felt for a pulse. There was none. Helen Payne identified herself as a medical doctor, explained that she had examined the victim, and officially pronounced her dead.

While the drama was unfolding in the Branion apartment, Detective Michael Boyle was sitting dejectedly out in the Cook County Morgue, waiting to testify at a homicide inquest. He was hardly in a festive mood. He had a throbbing toothache, for one thing, and was woefully behind in his Christmas shopping. Moreover, his annual pre-Christmas house party had been scheduled for that very evening, and he hadn't even picked up the food trays.

Boyle normally worked with Detective John Mannion. The two made a good team, having joined the department together straight out of military service in 1961. But Mannion, the lucky devil, was on furlough and wouldn't be back until after the holidays. Boyle was temporarily working with Detective James McGreal, and was griping to him about his sore tooth when they got the call to get over to the Branion address on the double.

The crime lab men were already working the scene when Boyle and McGreal entered the spacious apartment. Dr. Branion, his head buried in his hands, was seated on the living room couch, sobbing quietly.

In order to spare the dead woman's husband the discomfort of having to watch the crime lab men going about their work, the detectives suggested it might be more comfortable for them to talk in the old Washington Park detective headquarters. Branion agreed and went with the officers, accompanied by his wife's brother, Nelson Brown. Brown, an attorney who had arrived at the scene, said he wanted to be present during any questioning. He stressed that he was acting as a relative of the deceased, and not as his brother-in-law's lawyer.

Dr. Branion was not considered a suspect. It was he who had discovered the body, and he had witnesses. Police surmised the wealthy doctor's wife had been slain by an intruder—possibly a burglar who had slipped into the apartment in hopes of finding Christmas gifts under the tree waiting to be opened. But the detectives had to start at the beginning, and it would be necessary for the victim's husband to provide any background information that might be helpful.

While Boyle and McGreal talked to the grieving husband, mobile crime lab technician Alvin Karston recovered three expended bullets and four cartridge casings at the murder scene. Two of the slugs were found under the body after Donna Branion was lifted onto a stretcher. The third bullet lay on the floor near the body.

Karston also found a cord from an electric iron next to the deceased. It appeared the killer had first attempted to strangle Mrs. Branion, possibly in the bedroom. Police theorized she screamed, and tried to make her way out the back door, forcing the intruder to put the gun to her.

A postmortem examination at the county morgue, where the body was taken, indicated thirteen separate wounds—seven so-called "entry wounds" and six caused by bullets exiting. The three slugs that had been recovered at the scene had ripped through both her hands as she tried to protect herself from her attacker.

One of them then went through her head, one tore through her neck, and the third went into her shoulder and out her back. A fourth slug was recovered from the body during the autopsy.

Questioning the woman's husband produced nothing that might hint at the identity of the killer. Once the crime lab crew had left and the blood was mopped up, Boyle suggested that the doctor might feel more relaxed if they were to continue their chat in the apartment.

Boyle and another detective, Charles McMillan, accompanied Dr. Branion and his brother-in-law back to the scene. A thorough inspection of the apartment by the two detectives, the victim's husband, and her lawyer brother indicated that nothing appeared to have been taken. Furthermore, there was no sign of a forced entry. That suggested that Mrs. Branion had admitted the killer herself, and probably knew him.

As the two detectives continued to look around, the grief-stricken Branion retired to the sun porch where he sat sobbing into his hands. His teen-aged daughter had come home while he was out with the detectives and had joined her younger brother upstairs with relatives. He seemed alone, now, with the terrible realization of what had happened.

"Pssst, Mike! I want to show you something," McMillan whispered to Boyle as they moved through the apartment.

"What's up, Charlie? Find something?"

"No, it's the doc," McMillan said in a hushed tone. "Look at the guy, Mike. While he's sitting there crying he's been peeking through his fingers, watching every move we make."

"He sure as hell is," Boyle whispered. "He's playing peek-a-boo and he isn't missing a thing. He's following our every move."

"Think we ought to talk to him some more?"

"Right. It just might be that the doc's not as broken up about all this as he'd like us to think."

The two detectives walked casually out to the sun porch and asked Branion if he'd mind going over everything one more time, up to the discovery of his wife's body.

"Not at all," Branion said, stifling a sob. "I realize you gentlemen have a job to do and I want to help you all I can. Well, like I told you before, I left my office at 11:30 this morning and drove over to pick up my son at 5480 South Kenwood. I got there at about 11:35, and he was waiting out in front for me. Then I drove over to East Fifty-third Street to pick up Maxine Brown to have lunch with us. She couldn't make it, so we drove home."

Branion paused to wipe the tears from his eyes. "Go on, doctor. I know how tough this must be for you," Boyle said gently.

"When I entered the apartment I called out to my wife, and got no answer. I just sensed something was wrong. I told my boy to wait in the hall, and I went in alone. I went into the utility room and flicked on the light. I saw her lying on the floor."

"Did you go to her side?"

"No. I could tell she was dead. I could see the presence of lividity in her legs. I flicked off the light, then went through the kitchen and out the back door and called for Helen Payne."

While going over the apartment earlier the detectives had noticed an array of weapons in the laundry room. Boyle now inquired, "Tell us about the guns in the laundry room, if you will, doctor."

"Certainly. It's really a combination laundry and work-shop. I'm a gun collector, you see, and I make my own ammunition."

"How many weapons are in your collection, would you say?

"I have twenty-five—pistols, rifles, and shotguns in there."

"Let's go over your collection and see whether any of the guns is missing," Boyle suggested.

The trio went into the laundry/workshop and the two detectives stood by while the doctor examined his collection. "They're all here," he said. "All present and accounted for."

It was now nine o'clock at night. It had been a long day, and what's more, Boyle had to cancel his party. He still hadn't done any Christmas shopping, and he still had the damned toothache.

"I think we're going to call it a day," he said. "We're all pretty tired. You get a good night's sleep if you can, doc. We'll be back in the morning. Maybe by then you will have thought of something you can tell us that might be of help."

"I'll do my best, gentlemen. You have both been very considerate. Good-night."

What Branion really meant was good-bye. Detectives Boyle and McGreal were more than a little bit surprised the following morning to discover that Dr. Branion, along with his four-year-old son and thirteen-year-old daughter, had taken off for a ski vacation in Vail, Colorado.

"It's just two days before Christmas, the guy's wife's on a slab waiting to be cremated, and he hits the ski trails," Boyle remarked. "Just like that! You ask what I think? I think it's time we go out and talk to some of the good doctor's friends, Jim."

In talking to Mrs. Kentra in the adjoining apartment the detectives learned that the sharp sounds she heard, that could have been gunfire, occurred around 11:30 in the morning. It was only twenty minutes later that she heard Dr. Branion out on the back porch calling up to Helen Payne.

"Did you see the doctor's face? Did he appear to be distressed?"

"No, he did not," Mrs. Kentra affirmed.

The next stop was the nursery school. Dr. Branion had told police he arrived to pick up his son at 11:35 A.M. But an assistant teacher, Joyce Kelly, told the detectives she distinctly remembered seeing the doctor enter the building between 11:45 and 11:50. "Oh, this is so terrible. I couldn't believe it when I heard it on the radio," she added.

"Wait a minute. You say you saw him enter the club?" Boyle interrupted. "Wasn't his little boy waiting for him outside?"

"Oh, no. The boy was in the all-purpose waiting room, waiting for his daddy. I remember seeing his daddy help the boy on with his jacket." The detectives locked eyes for a brief moment, just long enough to register the teacher's comment. Dr. Branion had positively told them his son was "waiting out in front."

From the nursery school the doctor said he went to pick up Maxine Brown for lunch. The detectives followed the same trail, finding her in her office. "Yes, Dr. Branion telephoned me the previous evening, around ten or eleven o'clock, to make a luncheon engagement," she said.

"Did you have lunch with the doctor and his wife often?

"No. I've been working here at the real estate office since September, and this was the first time he'd ever called me," she said. "I thought it was rather strange."

As the detectives left the woman's office they compared notes. "It is strange, isn't it?" Boyle mused. "It's almost as though he wanted to make sure someone was with him, to give him an alibi before he discovered his wife's body."

"His time schedule doesn't add up, either," McGreal noted. "He says he picked up the kid at 11:35. The people at the nursery say it was ten or fifteen minutes later than that. And then this thing about him peeking through his fingers last night, when he's supposedly bawling his eyes out . . ."

The two went back to headquarters and typed up reports of the interviews while everything was still fresh in their minds. The following day, Christmas Eve, they talked to Dr. Helen Payne, the third-floor neighbor who had pronounced Donna Branion dead.

"As I understand it, Dr. Branion said he knew his wife was dead because of the lividity in her legs," Boyle said.

"He couldn't have. The blood does not settle for at least an hour or two after death," the woman doctor replied. "There was no lividity present when I examined the body. She couldn't have been dead an hour."

Another discrepancy. If lividity had set in, as Dr. Branion insisted, his wife would have had to have been slain while he was still at the hospital. But Dr. Payne, who said she pronounced the murder victim dead at 12:20 P.M., said she had not been dead an hour.

While Dr. Branion skied, police worked. During the week between Christmas and New Year's the results of various tests came back one by one.

The medical report confirmed that Donna Branion had died within the hour that her body was discovered. And a firearms expert from the crime lab, Burt Nielsen, told Boyle, "Your lady was knocked off with a James Bond gun."

"How so?" the detective asked.

"Well, the four slugs had a class characteristic of .380 caliber automatic ammunition with six lands and grooves with a right twist. This is characteristic of bullets fired by a Walther PPK and a few other weapons. But the cartridge casings had markings on their bases which signified that the weapon used to fire them had a loading indicator," Nielsen explained.

"Only one weapon which fires .380 ammo has both a loading indicator and leaves six lands and grooves to the right on the slugs. That's the Walther PPK—the same kind of pistol James Bond uses in the movies."

"What kind of person would have a James Bond weapon?" Boyle asked. "That sounds like a collector's item."

"Well, you said your doctor was a gun collector, didn't you?" responded the weapons expert.

"He sure as hell is," replied Boyle. "He even makes his own ammo."

Before ringing out the old year the detectives picked up one more juicy tidbit of info. Dr. Branion was a known philanderer with a bevy of girlfriends. From traffic police it was learned that Branion had been stopped for speeding several times, once for going 100 miles an hour, and on each occasion was accompanied by a beautiful woman—not his wife. His most recent companion had been his own nurse, Shirley Hudson.

The detectives also learned that Branion had asked his wife for a divorce just before Christmas, and that she had refused.

Monday, January 1, 1968: Back from furlough, Mannion rejoined his partner, Boyle, and together they sought out nurse Hudson in her high-rise apartment in the Hyde Park neighborhood near the University of Chicago.

Branion's nurse freely admitted a relationship with the doctor that was something less than professional. "In fact," she related, "we just got back from a skiing trip to Colorado." Incredibly, Dr. Branion had taken his girlfriend along on the junket to Vail with the kids, while their mother's bullet-riddled body was still being examined in the county morgue.

Another woman whose name had been linked to Dr. Branion's through gossip was Chicago society figure Anicetra Souza. She was next on the detectives' list. She explained that she and Branion had boarded their horses together in Indiana, but denied that her friendship with the doctor was anything more than equestrian.

"Well, I think we've got ourselves a red-hot suspect," Boyle told his partner. "The question is, could he have pulled it off?"

"There's only one way to find out," Mannion said. "We've got his time schedule. Let's see if it checks out."

Using a gold Swiss stopwatch belonging to Boyle's father, a former federal prosecutor, the two police detectives set out to retrace the route Branion said he drove on the day of the murder. Starting at square one, they left the Ida Mae Scott Hospital at Fifty-first and Prairie, drove past the Branion apartment on Woodlawn nine blocks away, then over to the nursery school on Kenwood, and from there to the insurance office where Maxine Brown worked on East Fifty-third Street. They then drove back to the Branion apartment.

The thorough detectives didn't do it just once. That could have been a fluke. Taking turns at the wheel, they drove the route six different times, in varying weather conditions, at the legal speed limit of thirty miles an hour. Then they tabulated the results.

The gold stopwatch had uncovered a fifteen-minute gap in Dr. Branion's timetable. "He sure as hell could have done it," Boyle said. "Our tests show that it would have been possible to drive straight to the apartment from the hospital, execute a well-planned murder, and then pick up the boy. And there was still time to stop by Mrs. Brown's office and return to 'discover' the body."

"We've given him a motive, and we've proved the doc could have done it in the time frame we now have," Mannion agreed. "How about the murder weapon? Do you supposed it could be in the doc's gun collection?"

"Let's ask him," quipped Boyle. They did just that. They called Dr. Branion and asked, "Do you have any weapons in your collection capable of firing .380 bullets?"

"Why, yes, I do own such a gun—a .380 Hi Standard pistol," he said. "Why do you ask?"

"Would you have any objections, doctor, if we ran it through some tests?"

"Ballistics tests? Not at all. Stop by and pick it up."

It was too easy. The detectives turned the gun over to a weapons expert at the crime lab who fired some test shots and compared the slugs to the murder bullets. "It's the same caliber, fellas, but not the same gun. No cigar."

In returning the .380 Hi Standard pistol, Boyle and Mannion asked Dr. Branion whether he also owned a Walther PPK, the so-called "James Bond automatic." The doctor replied, "No. I have never owned such a weapon as that."

The evidence against the gynecologist was convincing, but circumstantial. The detectives decided they had to move fast, however, since Branion was now aware they were trying to build a case and he might fly the coop.

They laid it all out before Thomas Hett, chief of the Cook County state's attorney's Criminal Division. "We're not done yet, Tom, but this is what we've got on the suspect so far," Boyle explained.

"You guys ought to be lawyers," said Hett, after poring over everything the detectives had put together, including the test runs with the stopwatch. "I'm going to authorize a warrant charging Dr. John Marshall Branion, Jr., with his wife's murder."

Boyle and Mannion served the warrant themselves, on January 22, 1968, exactly one month to the day after Donna Branion's body was discovered on the utility room floor. They found Branion at the hospital, where they confronted him as he emerged from the operating room, wearing his green surgical gown.

"Doctor, you are under arrest for murder," Mannion declared.

"What? Whose murder?" the astonished Branion asked.

"Your wife's."

The arrest of a suspect usually signals the end of a police investigation, but for Mannion and Boyle there were still a few miles to travel. For one thing, they still didn't have the murder weapon. Linking that particular gun to Dr. Branion now became a matter of top priority.

A tipster told police Branion had disposed of a weapon in the icy waters of Lake Michigan. The snitch could have been a crank, or someone with a grudge against the doctor, or maybe a jealous husband. The story fit right into the pattern of events, however.

If Branion had ditched the murder gun in the lake it might never be recovered. The floor of Lake Michigan off Chicago is probably dotted with hundreds of them. But there were still the bullets it had fired. The detectives paid another visit to the crime lab for a crash course in ballistics. From lab technicians they learned that "red dots" on the primers of the four recovered shell casings from the murder scene were common characteristics of German-made GECO ammunition. And this was the type of ammo used in the Walther PPK.

With Branion temporarily in custody pending a bail bond hearing, Mannion and Boyle returned to the apartment with a search warrant authorizing the seizure of any GECO type ammunition. The room where Donna Branion had fallen mortally wounded a month before was deathly quiet, save for the detectives' footsteps across the tile floor. The hands on the wall clock pointed to 7:00 P.M.

"Let's start with the doc's workshop in the laundry room," Boyle suggested. "This time, we know what we're looking for."

And they found it. The detectives couldn't believe their own luck. In a closet near the doctor's work bench was a box of GECO .380 ammunition with precisely four bullets missing.

"And look at this, Mike," Mannion said, holding up a box that had contained a Walther PPK. "The doc told us he never owned any such gun."

The box was empty, except for a paper target—but these cops were on a roll. Those meticulous Germans who had manufactured the Walther PPK that came in the box had included the gun's serial number on the target sheet, giving the detectives the number of the suspect murder weapon: 188274.

"The name of the importer who distributed the gun is on the box," Mannion noted. "Joseph Galeff & Sons, New York City."

"I think we're on our way," smiled Boyle. "Records have to be kept of gun sales."

A telephone call to the New York importing firm told the detectives that Walther PPK No. 188274 had been sold by Galeff & Sons to Bell's Gun Shop in the western Chicago suburb of Bellwood. A check of the store's records showed that the specific weapon in question had been purchased two months before the murder by James Hooks, who gave an address on Martin Luther King Drive.

From an earlier phase of their investigation, the detectives knew Hooks was a close friend of Dr. Branion. They wasted no time in driving to his South Side home. "Have you ever owned an automatic pistol, Mr. Hooks?" Boyle asked.

"No, I don't like automatics," Hooks said nervously. In fact, the presence of the two detectives so flustered him that he excused himself five times "for a glass of water" while they were attempting to pin him down.

"Look here, Mr. Hooks. We know you bought an automatic pistol, a .380 Walther PPK, as a matter of fact. Here's your name on the purchase order from Bell's gun shop," Mannion pressed. "We have the purchase order right here."

Hooks blanched, and stuttered, "Oh, yeah. I forgot."

The detectives told him they were willing to overlook the fact that an otherwise intelligent appearing person had "forgot" the purchase of the highly unusual James Bond-style gun just three months earlier. "What we really want to know is, where is that gun right now?" Boyle emphasized.

"Ahhh, I don't have it."

"If you don't have it, Mr. Hooks, where is it? What did you do with it?

"I gave it as a birthday gift to Dr. Branion."

Now the hunt was over. Through pit-bull detective work Mannion and Boyle, putting in countless hours of their own time, had finally placed the Walther PPK in Dr. Branion's gunhand. And the Walther's unique cocking indicator had left its telltale mark on each of the murder shells as it fed them from the clip into the firing chamber. The exclusive Walther "signature," visible to ballistics experts only under a microscope, had spoiled the perfect crime. There had been no prowler. The husband did it.

The chagrined Dr. Branion chose not to testify at his own trial. He denied nothing. A Criminal Court jury, after hearing the evidence amassed by Boyle, Mannion, and his stand-in, McGreal, deliberated seven hours before finding the Swiss-educated physician guilty of his wife's murder.

Judge Reginald J. Holzer, Jr., sentenced the defendant to not less than twenty, or more than thirty years in prison.

End of story? Hardly. Remember, this happened in Chicago. Dr. Branion, who had been free on bail pending trial, spent only a few days in jail before being released again on an appeal bond. Few, indeed, are accused murderers who are permitted to roam the streets free on bond while awaiting trial; and even fewer are those allowed to remain free on bond after being found guilty.

In Chicago it is what is known as "clout." Judge Holzer consented to an "in chambers" agreement to set a ridiculously low $5,000 appeal bond—pocket money for a man of Branion's means—and he walked out of jail after posting the customary 10 per cent.

Next, Branion petitioned the court for permission to move to Cheyenne, Wyoming. State's Attorney Edward V. Hanrahan vigorously opposed the move and requested that Branion's bond be revoked. But Illinois Supreme Court Justice Daniel P. Ward, a former prosecutor who once worked in the same building as Branion's father, allowed the move. A red-faced Hanrahan angrily denounced the fact that Branion was not in jail like other convicted killers as "a disgraceful example of special privileges granted by the Illinois Supreme Court."

So Dr. Branion waved bye-bye to Chicago and headed out west again, just like he did with Shirley Hudson when his slain wife was still laid out on a slab in the morgue. He took nurse Hudson with him this time, too, and married her once they got to Cheyenne. Police, who were keeping tabs on his moves, needed a scorecard for what would happen next.

While still free on appeal bond Branion divorced Shirley Hudson Branion and married Anicetra Souza, the Chicago socialite who had earlier told police she and the doctor were friends, and nothing more. Then he divorced Anicetra, remarried Shirley, divorced Shirley a second time, and remarried Anicetra. The marital box scores: Four marriages and three divorces with two women in just two years time, while appealing the conviction for killing yet another wife.

During his two years in Wyoming Branion was so busy getting married and divorced that he never did open a physician's office, as he promised the court he would do if permitted to leave Illinois. Nor did he find any other type of employment. He obviously did not lack for money. Then, in June 1970 he packed his bags and flew with Shirley, his wife of the moment, to Los Angeles.

"He blew Cheyenne without notifying us," Robert Novelle, chief of the Criminal Appeals Division of the State's Attorney's office, complained. Efforts were renewed to have Branion's bond revoked, but again the prosecution's request was denied. If you have clout, flaunt it.

The Illinois Supreme Court subsequently affirmed Branion's conviction by a six-to-one vote, ruling that the state had "woven a web of strong circumstantial evidence, strong enought to support a conviction."

But still the elusive gynecologist thumbed his nose at the law, remaining free on the paltry $5,000 bond while his case went to the U.S. Supreme Court. By December 1970 he'd had enough of the West Coast and flew to New York, where authorities were able to pinpoint him on the third anniversary of his wife's death. He'd taken a job as a business agent for the slain Donna's cousin, Oscar Brown, Jr.

That was the last they'd heard of the man in whom Judge Daniel P. Ward had placed his trust.

The highest court in the land ultimately refused to consider Dr. Branion's case and he was finally ordered to surrender in Criminal Court in Chicago on June 25, 1971, but by then he was long gone. His lawyer, Howard T. Savage, sheepishly told the court, "I do not know where my client is."

"I just sensed this guy was going to do this," fumed prosecutor Novelle. "What the hell did he have to lose? We'll find him sooner or later, but I think he'll give us a merry chase."

Branion's bond was forfeited and a warrant was issued charging the convicted killer with unlawful flight to avoid incarceration. The warrant was turned over to the sheriff's office to serve, but by now John Marshall Branion, Jr., was off to a running start.

How he got a passport no one knows, but he next surfaced in Khartoum, in the Sudan, where he was detained by African authorities in 1972 for carrying forged identity papers. By the time American police learned that the fugitive was in custody, however, Branion had again given the law the slip.

Interpol, the global police intelligence agency, finally traced him to Uganda, where he turned up—incredibly—as personal physician to the mad dictator, Idi Amin. One report relayed to investigators was that Dr. Branion was one of the few medical men available to treat wounded Ugandan soldiers after the 1976 Israeli commando raid at Entebbe.

The ruthless Amin had offered the madcap medico sanctuary, but Interpol files indicate it was anything but comfortable. Most of Branion's tenure in Uganda, from 1972 until Amin's ouster in 1979, was spent under "house arrest."

He fled with the crazed Amin when his dictatorship was overthrown, and was next reported in South Africa. But he again faded from sight.

Then, after a dozen years on the run while evading police in his intercontinental game of cat and mouse, the convicted wife slayer from Chicago was suddenly reported in far-off Malaysia. According to Interpol, he flew there from South Africa, and quickly lost himself in the racial melting pot of Kuala Lampur, under an assumed name.

Efforts to bring about his return to the United States were revived, but if he had indeed taken up residency in the former British possession, Malaysian authorities said they were unable to find him. It appeared that the doctor had finally found the prescription for anonymity.

Then, unexpectedly, his clandestine existence came to an abrupt end on September 27, 1983, when Ugandan officials revealed that the fugitive was back in the East African nation where he'd been taken into custody by police.

American authorities were advised, "If you want to get him, we are expelling him and you can pick him up at the airport."

Cook County Sheriff's Investigators Michael Blackburn and Albert Roth were on the scene at Entebbe on Wednesday, October 13, when Branion, who had been using the Ugandan name of Busingye, meaning "peace," was officially booted out of the country. As the former Chicago physician was escorted apprehensively to a waiting airliner Blackburn appeared at the hatch and greeted him: "Good morning, doctor. We have a warrant for your arrest."

Branion was flown nonstop to London, where he and his lawmen escorts boarded a TWA flight for Chicago, arriving the following day. On Wednesday, November 2, 1983, the fifty-seven-year-old globe-trotter was brought in manacles before Criminal Court Judge Maurice Pompey who ended the twelve-year odyssey with a rap of the gavel. He ordered that Branion be transported to the state penitentiary to begin serving his twenty-to-thirty-year sentence without further delay.

EPILOGUE

Three years after Branion was sent to prison, Judge Reginald Holzer, who had brazenly set the paltry $5,000 bond that allowed him to flee the country after his conviction, was himself convicted in federal court on charges of mail fraud, extortion, and racketeering. The judge was sentenced to eighteen years in a federal penitentiary. In 1987 documents filed in U.S. District Court in Chicago revealed that Holzer had accepted a $10,000 bribe to release the convicted Branion on bond, and solicited an additional $10,000 bribe from Branion's brother-in-law to overturn the conviction and free Branion completely. The judge reneged on the second offer after prosecutors got wind of the scheme.

Later that same year Judge Paul E. Plunkett in federal court ruled that Branion was not an innocent man and denied a new appeal by the disgraced doctor to be released from prison.

Branion served seven years of his sentence in the state prison facility at Dixon, Illinois, before Governor James Thompson—in the wake of pressure from civil rights activists—commuted his sentence on August 7, 1990, because of failing health. Dr. Branion, who suffered from a brain tumor and a heart ailment, died one month later in the University of Illinois Hospital at the age of sixty-four.

CHAPTER 8

DEATH ON A KING-SIZED BED

The idyllic village of Long Grove, with its picturesque wooden covered bridge at one end of town and the old grist mill with its water wheel anchoring the other end of the street, was settled in the early 1800s by German farmers who called it Mutterholz—the mother woods—because the northern Illinois countryside reminded them of the Saar Valley.

The devout Rhinelanders spoke Plattedeutsch, right up to World War I, as they toiled in their nearby fields. From time to time they came to the crossroads, where the Village Tavern still stands, to buy their supplies, weigh their milk, make their cheese, shoe their horses, and exchange the news of the day. On a hill just beyond the covered bridge they built a small church where services are conducted to this very day.

The quaint old village, a scant thirty miles northwest of Chicago, is right out of the pages of Washington Irving. And like his Rip Van Winkle, the tiny community fell into a deep and timeless sleep.

Through the War to End All Wars, the Roaring Twenties, the Great Depression and the stark days of World War II, its weathered clapboard buildings stood untouched as the rest of America went soaring by into the Space Age.

What a marvelous setting for a cruel and diabolical murder!

It was in the late 1940s that several women breathed new life into the community by opening a modest antique shop in one of the historic old buildings. Other shops followed, and Long Grove slowly awakened to the twentieth century.

The architecture of the town was faithfully preserved, but the old granary, blacksmith shop, general store, and cheese factory took on such trendy names as The Spicery, The Needle Case, the Coffee Bean LTD, and Crock N' Block.

Long Grove became the "in" place to live for wealthy Chicago suburbanites, with most of its 1,400 inhabitants putting up sprawling ranch-style homes on large multi-acre lots on the outskirts of town. The newest development was Country Club Estates, a luxury subdivision of white, brown, and tan brick homes and rustic wooden street signs, about two miles from the old covered bridge.

It was in Country Club Estates that boyish-looking Larry Weaver and his striking, athletic wife, Nola Jean, decided to settle as America moved into the mid 1970s.

They had grown up together in the little town of Camden, Arkansas, where doe-eyed Nola Jean was a cheerleader and member of the homecoming court at high school. Larry, two years her senior, played both basketball and football for the home team.

Nola Jean moved to California with her parents after graduation in 1961, but returned the following year to walk down the aisle with Larry after he bombarded the West Coast with love letters and phone calls.

They both chose academic careers, and by the time he was twenty-four years old, Larry had become superintendent of schools in the Arkansas town of Smackover, population 2,058. A few years later the couple moved to Chicago so Larry could work on his doctorate at Loyola University.

He landed a job as principal of Cooper Junior High in the northwest suburb of Buffalo Grove, and the slender, good-looking Nola Jean, with her curly brown hair, became a physical education teacher at nearby Elk Grove High School. In 1975, the thirty-three-year-old Weaver was elevated to assistant superintendent for administrative services for the Buffalo Grove-Wheeling School District.

The attractive young couple's future looked bright indeed. Weaver's father had sold his trucking business down south and divided a $104,000 nut between his son and daughter, Patricia. On top of Larry's $52,000 share, his father gave him another $34,000. With this $86,000 nest egg Larry and Nola Jean had no trouble purchasing a $100,000 ranch home with a sweeping semi-circular drive at Lincoln Avenue and Checker Road. They moved into their new home in Long Grove in 1976.

The Weavers knew they had "arrived" when their new neighbors in Country Club Estates invited them to the annual party at the exclusive Hillcrest Country Club.

"They're such dedicated people. I've never heard a cross word between them," one of their friends remarked. Larry was known as a taskmaster at school for his industrious ways, and Nola Jean, who taught dancing and girls volleyball, soon developed a reputation as "that nice gym teacher." She had always been a church-goer, and now both she and Larry took an active part in Long Grove community life, which centered around the church where their eight-year-old daughter, Tiffany, attended Sunday school.

It would seem that the tight little family had it made.

On Sunday night, December 4, 1977, just days short of Larry's thirty-sixth birthday, he and his thirty-four-year-old wife, along with little Tiffany, were nestled snugly in their new home. A light snow covered the ground outside. Their two dogs dozed lazily in front of the hearth.

Most of their neighbors kept dogs for security reasons. There was no police protection in the unincorporated community, and the sheriff's office in Waukegan was a good fifteen miles away. Weaver also kept a .22 caliber target rifle in the house.

Just two days earlier the Weavers' next door neighbor, Earl Goodfellow, had seen two suspicious-looking men in a green pickup truck driving slowly by the Weaver house as though they might have been casing it. When they spotted Goodfellow they hit the gas and sped away.

Goodfellow told his wife, Cindy, "I think we ought to ask the sheriff's office to send a patrol car through here from time to time. Burglars know people have a lot of Christmas presents piling up in their homes this time of year and they cruise around, looking for places where somebody might be away during the day, like the Weavers."

The neighborhood was as quiet as a Christmas card this Sunday night, however. At 9:30, after telling Tiffany a story, Weaver patted her on the bottom, kissed her good-night, and told her to scamper off to bed. Nola Jean tucked her under the covers, turned off the light, and gently closed the door.

After watching the ten o'clock news the Weavers, too, retired for the night. Monday was a working day for both of them.

Shortly after 1:00 A.M. the Goodfellows were awakened by a frantic pounding on their front door. Goodfellow pulled on his robe and slippers, flipped on the porch light, and peered cautiously outside to investigate.

Nola Jean, clad only in her nightgown, was standing in the snow, holding the sleepy-eyed Tiffany, who was wrapped in a quilt, in her arms. The Weavers' two dogs stood protectively at Nola Jean's side.

She screamed hysterically as Goodfellow swung open the door. "Call the police and fire department! There's been some shooting and a fire!"

"Come in, Nola. Hurry inside," he ordered, holding the door ajar. Then, calling to his wife to get up, Goodfellow grabbed the telephone. The call to the sheriff's office, which alerted the Long Grove Volunteer Fire Department, was recorded in 1:26 A.M.

Fireman Melvin Towner, a driver for the department, was still awake when the alarm phone rang in the bedroom of his home. He had just turned in from the last of six fire calls the department had answered that wintry night.

As Towner headed for the stationhouse at the town's crossroads for the seventh time, he radioed his dispatcher for details. "Burglary and fire reported at 99 Lincoln Avenue. Repeat—99 Lincoln Avenue. That's all we have at the moment."

Towner screeched up to the station, cranked up the fire truck and had it out in the street ready to roll as fellow firefighters clambered aboard. The Weaver house was totally dark and there were no outward signs of smoke or fire as Towner wheeled his rig into the circular drive.

A squad car, its red flashing lights announcing its presence, pulled in quickly behind the fire engine and two sheriff's deputies bounded out, shotguns at the ready.

"Stay with your rig," they commanded. "There's supposed to be two guys with guns inside there. Nobody goes in until some backup gets here."

The lawmen stationed themselves so that one could watch the front of the house while the other had a clear shot at the rear. They could hear more sirens wailing in the distance and they didn't have long to wait before four more squads converged on the driveway, turning the sleepy winter scene into a disco of flashing red and white lights with the static of police and fire radios crackling in the background.

The Long Grove volunteers stood by apprehensively as the heavily bundled police officers edged cautiously toward the darkened home, flashlights and weapons in hand. The sliding glass patio door at the rear of the house, from which Nola Jean had fled with Tiffany and the two guard dogs, was slightly ajar. A deputy quietly rolled it open.

The acrid smell of smoke hit their nostrils as the lawmen slipped into the house and proceeded to check it out, room by room. The door to the child's bedroom was open, but the door to the master bedroom was closed, and felt warm to the touch.

"Okay! Firemen inside on the double," a lawman beckoned from the front door of the home. After being quickly briefed on the situation the volunteers smashed a window from the outside to ventilate the bedroom and pushed open the door.

A king-sized bed—the eye of the blaze—loomed through the smoky darkness as a glowing, smoldering square in the center of the room. It hissed and steamed angrily when the firefighters turned their hand extinguishers onto it.

Poking their torches about the room, police and firemen observed that the fire and heat had caused considerable charring and melting of various objects, and had caused the ceiling tiles to loosen and fall to the floor.

But for the moment all eyes were riveted on the extensively damaged bed itself, and the grim object it now displayed. Lying on the left-hand side of the bed, clad in the remnants of his pajamas, was Larry Weaver. His face was partially burned away, causing his teeth to glisten in an eerie, taunting smile from his blackened skull.

"Call Mickey Babcox, and until he gets here don't anybody touch anything," ordered Sheriff's Lieutenant Eugene McGaughey, who assumed command of the situation. "And that includes the phone. There could be prints on it."

One of his men sprinted to his squad car in the driveway and radioed the dispatcher in Waukegan to "get on the horn and wake up Babcox."

Lake County Coroner Robert H. Babcox made it from his home in Grayslake to Long Grove, a straight shot down Illinois Route 83, in ten minutes. One of the best-known people in the county, Mickey Babcox was a former high school football star, and had been a deputy sheriff himself before being elected coroner in 1952 at the age of twenty-four. He was also a licensed mortician.

Because of his police background, and the professionalism of his office, which employed former lawmen as investigators, the fifty-year-old coroner had an excellent rapport with law enforcement agencies throughout the area.

"Well, what have we got here, Gene?" the hulking Babcox asked, striding past police lines and into the now brightly lit Weaver home. There wasn't a type of death he hadn't investigated in the past twenty-five years, and he was becoming a bit jaded.

"Looks like a home invasion, Mick," answered Mc-Gaughey, leading the way to the bedroom. "The dead guy seems to be Larry Weaver, a local school official. His wife and kid are next door at the neighbors'. She's giving a statement to the boys right now, but she's pretty broken up."

"Can't say that I blame her," mused Babcox, bending over the grisly remains on the mattress as he inhaled the odor of burnt flesh. "Poor devil's burned beyond recognition—over 90 per cent of his body it looks like. We're gonna have to do an autopsy to find out for sure what killed him. Could have been the fire; could have been something else, eh Gene?"

"The wife said he was shot, but you can't tell by looking at what's left of him," McGaughey volunteered.

"That's for sure. Let's go talk to her. Which way?"

Nola Jean was sitting on a couch in her neighbors' living room, nervously twisting a damp handkerchief in her hands. Because of her distraught condition she was able to provide only sketchy details as to what had transpired.

"We were awakened about 1:00 A.M. by the dogs barking. Larry got up to investigate. He came back and whispered that there were two people in the house. 'Honey, get the gun and make a run for it,' he told me."

Nola Jean tried to flee but was accosted just outside the door by two men, who wrested the .22 rifle away from her. They then called into the house and ordered her husband to surrender, she said. When Weaver appeared, with his hands up, they roughly shoved the woman back inside, and began demanding money.

She said the invaders insisted that Weaver turn over to them $750,000 they said he obtained from a hospital. They had apparently mistaken him for some doctor. "Larry said he didn't have that kind of money, but they wouldn't believe him," his new widow sobbed.

After some discussion, she said, Weaver told the men he knew where he could lay his hands on some cash. The older of the two held Nola Jean at bay in the house while his younger partner left and drove off with Weaver, who was still in his pajamas.

"When you say 'older' or 'younger' man, could you describe them for us?" McGaughey asked.

"They were both white men," she responded. "One of them looked like he was in his forties, and the younger one I'd say was in his middle twenties. They were wearing gloves, both of them, and one of them was carrying a gun."

She said that about fifteen minutes after Weaver and the younger man left they returned, and the intruder told his companion, "He's lying." The younger bandit roughly herded Weaver into the bedroom. "Then I heard one shot," she said. The man then raced into the room where she was being held and shouted to his companion, "We'd better get out of here!"

As soon as the men fled she said she awakened Tiffany and ran to the Goodfellow home. "You know the rest," she sobbed.

Sheriff's investigators checked the two cars parked in the attached garage and found one of the hoods still warm. It had, indeed, been driven recently.

Babcox ordered Weaver's body removed to the Lake County Morgue in Waukegan, and directed that the home be sealed pending further investigation. Nola Jean and her daughter, along with their two dogs, spent the remainder of the night with the Goodfellows.

An autopsy on Larry Weaver was performed first thing in the morning after his identity was positively established through dental charts. People have been known to fake their own deaths for insurance purposes, but that was not the case here.

The postmortem examination revealed that Weaver had been shot twice in the head with a small caliber weapon. After he was dead his body was doused with a flammable liquid and set afire.

While the coroner's pathologist was examining Weaver's charred body in Waukegan, six detectives under the direction of Louis A. Harceg, chief investigator for Sheriff E. J. "Chick"

LaMagdeline, returned to the Weaver home. Harceg and Detective Kurt Proschwitz had been among the first investigators on the scene the night before.

They definitely established that there was no evidence of a forced entry. Every window and door in the house was locked from the inside except the patio door through which Nola Jean and her daughter had fled. Possibly they had carelessly left it unlocked, living in a relatively crime-free area.

Nothing in the house appeared to have been disturbed. There was no evidence of ransacking. Even the papers on Weaver's desk were in neat piles. If the intruders were after money, they were evidently satisfied none was hidden in the home.

State Arson Investigator Harry Schaefer determined that some type of accelerant had been spread on the right side of the oversize double bed and ignited. The condition of the bed itself, and an unburned spot where the body had lain, indicated that Weaver was *under* the covers when he was set afire.

Nola Jean, meanwhile, had taken little Tiffany and gone to the home of relatives. Harceg and Proschwitz drove over to talk to her in hopes that she had regained her composure enough to provide them with a better description of the killers.

She said the older suspect was a stocky man about forty, and five-feet-ten to five-feet-eleven-inches tall. He had shaggy light brown hair, cut short, dark eyes, and a "weathered" complexion. As best she could recall, the man was wearing dark trousers, and a fingertip-length coat with flap pockets. "It was a canvas coat with a green splotchy design," she said, indicting it might have been a camouflage hunting jacket.

"Oh, yes," she remembered. "He was the man with the gun in his right hand. He was wearing dark leather gloves with short fingers."

The other man appeared to be in his late twenties. She said he was about six-feet-two-inches tall, of medium muscular build, and had dark blond to light brown shoulder-length hair with reddish streaks. "He had bushy eyebrows, and acne scars on his face," she added. He wore a fingertip-length dark blue or black coat and dark blue or black trousers, and had a pullover sweater under his jacket. He wore knit gloves, dark blue or black around the hands but of lighter material around the fingers.

The younger man, the apparent killer who had yelled, "We'd better get out of here," spoke with a Southern accent.

Nola Jean had been remarkably observant. Her detailed descriptions enabled sheriff's artists to prepare composite drawings of the murder suspects, which were distributed to police agencies throughout the area the following day.

Armed with copies of the drawings, a dozen detectives were assigned to question friends, neighbors, and relatives of the Weavers in an effort to determine whether there was anything in the couple's background that might have precipitated the killing—although it appeared now to have been a case of mistaken identity.

The murder victim seemed to have led an impeccable existence. "He was a very hard working, competent person. He moved up through the ranks of our district," Superintendent Kenneth Gill told investigators. "Larry challenged people to do their very best all along."

Nola Jean, meanwhile, accompanied several sheriff's men to Libertyville, where she voluntarily submitted to a lie detector test to remove herself from suspicion. The test proved inconclusive, and she surprised her questioners by refusing to take a second examination, on advice of her attorneys. "We wanted to retest her to clear up some discrepancies, but her lawyers took her off the machine," the polygraph examiner told investigators.

State's Attorney Dennis P. Ryan entered the case on the third day, Wednesday, December 7. He assigned the chief of his criminal division, thirty-year-old Ann Regan, to coordinate the sheriff's investigation. Regan immediately went to the Weaver home with Harceg to familiarize herself with the surroundings.

While she examined the scene of the crime, Harceg's men fanned out through the spacious yard and the acres of cultivated fields across the street. They were looking for Weaver's missing .22 rifle. They were also hopeful of recovering any spent bullets Weaver might have used in target practice, to compare with the two slugs found in the victim's head.

Services for Weaver were held that same morning in the First Baptist Church in neighboring Palatine. His remains were then shipped to Magnolia, Arkansas, where his mother lived, for burial. Nola Jean accompanied the body, and spent the next week there with her mother-in-law, Vida Weaver.

During her absence investigators searched in vain for the stocky murder suspect and his acne-faced companion. Detectives talking to close friends of the Weavers, however, were slowly piecing together a seamy story of sex on the sly and unspeakable family secrets.

When Nola Jean returned home to pick up the pieces of her shattered life she left eight-year-old Tiffany behind with the child's grandmother. "I'll pick her up when I come back to spend the Christmas holidays," she told her husband's mother. "It's best that she's away from things up north for awhile."

The first day back at work in Elk Grove High, where she had taught for nearly eight years, was the most difficult for Nola Jean, but she decided to face her colleagues and students head-on on Friday, December 16. Her first day back to school also proved to be her last.

The morning session went surprisingly well. Shortly after noon, while she was conducting her modern dance class, she was summoned to the nurse's office. A rejuvenated Nola Jean, wearing a red jogging suit, bounded into the room and flashed a greeting smile at the two sheriff's investigators who'd been waiting for her.

"You gentlemen wanted to talk to me?"

"No, Mrs. Weaver. We've come to take you back to Waukegan with us."

"Have you found the men who . . ."

"We don't think there were any men, Mrs. Weaver. We have a warrant for your arrest, charging you with the murder of your husband, Larry Weaver. Anything you say from here on out may be used against you."

Nola Jean's sexy jaw dropped as she looked at the two deputies in utter astonishment. They weren't kidding! She was handcuffed and led quickly from the school in her red jogging togs as stunned students and faculty members looked on. It was Larry Weaver's thirty-sixth birthday.

The widow Weaver was speechless on the short ride to the county seat. She was taken directly to the courthouse where she was arraigned before Circuit Judge Charles F. Scott, who set bond at $100,000. She had no trouble coming up with the 10 per cent in cash required by Illinois law. She left the courthouse in a daze, repeating over and over, "I didn't do it. I just didn't do it."

But Sheriff LaMagdeline and Prosecutor Ryan felt otherwise. There were no two mystery men as far as they were concerned. Nola Jean had concocted the story after hearing her neighbors tell of the two strangers driving suspiciously past the house several days earlier.

"Mrs. Weaver's arrest was based on the fact that physical evidence found at the scene contradicted statements she gave to investigators," said LaMagdeline, who had played low-key during the ten-day homicide probe. Although entirely circumstantial, his men had built a convincing case against the attractive young schoolmarm.

She had been a suspect from the very beginning, when Coroner Babcox pointed out that Larry Weaver's nearly incinerated body had been lying under the covers, indicating he'd been asleep when the two bullets were fired into his temple.

And then there was the condition of the house. No forced entry. No sign of tampering with doors or windows. No ransacking. No signs of a struggle.

What capped it was Nola Jean's story about Larry, in his pajamas, driving off somewhere with the six-foot-two-inch killer in search of money. Detectives checked both cars in the Weaver garage while Nola Jean was next door talking to Babcox and McGaughey. Although the garage was unheated, the engine block of Nola Jean's blue car was warm, indicating it had been driven a short time before. Larry Weaver's car was ice cold.

Could Larry have taken his wife's car when he went off with one of the killers? Investigators did not overlook that possibility. In addition to finding water from freshly melted snow on the floor mat in the front seat of Nola Jean's car they noted that the driver's seat was in the full-forward position. Larry Weaver stood six feet tall. He would hardly have driven with the seat full-forward, especially in company of a six-foot-two-inch stranger.

Furthermore, Nola Jean's purse and car keys were found on a counter beside the door leading to the garage where she had apparently dropped them after disposing of the .22 rifle. The gun was never found.

And why did Nola Jean's lawyer suddenly refuse to let her take a second lie detector test? There were a few discrepancies in her stories that authorities wanted to clear up. On the night of the murder, for example, she said that after hearing gunfire in the bedroom she awakened Tiffany and fled to the neighbor's home. On a subsequent occasion she told investigators one of the invaders held her and Tiffany in one room while the man with the gun marched her husband into the bedroom and executed him.

Finally there was the thing that caused the sheriff and coroner to become skeptical of her story in the first place. There were no footprints in the new-fallen snow, other than Nola Jean's and those of the dogs leading to the house next door.

"The fellows from the crime lab did an excellent piece of work putting it all together," LaMagdeline's chief deputy, Robert Corder, one-time police chief of Zion, Illinois, declared.

But the question remained: Why would anyone want to kill Larry Weaver, the epitome of virtue in the eyes of his friends? In trying to establish a motive for the killing investigators uncovered a bonanza. The more friends and relatives they talked to while Nola Jean was playing the grieving widow's role down Arkansas way the more it became apparent that family life was something less than utopian under the Weaver roof.

Investigators learned that Nola Jean was having extramarital affairs with at least two men—her boss at Elk Grove High School and her own brother-in-law.

It was no secret among her students that the vivacious young gym teacher had something going with athletic director Robert Tipsword. One student told investigators she had surprised the couple on a wrestling mat, and they weren't practicing arm locks.

The sheriff's office had put a tail on Nola Jean after the murder, and she seemed blissfully unaware that Proschwitz was seated behind her on the plane when she accompanied her husband's body back to Arkansas. Tipsword flew with her, Proschwitz reported, and the two of them "nuzzled" in their seat on the flight to bury Larry.

A female friend of Weaver's told police he had confided in her about his wife's affair with yet another man, Dennis Johnston, the husband of Nola Jean's younger sister, Judy. Johnston, a divinity student no less, and his wife were living in the Weaver home at the time.

About six weeks before he was murdered Weaver told the friend he and Nola Jean had argued violently over her involvement with her sister's husband. Weaver said he was so angry he beat Nola Jean, and she retaliated by getting his .22 from the bedroom closet. A shot was fired into the ceiling as they struggled over the rifle.

Several weeks later, police learned, Nola Jean purchased ammunition for the weapon while visiting in Arkansas.

Detectives also were told that Weaver, frustrated and disgusted over his wife's personal habits, had taken over most of the household chores. In searching the home investigators found angry notes in Weaver's hand asking about Nola Jean's sexual partners, and her responses. There were also erotic poems about sexual encounters with women found among Nola Jean's possessions.

Furthermore, investigators found that Weaver was heavily insured, had liberal employment death benefits, owned a condominium in Florida in joint tenancy with Nola Jean, in addition to the Long Grove estate, and stood to inherit a considerable sum from his parents.

With Larry out of the way, Nola Jean would get it all. And sleepy little Long Grove, where absolutely nothing ever happened bigger than an antique sale, not only had a ghastly midnight murder to buzz about but a first-rate sex scandal to boot. The kids at Elk Grove High School winked slyly and chortled as they talked about their popular gym teacher, "Nola Jean, the sex machine."

For a woman who insisted she was innocent, Nola Jean went all the way to the top for help to prove it. She hired Sam Banks, one of Chicago's premier criminal lawyers.

Banks' first move was to ask permission for Nola Jean to leave the state so she could celebrate Christmas with her family in Arkansas.

In a highly unusual action, under the circumstances, the court agreed she could leave Illinois from December 23 through January 5, provided she travel only to Magnolia, Arkansas, where Tiffany was staying with Larry's parents, or to nearby Camden, where Nola Jean's family still lived.

After the holidays she returned home, alone, and spent the next ten months free on bond until October 18, 1978, when she went on trial for her husband's murder.

Prosecutor Ann Regan told the jury of six men and six women the murder was "the product of adulterous love affairs . . . and resentment built on seven years of discontent." In her opening statement she asserted, "Larry Weaver had been a good provider for Nola Jean . . . but for affection she went somewhere else."

The affair with Tipsword went on for seven years, Regan told the court. The affair with Johnston blossomed while

Nola Jean's sister and brother-in-law were living with the Weavers, and ended on October 15, 1977, when Larry learned of the cuckolding and the Johnstons moved out.

Defense lawyer Banks scoffed at the state's case, saying he would prove Nola Jean's story that Weaver had been killed by home invaders. "The police did absolutely nothing to find and locate and prosecute the real murderers," he told the jury.

Little Tiffany, now nine years old, was called to testify for the prosecution. She remembered little of the night her father was killed. "I put on my jamas and watched TV with my daddy," she said. "Mommy was working in the kitchen." After being tucked into bed she knew nothing more until her mother awakened her. "I asked mommy what was going on, but she said, 'Shhh. I'll tell you later.'"

Larry's unmarried sister, Patsy, forty-eight, an education administrator, said that she learned of Nola Jean's seven-year affair with Tipsword while the widow was spending the Christmas holidays in Magnolia with Larry's family. It was Nola Jean, herself, who told her in-laws about it.

"I asked if Winnifred (Tipsword's wife) and Larry knew about it and she said, 'Yes—since last summer—and they understood,'" Pat Weaver testified.

Did Winnifred Tipsword really know? She testified that she and her husband had been "very close" to the Weavers, often seeing them four or five times a week. "But I didn't know that my husband was seeing Nola Jean until after the murder."

Nola Jean's other paramour, Dennis Johnston, testified for the prosecution as a hostile witness. Her brother-in-law told the jury that he and his wife, Judy, both twenty-seven, lived in the Weaver home for several months while he was studying at Trinity Evangelical Divinity School in nearby Deerfield. During that time Johnson admitted becoming "infatuated" with Nola Jean, but he vigorously denied any "sexual conduct."

Banks called no one for the defense, and chose not to put Nola Jean on the witness stand where she might be subjected to cross-examination. "We feel the state has not met their burden. They have not proven their case. We wouldn't dignify it with a response," he declared smugly.

On Wednesday, November 1, after ten hours of deliberation, the jury of Nola Jean Weaver's peers found her guilty of murdering her husband, Larry. The verdict inspired a bit of doggerel reminiscent of the Lizzie Borden murder case in Fall River, Massachusetts, so many years ago.

> Nola Jean Weaver,
> Nola Jean Weaver
> "Not Guilty," she said,
> But they didn't believe her.

Despite her conviction she remained free on bond for another two months. Finally, on January 3, 1979, after one more Christmas on the outside, Judge John L. Hughes sentenced her to forty to sixty years in prison.

"I just want to say that I did not choose murder," she protested. "I am innocent. I lost Larry. I lost my freedom. And I lost my child."

"Only God and the defendant will know for sure what happened that night," Judge Hughes replied from the bench. He then ordered her transferred to the women's penitentiary at Dwight, Illinois.

But the world had not heard the last of Nola Jean Weaver. From her prison cell she continued to battle over custody of Tiffany, all the while proclaiming her innocence.

The daughter had been sent to live with Dr. and Mrs. Jerome Head, former neighbors of the Weavers, in Long Grove. But Larry's sister, Pat, now dean of women at Southern Arkansas University, wanted Tiffany to come to live with her in Magnolia. And Nola Jean wanted the child to be cared for by the Goodfellows, who had moved to Texas. The family won out, and after two months of hearings Aunt Patty took Tiffany to Arkansas to live with her and the paternal grandparents.

Nola Jean took on prison life like she had done everything else in her thirty-five years—as a challenge. She became a modern dance instructor and a behind-the-walls community leader. She taught less fortunate inmates to read, inaugurated a Sesame Street program and Easter egg hunts for visiting children, organized Christmas caroling, and was elected president of the Dwight Jayceettes.

The prison newspaper even featured her as its "Interesting Inmate of the Month."

Under Illinois law, she would have to serve eleven years and three months before becoming eligible for parole. That was not for Nola Jean. She continued to protest the guilty verdict and on November 6, 1980, the Illinois Appellate Court overturned the murder conviction and granted her a new trial.

The court did not agree that she was innocent. A three-judge panel determined, in fact, that "evidence was sufficient to find the defendant guilty of murder beyond a reasonable doubt." But the court also ruled that she had not enjoyed a fair trial.

The high court listed two points. In a twenty-one-page decision the judges ruled that prosecutor Ann Regan made an improper reference to Nola Jean's extramarital affairs during closing arguments to the jury; and the trial judge failed to poll jurors on whether they had been prejudiced by media coverage of the murder. The judges said:

"Despite our determination that the evidence was sufficient to convict, the defendant did not receive the fair trial to which she was constitutionally entitled. Therefore, her conviction for murder is reversed and the cause is remanded for a new trial."

So three years and one conviction after Larry Weaver was found shot to death on his flaming connubial cot, his attractive widow walked out of jail free—for the time being, at least.

She posted bond with a $15,000 "widow's award" she was permitted to draw from her late husband's estate, moved in with a female friend in the Chicago suburb of Schaumburg, and severed all her old ties.

"I did not kill my husband," she insisted. "Those two men did it."

Nola Jean's second trial, which was scheduled to begin June 27, 1983, never got off the ground. On June 9 she stunned her believers by doing a reverse-play, and walking into Lake County Circuit in Waukegan to plead guilty as charged.

Judge Harry D. Strouse, Jr., as surprised as anyone else, asked whether any threats, promises, or inducements had been made to persuade her to come forth and admit her husband's murder. "There have not been any threats," she replied in a strong, calm voice. "It's just . . ." Sam Banks, still her lawyer, cut her off with a gentle pressure on her arm.

The charade was over. Under terms of a plea bargain agreement negotiated with Assistant State's Attorney Raymond McKoski, Nola Jean was sentenced to fourteen years and one day in prison. With credit for time already served, she would become eligible for parole in two years.

Nola Jean actually served four years and nine months, but it wasn't what one would call "hard time." After two years and eleven months at Dwight she was transferred in May 1986 to the Jessie "Ma" Houston Community Correctional Center, a halfway house on Dearborn Street, just north of Chicago's Loop. For the next twenty-two months she participated in a work-release program, holding an outside job and returning to the center at night. She was placed on three years parole on March 23, 1988, to begin a new life at the age of forty-four.

EPILOGUE

After her release from confinement, Nola Jean moved in with a close friend, Dorothy Evans, who had been a counselor at the school where Nola Jean taught. Evans, who was ten years her senior, "adopted" Nola Jean, who changed her name to Jean Roberta Evans. Dorothy Evans died a short time later and Nola Jean inherited the Evans family soybean farm in Missouri. She took a new husband in 1989.

The victim's mother, Vida Weaver, was not happy about Nola Jean's early release. "I don't even want to think about it. I wish they'd keep her," she said. "She hasn't been punished." Larry's sister, Patsy, added, "It's not fair, but then I don't suppose anybody said the judicial system would be totally fair."

Tiffany remained with her aunt, Patsy Weaver, in Magnolia, Arkansas. She graduated from college with a degree in business administration in May 1991, at the age of twenty-one, and one month later became a June bride.

CHAPTER 9

████████████████████████████████

EVERYWHERE THAT CLARENCE WENT

One woman's uterus was surgically removed by a madman. Two other women's breasts were hacked off. Another had a wooden pole rammed into her vagina. One had her throat cut from ear to ear—and lived to point her finger at the fiend who did it.

In all, thirteen women and girls ranging in age from seven to sixty are believed to have died horrible, agonizing deaths at the hands of one bloodthirsty butcher. Through faith, hope, determination, and clairvoyance authorities in Ohio, Michigan, Illinois, and Indiana have tied all thirteen of the hideous, senseless sex murders to one quiet man. Yet he has never been charged with any of the slayings.

When one lawman tracked him to a prison cell in Illinois and confronted him with the skein of killings he responded calmly, "Charge me or get off my back, man."

No hurry. He is currently doing 320 years for a terrifyingly bloody attack on a young housewife he left for dead, but who miraculously clung to life and testified against him.

He comes up for parole every few years. There is little likelihood he will ever be released, but if by chance some do-good review board does one day decide to return him to a place in society, police and prosecutors from three states are ready to move in with enough evidence, they hope, to keep him behind bars forever.

This man is wanted in Cleveland, Ohio, for the sex murders of Mary Branch, Fay Chandler, and Arotha Hawkins.

Authorities in the St. Joseph-Benton Harbor area in Michigan want him for the slayings of Amelia Boyer, Mary Esther Jones, Diane Carter, and Delores Young.

And police in Chicago and the nearby suburbs want him for the wanton killings of Audrey Ellis and five Jane Does—identities unknown—whose mutilated remains were found in various Cook County forest preserves.

The string of homicides attributed to this one man began in Cleveland on the night of November 28, 1963. Arotha Hawkins, a twenty-six-year-old housewife, disappeared on the way to her neighborhood grocery on the city's East Side. Her maimed and disfigured remains were found six weeks later in a wooded area not far from town.

Two months later the stabbed and mutilated bodies of Annie Fay Chandler, thirty-five, and Mary Branch, thirty, were found stacked, one on top of the other, in the basement rubble of an East Side apartment building that was being demolished. Both women had been stripped naked and their clothing was nowhere to be found. Both women's breasts had been sliced off.

The victims were hardly choir girls. Both suspected prostitutes, they had been known to frequent bars on Cleveland's East Side. Mrs. Branch had been dead only hours before her body was found on January 29, 1964. Mrs. Chandler had been dead for about two days. In addition to being stabbed and mutilated, Mrs. Branch had been strangled.

Due to the absence of blood at the scene, Detective Frank Moss surmised that both women had been killed somewhere else, sexually mutilated, and then dumped in the basement of the abandoned building.

Lieutenant Carl Delau, Cleveland homicide chief, noted the perverse similarities in the three killings and warned residents of the community: "A vicious, sadistic man is roaming the East Side. His victims apparently are women frequenting taverns, or out on the street at night."

Homicide investigators, led by Lieutenant Ralph M. Joyce, learned that Fay Chandler had been keeping company with a black man, about thirty-five, who had not been seen since her disappearance. From another witness, a local pimp, investigators learned that a man answering the same description—tall and lanky—had been seen forcing Mary Branch into an old model car several hours before the two women's bodies were found in the abandoned building at 2562 East Seventy-fifth Place.

Police were unable to locate the suspect for questioning, however, or even establish his identity. Every lead took them to a dead end, and Cleveland authorities found themselves confronted with a stubborn triple murder case they simply could not solve.

A year later, almost to the very day—February 1, 1965—the naked body of nineteen-year-old Delores Young was found in the ruins of an old fire-gutted home in Benton Harbor. Her body had been mutilated, but an autopsy showed she had actually died of shock while being raped, and possibly tortured, with some type of wooden instrument. A coroner's pathologist told police he found wood slivers in her torn vagina.

The lack of blood at the scene indicated the teen-aged girl had been murdered elsewhere. Then her body was taken to the old house and dumped in the ruins.

Two months later, on Sunday, April 4, twelve-year-old Bruce Hyler made a macabre discovery while playing in a patch of woods near his home in the Watervliet area, fifteen miles northeast of Benton Harbor. It was the headless, decomposed body of a naked black woman.

The terrified youngster tore home and blurted out the story to his parents, who contacted the Berrien County sheriff's office. Within minutes the area was swarming with police.

Among them was Andrew Novikoff, chief investigator for the county prosecutor's office. Before taking that position in 1961 he had been a sheriff's detective for fifteen years. The sheriff's men were not unhappy to see their former colleague, since Novikoff had a reputation for being one cop who never gave up on a case.

"It's a real messy one, Andy," he was advised. "Whoever the hell did this did a pretty thorough job of mutilating her, too. A real sadist."

"Any idea who she was?"

"Hell no. We'd have to have her head for that. No sign of it anywhere. No sign of her clothes, either."

"Yeah, she could have been killed somewhere else and tossed in the woods," Novikoff said, bending over the victim's remains. "It's a clean cut. Markings on the neck bone look like her head was severed with a saw."

"Hey! Hey! Over here! There's another one!" a voice called out.

"Another what?" Novikoff shouted.

"Another dead woman, for chrissake!"

It was a deputy coroner who had been called to authorize removal of the headless corpse. Taking a shortcut through the weeds on the way back to his car he stumbled on the body of a middle-aged white woman, partly obscured by brush and a small stand of scrub pines.

Like the other woman, she was naked, and her clothing was nowhere around.

"Oh, my God!" Novikoff gasped, pulling the bushes aside to get a better look at the body. "This is the most grotesque thing I've ever seen."

The victim had been stabbed in the heart three times, her abdomen had been slashed open and her uterus had been skillfully removed. "This is absolutely ghastly," Novikoff said, shaking his head in disbelief. "The surgery was done right here at the scene. One woman's head sawed off, another woman's female organs cut out—it's absolutely horrifying to think what we might have running loose around here."

"Do you think there might be more bodies around?" one investigator asked.

"It's enough to make your skin crawl," Novikoff answered. "What if we've stumbled onto a mad dog's burial ground? It's a possibility I don't even want to face."

A sheriff's investigator gave the order to fan out over the entire area. "Look for clothing, look for footprints, look for purses or anything that might have belonged to these women. And, for God's sake, let's hope we don't find another one."

Novikoff's worst fears were realized a short time later when a deputy came upon the body of seven-year-old Diane Carter. Police had been looking for the child since the previous Tuesday night when she disappeared while playing near her home on the western edge of Benton Harbor.

When they found her one of her red stockings was knotted tightly around her neck. Otherwise, like the two older victims, the young black child was naked—and she had been raped.

All three of the bodies had been similarly slashed. They were found about 150 feet from one another, in a triangular pattern.

The little girl appeared to have been strangled right where they found her, since grass from the scene was knotted in the stocking around her neck. The other two victims appeared to have been killed somewhere else and their bodies dragged to the "burial ground" where the mad butcher performed his surgery.

Sheriff's investigators roped off the area, in a grove at the edge of an orchard, which was used as a lovers' lane and by hunters after small game. It was covered now with a light dusting of snow—almost postcard pretty. But detectives referred to the grisly scene as "the madman's graveyard."

Despite her missing head, the first victim was identified as thirty-seven-year-old Mary Esther Jones. She lived alone. Police just happened to have her fingerprints on file from a drunk and disorderly arrest three years earlier. She had been dead about a month, but crime lab technicians were still able to lift enough prints to effect a positive identification.

The woman whose uterus had been cut out was Amelia Boyer, sixty. She had disappeared a week earlier from a

Benton Harbor laundromat where she worked from 4:00 A.M. to 6:00 A.M. as a cleaning lady. She and her husband lived in the rear of the self-service laundry. He reported her missing when she failed to return to their rooms at seven o'clock that morning.

Her purse had been found in the the laundry, along with her dustpan and broom. The place had been only half swept. Mrs. Boyer's husband told police, "She was complaining a little while ago about some black fellow called Tennessee Tom who was annoying her." Tennessee Tom—for now that would be the only clue.

All three of the victims lived within eight blocks of one another, and nineteen-year-old Delores Young had resided in the same general area.

Novikoff was on the scene the following day, April 5, when investigators returned to go over the "madman's grave-yard" inch by inch. "What do you make of this, Andy?" a sheriff's deputy asked, pulling a partly-burned Christmas card out of the snow and handing it to him.

Novikoff looked at the soggy greeting in his hand. It had been addressed to the young woman whose mutilated body was found a month earlier in the abandoned house in town. "Delores Young . . . so, he did that one, too," he mused.

Sheriff Henry Griese agreed that there was little doubt all four females had been slain by the same sex maniac, and promised full cooperation with Benton Harbor police. Although the last three victims had been found in his territory, they had most certainly been abducted in the city.

The teen-ager and the headless woman had been killed about a month apart, according to pathologists. Mrs. Boyer disappeared three weeks later, followed shortly by the little girl. The killer was stepping up his pace.

Police Chief Merle C. McCarroll declared the situation an emergency and cancelled all leaves and days off for his forty-eight-man force.

Fear gripped the female population of the Michigan community, and many women who held night jobs elected to call in sick, or simply stay home behind locked doors, rather than venture out onto the streets after dark. Within two days after the bodies were found in the "madman's graveyard" more than 100 people in Benton Harbor sought gun permits or inquired about permission to carry firearms.

Chief of Detectives Ronald Smith presided over a meeting in City Court chambers of thirty investigators assigned full time to the case. In order to avoid duplication or wheel-spinning, he divided them into groups to facilitate the investigation.

Lacking any clear leads, they spent their time running down more than 150 tips from apprehensive citizens. Many were only vague reports of "strangers" seen around town. Anyone could be a suspect.

A ten-year-old boy who had been playing with Diane Carter on the night she disappeared provided police with their best lead. "She went away with a man who came up and talked to her while we were playing in the park across from Diane's house," he related.

"Did he pull Diane into a car, or drag her away, or anything like that?"

"No, the man, he just talked to her and she went with him."

Diane's mother, Vervina, suggested that since her daughter, a pupil in the Sealy-McCord Elementary School, went willingly she might have recognized the man. The boy who observed the incident described the suspect as a tall Negro.

A thaw on Tuesday, the second day after the bodies were found, melted the light snow that had covered the scene and police found a stained hunting shirt and a pair of men's trousers. Sheriff Griese sent the items to the crime lab to determine if the stain might be human blood. The clothing, which could have belonged to the killer, was uncovered about eighteen feet from where Diane's body had lain.

Two weeks later, the severed head of Mrs. Jones was found in a field several miles away, across the street from an old house occupied by a family by the name of Haynes.

There were no more murders, and eventually the women of Benton Harbor resumed venturing out at night. The number of detectives spending time on the investigation gradually dwindled until there were none, and the case became only an "open file" in the office of Andrew Novikoff.

The stained men's clothing, the ten-year-old boy's description of the tall black man, and the nickname "Tennessee Tom" were all police had to go on. "The file remains open," Novikoff emphasized. "As long as I'm alive, it stays open."

Lieutenant Jerry Harmon, commander of the Cook County Sheriff's Police station in Burbank, a southwest suburb of Chicago, was known as a tireless detective who, like Andy Novikoff, would pursue a case far beyond the limits of most men. If need be he would even resort to the occult to bring criminals to justice, and nobody laughed at him because he produced results.

Harmon's first encounter with the supernatural came in 1960 while he was hot on the trail of a pair of torture bandits, Nick Guido and Frank Yonder. He got a tip that the fugitives were holed up around Fox Lake. It was out of his territory, but Harmon drove up there, in plain clothes, and sauntered nonchalantly into a local restaurant to sip a cup of coffee while pondering his next move.

A waitress who brought the coffee stared inquisitively at him as he raised the cup to his lips. "You're a policeman and you're looking for somebody. They're not here. The two men you're after are no longer in town," she discreetly whispered. Harmon gaped at her, speechless, as she continued. "I see them running from a car, near water. They're going to be captured, but it's in another state." Harmon gulped down his coffee and left. The waitress gave him the creeps.

But a year later the two suspects were captured in Michigan. They had abandoned their car during a police chase and were fleeing on foot when the pursuit ended at a river. It was exactly as the waitress had forseen. Harmon confided to his commanding officer, Captain Thomas R. Brown, about the incident and they joked about it. "You just might be receptive to this kind of mumbo jumbo," Brown laughed. "Get back to work."

The matter was all but forgotten. Then, in the summer of 1965, several months after the four unsolved Michigan murders, a woman's skull was found in one of the Cook County forest preserves ringing Chicago.

All efforts to identify the person to whom it belonged were met with failure and frustration. Brown, an old-school cop with more than forty years as a Chicago policeman and sheriff's deputy, refused to admit defeat and did something completely out of character. Calling Harmon to his office in the Homewood station he asked, "Jerry, have you ever heard of Irene Hughes?"

"Yeah. Isn't she that psychic?"

"She's an astrologist, but she's into this clairvoyant stuff on the side," Brown continued.

"So? Has she got a problem?"

"No, Jerry. We have. We've been busting our asses trying to come up with an ID on that skull, and in the back of my mind I've been thinking about you and that goofy waitress you told me about in Fox Lake."

"I never could explain that one, Tom."

"I know, and we laughed about it. Now I'm serious. Jerry, you're an outstanding investigator—as good as I've seen. Now I don't go in for this psychic business at all. I'm frankly skeptical as hell, I don't mind telling you. But there are some things we just can't explain, right? What I want you to do is get that skull we found in the preserves and take it to this Hughes woman."

"Chief, you've got to be kidding!"

"Like hell I am. Look. We've tried everything else. What the hell have we got to lose? I could ask someone else, but I want you to do it because of what happened with that waitress in the Guido-Yonder case. Maybe you're sensitive to invisible waves or something."

"Tom, I'll get my ass laughed right out of the department."

"No, you won't. This is strictly between you and me, Jerry. I want you to do it."

Harmon agreed, but only if Brown would go along as a witness in case anyone got wind of it afterward. Brown set up the appointment with Mrs. Hughes, and the two lawmen brought her the human skull.

Harmon gingerly handed it to the woman as Brown sat back and observed, trying to pretend he wasn't even in the room. Mrs. Hughes accepted the macabre object without hesitation, placed it in her lap, and tilted back her head and closed her eyes.

"Why am I getting the name Walker?" she asked, breaking a long silence.

"I don't know. It doesn't mean a thing to me," Harmon said. "How about you, Tom?"

"I draw a blank, too. Walker means nothing to me," Brown answered somewhat self-consciously.

"I'm getting very strong vibrations," the psychic continued. "This skull. It definitely has something to do with the name Walker."

That was the end of the "seance," as Brown called it: The name, Walker. But it was more than they had before. The two lawmen quietly checked missing person files throughout the area—without telling anyone why—but nobody had any reports on a missing female by the name of Walker.

One year later, on the Fourth of July, a group of holiday picnickers in a forest preserve near northwest suburban Palatine came upon the naked body of a woman. Her throat had been cut, her abdomen was slashed, and she had been raped and mutilated. Incredibly, she was still alive!

The mystery skull was abruptly forgotten, and Harmon was assigned to devote all his energies to solving this new atrocity. From her hospital bed the half-dead woman, a twenty-two-year-old Chicago housewife, told Harmon an almost unbelievable story of having lain in the woods about fifty yards from Higgins Road, hovering between life and death for three days and nights before someone found her.

Her nightmare began the previous Friday, July 1, when she had gone to Chicago's Central Police Headquarters in connection with a domestic complaint. While in the police building she encountered a tall black man who offered to help her.

"He told me he knew a judge in Skokie who could help me. We got into his car and headed north," she whispered through her bandages. "He stopped once along the way and bought some beer and some double-edged razor blades."

As they neared the northern suburb, however, the good Samaritan swung west, past O'Hare International Airport, and into the Busse Woods. He pulled into a parking lot, dragged the struggling woman from the car and forced her into the underbrush, all the while shouting, "I am a maniac!"

"He said that if I made a sound, only my bones would be found," she told Harmon.

The crazed stranger tore her clothing from her body, flung her to the ground, and brutally raped her. After the attack he took one of the double-edged razor blades and slit her throat, cutting the windpipe. As she lay gasping for air he slashed her stomach. Then, while blood oozed from her throat and abdomen the madman leaped atop her and raped the dying woman a second time.

He wasn't through yet. His passion spent, he pulled off the woman's ring and her watch and took $10 she had hidden in her shoe. Then he picked up a broken bottle and beat her unconscious with it, before abandoning her for dead.

To this day the woman bears a horrible scar, from ear to ear, to forever remind her of the terrifying experience. Harmon, sickened by the story, told her, "You might have been luckier than most. You know what the man looks like, and I swear to you that, somehow, we are going to catch this maniac and bring him to justice."

He was on the case for only a week, however, when on July 12 the decomposed remains of another young woman were found in a forest preserve near Lyons, just west of Chicago. She too, was naked, and her body had been slashed, stabbed, and mutilated.

"We can't seem to come up with an identity for the victim. Another Jane Doe, just like our skull," he told Brown. "This woman was cut and slashed just like the girl last week. Could be the same guy did them both—or maybe all three."

Harmon took photographs of the body and paid another call on Irene Hughes. She pressed the gruesome picture to her breast and began to tremble. "Jerry, do you remember that skull you brought me a year ago? I'm getting the same name. Walker! Walker! Walker! I get sick with the name."

"Are you telling me we've got another dead girl named Walker?" he asked incredulously.

"No, I don't think so, Jerry. I have this horrible, sick feeling about the name. Walker is not the victim. He is the murderer. Walker is the name of the murderer."

Harmon, somewhat doubtful, ran a routine check on the name but came up with nothing that would fit into the puzzle that now confronted him: Two women, dead. The name, Walker. And a twenty-two-year-old woman who lived. The same vicious type of attack. Could there be a madman loose in the area?

He did not have to wait long for the answer. Five days later, on July 17, another naked and mutilated body was found. This one was in Calumet Township, south of Chicago. Victim number four. The only possible clues to her identity were a high school class ring found at the scene and several articles of clothing.

Harmon checked out the ring, only to discover it had been lost by its true owner in Chicago four years earlier. Frustrated, he decided to pay another visit to Irene Hughes. He brought along a photograph of the latest victim's body, and the items of clothing found at the scene.

"Jerry. Jerry. I'm getting vibrations of the name Walker again," she said excitedly. "Oh, they're very strong. Walker. Walker. He has killed in other states, Jerry. He's a mass murderer. He killed this girl, too."

Could Jerry Harmon be sitting here listening to this, he asked himself. It taxed the trained investigator's imagination. How could someone look at a photograph of a murder victim and pick up thought waves broadcasting the killer's name? He reported back to Brown, shaking his head as he spoke. "Hell, Jerry. I'm damned if I know what to think," Brown said.

"Nor do I," Harmon sighed. "But I do know this, Tom. We've got a real crazy out there somewhere. He's killed three women that we know of, and damn near murdered a fourth. And Irene is so positive. So positive! Tom, I think she's actually got me convinced. We are looking for a tall black man named Walker."

Or was he looking for a will-o'-the-wisp, with nothing more to go on than a figment of a psychic's imagination?'

Victim number five was found in the forest preserve on Labor Day, September 5, when picnickers turned out in droves for the last big holiday weekend before saying farewell to summer. Her naked body was lying face down, and she had been raped. Her clothing was scattered nearby, where her attacker had flung it as he tore it from her body.

She was young and attractive, and had not been dead so long that her fine features were not recognizable. There was no purse and no identification. Police checked their usual missing person sources, but no one of her description was unaccounted for.

Then Harmon went back to his "usual" source. He took the dead girl's garments to Irene Hughes.

"Walker," she told him, as she ran her hand over the victim's clothing. "Jerry, it's Walker again. This girl . . . the vibrations tell me she was from Indiana . . . Walker picked her up in a bus depot. Try Northern Indiana, Jerry. Try Northern Indiana."

"I'm starting to think I'm a little cuckoo myself," Harmon told Brown. "But that psychic is so convincing she's actually got me thinking I ought to call Northern Indiana. Why the hell not? We've tried everything else. What the hell!"

What the hell. He did it. Harmon sent a description of the dead female to every police department in the northern part of the neighboring state—and the psychic proved right on target! He heard back almost immediately from police in Gary.

Authorities in the Northern Indiana steel town had a missing person report on a nineteen-year-old named Audrey

Ellis. She worked as a maid in the Chicago suburbs, and commuted to her job by bus.

Harmon was dumbfounded. Irene Hughes had suggested that "Walker" had picked up his latest victim in a bus depot. Harmon contacted relatives of the missing woman and brought them to the Cook County Morgue to view the body. "That's Audrey," they told him. "Sure enough, that's Audrey."

At last Harmon had one Jane Doe identified. The next step was to try to reconstruct Audrey Ellis' life, in an effort to determine what might have brought her and the killer together.

"I swear to you, this is the most bizarre case I've ever worked on," he told Brown. Little did Harmon know that an even more bizarre development was about to unfold, a turn of events he could only attribute to an "unknown power."

On September 20 the twenty-two-year-old housewife who had survived the July attack in the forest preserve, after having her throat slashed, was riding on a bus on Chicago's South Side. As she stared idly out the window, she was startled to see a tall black man standing on the corner—and he was no stranger. Although she got only a fleeting glance at him as the bus rumbled by, the whole awful episode of the July 1 rape and slashing flashed before her eyes as she recognized the face of the monster who had left her for dead nearly three months earlier.

Exhibiting the same pluck and presence of mind that had helped keep her alive for three days and nights after the near-fatal attack, she got off the bus at the very next corner, stepped into the street, and flagged down a passing squad car. Quickly explaining the situation she directed the officers to the corner of Forty-seventh Street and Cottage Grove Avenue, where a tall man in his middle thirties was lounging against the side of a building.

"Do you see this?" she asked the patrolman, baring the ugly, red scar running across her throat. "That's the man. That's the son-of-a-bitch who did this to me."

The suspect did not try to run. He offered no resistance, and almost seemed amused as he was placed under arrest and taken to the area police headquarters for questioning. The first thing his interrogators asked was, "What is your name?"

The tall, lanky man looked at the police officers through soft, brown eyes as he replied calmly. "Walker. My name is Clarence Walker."

Jerry Harmon's blood ran cold when Chicago police notified him that an arrest had been made in the forest preserve attack, and that the suspect's name was Walker! He sped to the station to see for himself. There it was on the arrest sheet: Walker, Clarence; Date of Birth, 25 February 1929; Address, 1026 E. 47th St., Chicago, Ill.; Male; Negro.

"Good God almighty, Irene, you've made a believer out of me," he said to himself, noting that his hands were trembling as he read the report.

Walker was turned over to sheriff's police, and was charged with attempted murder, rape, and robbery in the attack on the housewife who lived to tell about the razor-blade slashing.

Harmon questioned the suspect for hours about the other forest preserve victims but got nowhere. There were no witnesses to those killings, and he did not even know the victims' names. How do you question a man about the murder of Jane Doe No. 1, Jane Doe No. 2, Jane Doe No. 3, and so on? The only name he had was that of No. 5, Audrey Ellis, the nineteen-year-old from Northern Indiana.

Once they had the name, and a suspect, police were able to link the two. Sheriff's Sergeant Ronald Jackson, making the rounds of pawn shops on Chicago's South Side, found Audrey's high school ring. It had been pawned by Walker's wife. Yes, he had a Mrs. at home despite his suspected extracurricular activities.

Harmon talked to Mrs. Walker, who candidly admitted that her husband had boasted to her of killing numerous women in the forest preserves. "But I ain't never gonna testify against that man in court," she stressed. "No way, man. Nobody can make me, either." This was one woman who wanted to stay alive.

The skein of killings ended with Clarence Walker's arrest; but there were still two more bodies yet to be found.

On November 12, 1966, the remains of a young woman were discovered in a farm field. This brought the suspect's victims to six—five dead plus the woman who survived. Like the previous victim, Irene Hughes believed the girl was from Northern Indiana, but Harmon was never able to identify her.

The seventh, and last known victim was found November 26, two days after Thanksgiving, in a field near the south suburb of Lansing, along the Illinois-Indiana border. She, too, remains unidentified to this day.

But Sheriff Richard B. Ogilvie, a World War II tank commander who later went on to become governor, had had enough. Ogilvie ordered a special ten-man investigative unit to get to the bottom of the string of mutilation murders. In an effort to identify the victims, investigators purchased clothing similar to that found near some of the bodies, dressed up department store mannequins, and photographed them. The pictures were released to the news media, but no one came forward to say they recognized anyone.

The sheriff also engaged the services of Ray Shlemon, a *Chicago Tribune* airbrush artist and wartime OSS agent, to study the remains of the victims and prepare composite facial drawings. A noted anthropologist was called in from Pennsylvania to help establish the victims' ages.

It was all to no avail. None of the dead women have ever been identified except Audrey Ellis. And doe-eyed Clarence Walker has never been charged with any of the murders.

He went on trial, instead, for the maniacal attack on the twenty-two-year-old housewife. She took the witness stand against him in March 1968, and described in lurid detail how he had raped her, slashed her throat, cut and disfigured her, raped her again, and left her for dead in the woods.

Walker was found guilty on all counts. Criminal Court Judge Reginald J. Holzer sentenced him to 100 to 150 years for rape; 100 to 150 years for armed robbery; and 19 to 20 years for attempted murder. The sentences were to run consecutively, for a maximum of 320 years.

Holzer explained that the stiff sentences were imposed because of Walker's past record. He had killed before, police discovered. In checking out his background after his arrest, investigators learned that he had shot a fourteen-year-old boy to death with a rifle back in Tennessee in 1945, when he was only sixteen years old. He was convicted for manslaughter and sentenced to seven years in the Tennessee State Prison.

Now, twenty-three years later, Walker was on his way to prison again. "I hope that this time it will be for keeps," Holzer commented.

Back in Michigan, Andy Novikoff was still stewing over the unsolved murders of three women and the little girl in Berrien County. He had never given up on the case, and vowed he never would. He was convinced all were the work of one man.

One day, while reading a book about unsolved homicides across the country, he came upon a chapter recounting the mutilation murders of the three women in Cleveland in 1963 and 1964. A strange feeling came over him, and on a hunch he telephoned Ohio to talk about the murders with homicide investigators who had worked on the case.

The chance phone call turned into an enthusiastic exchange of information, in which police in the two states discovered a number of startling similarities in the seven slayings. They came to the conclusion that the three women in Cleveland, and the four victims in Benton Harbor, were quite possibly killed by the same person.

"If this is true, the guy traveled," Novikoff speculated. "He could have roamed the country, killing wherever he stopped. I'm going to check around." He then contacted other major police departments inquiring as to whether there had been any unsolved mutilation murders in their jurisdictions.

Jerry Harmon read the message in Chicago. He got on the phone with Novikoff and told him about the six murders in the surrounding area—and about Clarence Walker.

"It sure as hell sounds like the same guy," Novikoff told him. "Walker! Now maybe we'll get somewhere with this investigation."

But he didn't. Try as he might, he was unable to place Clarence Walker anywhere near Benton Harbor, before or after the murders, or ever. He relayed the info to Cleveland authorities, but there was no record of Clarence Walker ever having been there, either.

Then came another bizarre break in the case, as unexplainable as the day the twenty-two-year-old woman in Chicago glanced out of the bus window and saw Walker standing on the curb. A teen-aged boy was stopped for a traffic violation in Benton Harbor and police found him carrying a fictitious driver's license.

The license had been issued in the name of Clyde Haynes, who was twice the age of the youth who carried it. Thinking it might have been stolen, a probation officer questioned the boy's mother, who also went by the name of Haynes.

"Clyde Haynes? Oh, that's the boy's uncle. That's not his real name, you see, but he was using it when he lived here with us. My son, he didn't see any harm in using his uncle's old driver's license. He's not here anymore anyhow."

"The boy's uncle just used the name of Clyde Haynes? What's his real name, and where is he now?" the officer asked curiously.

"Oh, he's doin' time in prison over in Illinois," she said, shaking her head from side to side. "My brother's real name is Clarence Walker. Don't know why he used my married name while he was here."

The youth officer relayed the information to police, who passed it on to Novikoff, since they knew he had been checking on a man by the name of Walker some time earlier.

The excited Novikoff wasted no time in questioning the youth's family. He learned that Walker—using the name of Haynes—had been in Benton Harbor at the time of the four murders. Furthermore, he had briefly lived in the Haynes home near where Mary Esther Jones' severed head was found.

Novikoff reactivated the homicide investigation, and he and other detectives set out to establish the suspect's every movement while in the Michigan community.

The detective had already learned from Harmon of the murder in Tennessee, when Walker was a boy. The Tennessee angle took him directly to the laundromat where Amelia Boyer had worked. He not only determined that Walker had frequented the laundry, but a friend of the murdered woman identified a police photo of Walker as the elusive "Tennessee Tom"—the man Mrs. Boyer had complained was pestering her.

Novikoff also learned that Clyde Haynes, as Walker was known in the community, had socialized with Mary Esther Jones, and had been seen in a tavern with her shortly before she disappeared.

The investigator further learned that at one time during his stay in Benton Harbor the man known as Haynes had lived across the street from nineteen-year-old Delores Young, the girl whose mutilated body was found in the burned-out house.

Novikoff then went to the neighborhood where little Diane Carter had lived. Showing Walker's mug shot around, he found several witnesses who had seen the suspect loitering in the playground from where the little girl had vanished.

Walker, alias Clyde Haynes, had now been linked to all four murder victims in Michigan. Novikoff traveled to Tennessee to learn all he could about the suspect's childhood. He also made two trips to Stateville Penitentiary near Joliet, Illinois, to interview Walker, but was rebuffed both times. "Charge me or get off my back, man," Walker coldly challenged him.

Armed with a thick dossier on Clarence Walker, Novikoff went to Cleveland to personally discuss the case with homicide investigators in the three unsolved Ohio murders.

While Ohio authorities had been unable to place Walker in Cleveland at the time of the slayings, they did have a record of one Clyde Wesley Haynes. The man known as Haynes had been sentenced to one to twenty-five years in prison for armed robbery in Cleveland in 1954, and one to seven years for grand larceny in 1959. Furthermore, Haynes' arrival in Cleveland coincided with Clarence Walker's release from the Tennessee prison at the end of his manslaughter term.

"We're rolling. We're rolling," Novikoff said elatedly. "We're all talking about the same guy."

It was now November 1970, almost seven years after the triple murders, but after talking to Novikoff, Cleveland authorities decided to reopen their investigation. "I've had some extra pictures of Clarence Walker made. The mug shot was sent to me by Lieutenant Harmon in Chicago. I'm going to leave them with you," Novikoff said.

Cleveland police discovered that Walker, calling himself Haynes, had lived across the street from one of the murder victims shortly before he took off for Michigan. They showed his photo to friends of the homicide victims, Mary Branch, Arotha Hawkins, and Fay Chandler. The Michigan investigator's hunch had paid off.

On December 2, 1970, Cleveland Detective Carl Roberts and Lieutenant Ralph Joyce sent Novikoff an official departmental memo, notifying him of their findings:

1. For a period of three months, right up to the day she disappeared, Fay Chandler had been keeping company with the man known as Clyde Wesley Haynes. Roosevelt Chandler, twenty-two, a relative of the slain woman, identified the police photo of Clarence Walker as that of Haynes.

2. Buster Young, forty-five, and Katie McMillin, twenty-eight, both identified Walker's photo as that of the man seen chasing Mary Branch, and forcing her into a car just hours before the two women's bodies were found.

3. Fay Chandler's daughter, Ethel Smith, identified the photo of Walker as that of the man she had seen with her mother, although she never knew his name.

4. Clyde Haynes had worked in Dude's Garage on Outhwaite Avenue, where he had access to several old model autos of the type Mary Branch was seen being driven off in.

In conclusion, Roberts wrote Novikoff: "Since Clyde Wesley Haynes was in Cleveland during these mutilation murders, and has been positively identified as having had personal contact with these victims, we are satisfied that he is the person responsible for same."

Novikoff was satisfied that Walker was, beyond all doubt, the slayer of the four Benton Harbor victims as well. The case was solved, as he had vowed it would be, although no public announcement was made. Walker had not officially been charged with any of the homicides.

In August 1971, another woman was found slain in Benton Harbor and rumors spread like wildfire that the mad killer was on the loose again. It was not a mutilation murder, and bore no similarity to any of the four earlier killings, however.

To allay fears in the community, Novikoff and Berrien County Prosecutor Ronald J. Taylor issued a joint announcement, assuring the public that Clyde W. Haynes, also known as Clarence Walker, had been determined to be the killer of the three women and the little girl in 1965, and was safely behind bars in Illinois.

Four murders in Michigan and three in Ohio were marked "solved" because of the aggressive work of Andrew Novikoff, an old-time cop who didn't know the meaning of giving up. And six similar slayings were believed solved in the Chicago area because of Jerry Harmon, a lawman cut from the same cloth.

After sending Walker to jail for 320 years, Harmon teamed up with Irene Hughes to solve several other murder cases.

"I feel this way. When a person has been murdered, and we can't solve the crime, I will take help from anyone who will offer it," he said. "If you can't help a person who is no longer on this earth you will never amount to a good investigator."

Clarence Walker, meanwhile, has been quietly doing his time in Stateville. Though he still technically has 297 years to go at this writing, he became eligible for parole in 1977, and has since appeared regularly before the Illinois Prison Review Board. He has been accruing "good time" at the rate of about thirty days a year, which means he gets to see the review board a month earlier each year. His next scheduled appearance is February 1992.

The tall, gangling prisoner is known to fellow inmates as "High Pockets." Prison officials say he keeps to himself, and passes the years on a jailhouse work detail, painting and repainting cellblocks their drab institutional colors. His record, for the most part, is one of good conduct.

EPILOGUE

Novikoff retired from police work in 1976, and Harmon turned in his badge in 1984. Both men believe there are more than thirteen killings involved here. They are convinced that if Walker's travels around the country could be chronicled they would also find a trail of unsolved disappearances of women of all ages.

When Novikoff retired to California he took with him a complete copy of all of the murder reports, and he continues to closely monitor Walker's prison stay. He has been putting together a book about the string of murders attributed to Walker in Ohio, Michigan, and Illinois, as well as the one for which he was convicted in Tennessee. He calls his story, "And Everywhere that Clarence Went . . ."

CHAPTER 10

THE PHANTOM OF THE RAIL YARDS

Thunder boomed off the horizon and lightning cracked across the midnight sky over Hammond, Indiana, as switchman Virgil Terry punched in for work at the sprawling Indiana Harbor Belt rail yards. Saturday, August 3, 1963, was only a few minutes old, and already it was uncomfortably hot and sticky as the fifty-two-year-old railroader carefully picked his way across the ribbons of steel tracks with fellow crewmen Kenneth Dibble and James Crane.

Amid the eerie, distant glow of blast furnaces and oil refineries, the trio headed toward the giant diesel locomotive droning alongside the switchman's shanty. Engineer Roy Bottorff, sixty, and Fireman Paul Overstreet, forty-five, were already waiting in the dimly lit cab.

It was just two nights shy of the full moon.

Terry got a firm grip on the hand rail and pulled himself up onto the engine as Crane and Dibble climbed aboard the caboose. As soon as every man was in his place Bottorff eased out the throttle. In less than an hour the crew had coupled up their fifty-five car freight train and pulled it to the far end of the yards.

At 1:05 A.M. Terry swung down off the locomotive and walked to the west end switchman's shack, where he called the Hammond tower for clearance to head for the Calumet City yards just over the line in Illinois.

"You're on hold until the Blue Island train clears, Virg. It'll be coming through any minute now," he was advised. "Then you've got a highball."

As soon as the Blue Island rumbled past the Columbia Avenue crossing Terry threw the switch to the main line and waved his lantern to signal Bottorff to bring the train ahead. There was no acknowledgment. The mighty engine, its bright headlight cutting through the darkened yard, did not move.

Terry walked toward the train, preparing to jump aboard as it pulled abreast. He gave the "come-ahead" signal several more times, but the locomotive seemed glued to the spot.

As he came up alongside the diesel he noticed that Bottorff's head was lying part way out the side window. The switchman would later tell police: "I climbed up on the engine and touched Roy on the arm, and then I noticed blood on his face and neck. I turned around and saw that Overstreet had blood on his face, too. I jumped off the engine and ran to a yard speaker and called to the yardmaster to contact the police and railroad officials, and to send an ambulance right away."

Bottorff and Overstreet were dead at the controls. Each had been shot twice in the back of the head. Two .22 caliber shell casings were found on the floor of the cab. Another had fallen into the engineer's open overnight bag, and the fourth was lying on the ground alongside the locomotive.

Paul Overstreet and Roy Bottorff were but the first to die.

That humid August night marked the bloody beginning of an eerie succession of train murders at the hands of a phantom stalker. Over the next fifteen years a total of seven trainmen would be ambushed and shot to death along 200 miles of the same track system between the Hammond yards and Jackson, Michigan.

The third victim would be Engineer John W. Marshall, fifty-one, of Niles, Michigan, cut down by withering shotgun blasts at 4:38 A.M. on August 6, 1968, as he stood alongside his diesel in the yards at Elkhart, Indiana. He was struck once in the midsection, once in the side, and twice in the head by a 12-gauge weapon fired at close range.

Victim number four was Engineer James "Tiny" Mc-Crory, also fifty-one, of Niles. A deer slug from a 20-gauge shotgun slammed him in the head at 1:08 A.M. on April 5, 1976, as he sat in the cab of his locomotive parked near the diesel house in the same Elkhart yards.

Then, on New Year's Eve 1978 the killer scored a horrifying triple-header. Victims five and six were Conductor William Gulak, fifty, of Lincoln Park, Michigan, and Flagman Robert Lee Blake, forty-two, of Southgate, torn apart by blasts from a 12-gauge shotgun as they sat in the trainmen's locker room at the depot in Jackson, Michigan, at 6:44 P.M.

As the phantom killer whirled about to leave the depot he bumped into Fireman Charles Lee Burton, thirty-two, of Jackson, who was heading for the so-called "hot room" to warm up, and caught him with another deadly blast on the station platform. Burton became number seven.

Through all the killings, police had been working intensively since day one. The Federal Bureau of Investigation was also in on it right from the start, assisting Hammond detectives in their investigation of the Bottorff and Overstreet homicides, since the victims were engaged in interstate commerce at the time they were gunned down.

There was nothing in the background of the Hammond victims to target them for murder, nor could police uncover any involvement in union problems.

Detective Sergeants Frank Bogielski, John Foschaar, and William Blaemire, who dug into the victims' personal lives, found nothing but two well-liked family men who neither drank nor gambled.

Both were veteran trainmen. Bottorff had built up a respectable forty-three years of seniority, and Overstreet had put in twenty-two years on the job. Each was a homeowner with a wife and four children. The engineer, a World War I aviator and former Moody Bible Institute student, wrote poetry and painted religious scenes as a hobby. The fireman was a dedicated gardener.

Motive? The Hammond detectives and FBI agents were baffled.

The only thing they were sure of was that the killer had to know something about railroading himself, since he seemed to know exactly when to climb aboard the midnight diesel and carry out his fatal mission unobserved.

More than 100 individuals were questioned in the course of the police investigation, and at least 42 railroad men who had been associated with the slain men submitted to lie detector tests. All were cleared, according to Raymond Johnson, chief of detectives.

Up to this point each of the murders was being investigated independently, and a pattern had not yet been established. It was Detective Sergeant David Keck in Elkhart who initially drew the pieces together while working on the 1976 shooting of Tiny McCrory.

Digging out the 1968 file on the John Marshall homicide, he found a common denominator. Both Marshall and McCrory had been engineers, both lived in Niles, Michigan, and each had been shot down in the Elkhart rail yard in the middle of the night while working on or near his locomotive.

Was it a coincidence, or could the two slayings be part of a bizarre pattern?

Another piece of the puzzle was provided by Elkhart Detective James Bowlby during routine questioning of Leo Fawley, a railroad union representative. Fawley recalled working as an engineer some years earlier on a run through the Hammond yards when his fireman, who was not normally a talkative man, commented, "You know, there was a couple of guys killed here. Do you remember that?"

"I had only a vague recollection," Fawley told the detective. "In fact, I didn't think anything of it at the time."

Bowlby reported the conversation to Sergeant Keck, who contacted Hammond authorities and inquired as to whether they had any railroad yard murders there.

"Yes, we had two men killed in 1963," Hammond police replied.

No doubt about it. The pattern was there. All four slayings involved railroad men, shot in the back while working in the yards in the middle of the night.

The original Hammond investigators by now had retired, but the case was reopened with Keck's help by Detectives John Baron and Walter Murray.

Keck, meanwhile, told Detective Bowlby, "Jim, see if you can get hold of Fawley again and find out if he can remember the name of that fireman who mentioned the Hammond murders to him." Keck made the contact. "Oh, yeah, I remember the guy well, because I once represented him in a union grievance," he told the detective. "His name is Rudy Bladel."

The name rang a bell with Sergeant Keck, too. A man named Bladel had been involved in an Elkhart shooting incident some years before and, if memory served correctly, it had been in a rail yard.

The sergeant rummaged through five years of closed case records until he found the file he was after—the Louis Sayne ambush. The meager report was dated March 30, 1971. That was eight years after the two Hammond killings, three years after the Marshall murder in Elkhart, and five years before the slaying of McCrory.

The incident attracted little attention at the time because the facts were cut and dried, but suddenly it looked very, very big. Keck's memory was correct. It had happened in a rail yard.

It was 3:55 A.M. when a bearish figure of a man stepped from behind a darkened oil storage tank in the Elkhart yard and commenced blasting away at Engineer Louis John Sayne, forty-seven, with a .357 Magnum. Sayne, who had just reported for work, was struck twice in the back. Despite his wounds he managed to wrest the weapon from his assailant and shoot him in the stomach with it.

Sayne, a railroad veteran with the old New York Central

and later Conrail and Amtrak, vividly recalled the night when detectives questioned him about the ambush.

"I was in a happy mood because there were two train jobs that night, and I got the good one—going to Chicago. It paid more. I just finished a cup of coffee at a nearby all-night restaurant and I was walking toward the roundhouse to climb aboard a Burlington Northern freight engine when I heard two quick shots. I was hit in the back and hip. I thought to run, but hell, I couldn't outrun bullets so I turned around and faced him. We wrestled. He tripped on my overnight bag and fell down. I fell on top of him, grabbed the gun and shot him."

As it turned out, neither man was mortally wounded because the gun had been loaded with homemade bullets fashioned from a welding rod and coated with wax. The two gunshot victims were rushed to the Elkhart hospital, and as surgeons worked over them in the emergency room Sayne turned and recognized his assailant as a locomotive fireman who had once worked with him.

"Why did you shoot me, Rudy?" the puzzled engineer inquired.

The dour-faced Bladel, then thirty-eight, and a career railroader like Sayne, replied, "I did all I could to get the Niles men out of Elkhart," as if that explained everything.

Bladel was charged with attempted murder. Prosecutors agreed to a guilty plea to a reduced charge of aggravated battery, and on December 31, 1971, Bladel was sentenced to one to five years in the Indiana State Prison at Michigan City.

Bladel served eighteen months. In discussing the Sayne shooting with a relative after his release, he commented, "I only wanted to dust his pants off."

The shooting incident cost Bladel his job. After his release in 1973 he appeared at a union hearing in an unsuccessful appeal to get the railroad to take him back.

"He came up to me and shook my hand," the baffled Sayne recalled. "He said the reason for shooting me had nothing to do with me personally, 'Just the Michigan men.' Imagine that!"

Murder victim Christine Schultz was found by her two sons shot to death.

Laurie Bembenek as she appeared in an ad for Schlitz beer. The ex-policewoman and Playboy bunny was convicted of killing her husband's ex-wife.

Famed Chicago radio personality Everett Clarke goes over script parts with student actors. Clarke would play a crucial role in the solving of his own murder.

Acting student Paul DeWit murdered Everett Clarke on the same stage where DeWit had taken lessons from the familiar radio personality.

Marion K. Mueller; police say her son-in-law killed her and two others with arsenic.

David Hoffman with his wife Carol, and daughter Heidi in 1977; three years later, Hoffman brutally murdered his wife, disposing of her remains in a kitchen trash disposal.

Courtesy Chicago Tribune

Charles Albanese sits stonily in police car while enroute to courthouse to face charges of triple murder by arsenic poisoning.

Mary Lambert; police say she was slain with arsenic by her granddaughter's husband.

Yvonne Kleinfelder, who dubbed herself "Satan's Voodoo Dancer," reportedly boiled her live-in boyfriend to death.

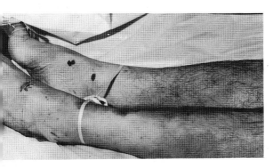

The witch's victim, John Comer, was described by friends as well-educated. This morgue photo shows the cigarette burns on Comer's ankles inflicted by Kleinfelder after she had bound him to her kitchen table and boiled him.

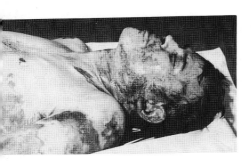

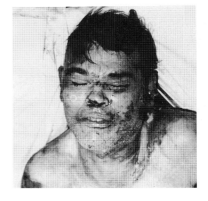

Morgue photographs of John Comer. He reportedly spent six days in excrutiating agony, bound naked to Kleinfelder's kitchen table after she had boiled him from head to toe.

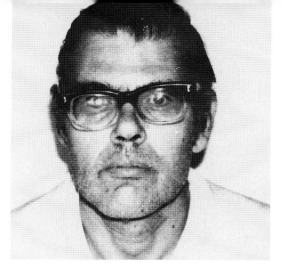

Shortly before his death, one of Comer's co-workers said, friends were telling him to "get the hell out of that house."

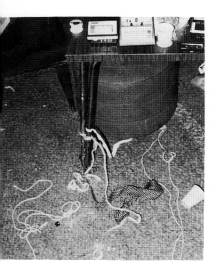

"The witch" used lengths of rope and a necktie to hogtie John Comer to a table in the apartment. Police have yet to explain how the 125-pound Kleinfelder overcame the strength of John Comer who, at 175 pounds, regularly lifted weights up to 200 pounds with little effort.

"The walls were too thick for anyone to hear his screams," said police of this apartment building wherein John Comer was boiled to death by Yvonne Kleinfelder.

Joe Ramos, the "Latin Lover," was shot to death by his married girlfriend, Patricia Gil.

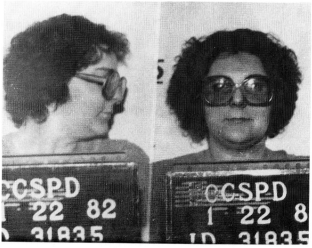

Patricia Gil—her attempt to dispose of the body of her victim, Joseph Ramos, was botched by the telltale odor of decomposition.

This ammunition box was a crucial piece of evidence against Chicago physician John M. Branion. He was convicted of firing the four missing rounds into his wife just days before Christmas, 1967.

Dr. John Branion shot his wife and fled from police to sanctuary as Ugandan dictator Idi Amin's personal physician.

"I've never heard a cross word between them," a friend said of the Weavers. Yet shortly after Larry Weaver's murder by supposed burglars, Nola Jean Weaver pleaded guilty to his murder.

Nola Jean Weaver leads other women in a prison exercise class. She was photographed while doing time for the murder of her husband.

LAKE COUNTY SHERIFF'S OFFICE
WANTED INVESTIGATION OF HOME INVASION-HOMICIDE
Reference Report 77-53981
CONTACT: Chief Investigator Lou Harceg   (312) 698-6300

LAKE COUNTY SHERIFF'S OFFICE
WANTED INVESTIGATION OF HOME INVASION-HOMICIDE
Reference Report 77-53981
CONTACT: Chief Investigator Lou Harceg   (312) 698-6300

Police sketches derived from the descriptions given by Nola Jean Weaver of the intruders who she claimed killed her husband, Larry.

Lt. Jerry Harmon of the Cook County sheriff's department. His use of mystic powers to solve several murder cases amazed fellow lawmen in Illinois.

Courtesy Chicago Tribune

Five women were brutally murdered in forest preserves of Cook County, Illinois, in 1966. The victims, including one found on July 17 (below) and another (left) found by picnickers on Sept. 5, were tortured, raped and strangled to death.

Lawmen and anthropology experts discuss evidence in the baffling case of the murders of unidentified women. Knotted nylons, shown in photographs below the victims, were used for strangling the victims. Lt. Jerry Harmon (left) examines a photo of one of the women, all of whom were sexually assaulted and stabbed.

Clarence Walker, the multi-state killer who brutally raped, tortured and murdered numerous women and young girls. Walker's future was sealed behind Illinois prison gates when a psychic tipped off Lt. Jerry Harmon.

Trainman Rudy Bladel challenged police to come up with evidence against him. "You're a cop," he said. "Prove I did it." The cops did, putting Bladel behind prison bars for three rail killings.

Shirley and Alan Rhodes' brief marriage ended in murder. After her body washed up on a Florida beach, police went looking for her husband.

His hands manacled, murder suspect Chester "Rocky" Weger is led to cave opening where bodies of three women were found.

Courtesy Chicago Tribune

Murder victim Lillian Oetting—just moments before her death she snapped a mysterious picture.

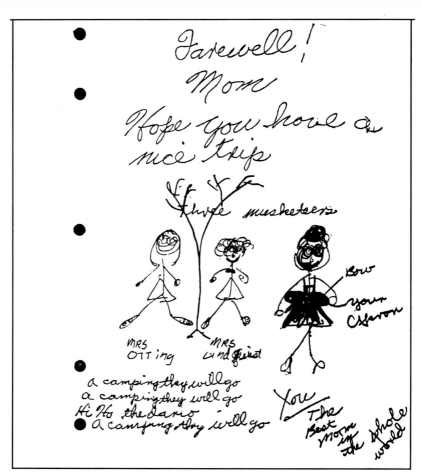

"Farewell!. . . you're the best mom in the whole world." Farewell note from Frances Murphy's twelve-year-old daughter.

Murder victims Frances Murphy and Mildred Lindquist, in photo taken by companion Lillian Oetting.

Hilma Marie Witte with her son, confessed crossbow killer John "Butch" Witte. The solving of this case sparked questioning of yet another death in the Witte family years earlier.

Entertainer Walter Scott and his wife, Jo Ann Notheis. She was charged with her husband's murder after police found his body in James Williams' cistern.

James Williams was charged with killing his former wife, Sharon, shown here with him, and trying to make her death look like an auto accident.

Egyptian Ibrahiem Allam, wanted for the murder of a man who had sex with his wife, was arrested for fighting on a street in Chicago. The murder took place in Vienna, Austria.

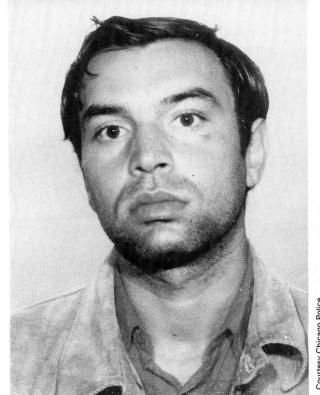

Dalia Allam, whose husband forced her into prostitution. Police said her husband killed one of the paying lovers in Austria.

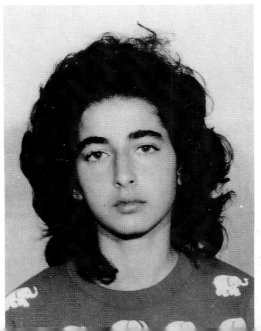

Belle Gunness, with children, perished in her farmhouse fire. Gunness herself escaped the flames, leaving behind a barnyard filled with murdered suitors.

This partially decomposed man's body was one of many dug up in LaPorte, Indiana, barnyard of "Lady Bluebeard," Belle Gunness.

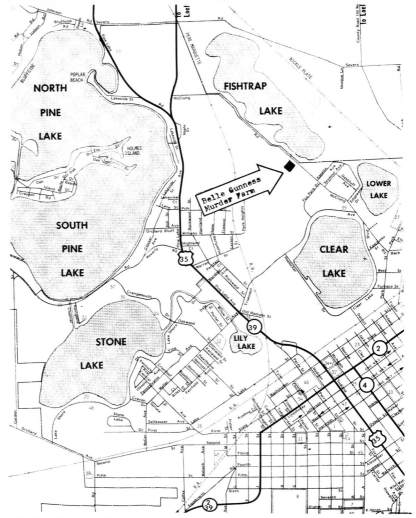

Belle Gunness' mantrap, located just below Fishtrap Lake in LaPorte, Indiana. Belle's barnyard was a grisly graveyard for her lovesick victims.

Nothing pleased Belle Gunness more than the sight of a lonely, love-starved suitor arriving at her farm "graveyard" with money to pay her mortgage. Few of such men were ever seen again.

Bladel's remarks after the shooting, and again at the hearing, held little significance at the time. But now, as Sergeant Keck went over the old file it began to make a lot of sense. Bladel's words were the basis of one man's fanatical grudge against the railroad industry:

In the late 1950s the New York Central shifted most of its operations from Niles, Michigan, to the new rail yard in Elkhart. The move resulted in the layoff of more than seventy-five trainmen in Niles, where the number of train crews was cut from twenty-two to five.

"There were strong feelings, and the railroad let the unions fight out a solution," Sayne explained.

Eventually the unions ruled that 52 per cent of the personnel needs at the expanded Elkhart yard would be filled by Elkhart men; with the other 48 per cent, the so-called "Michigan percentage," being provided by railroaders from Niles.

The ruling caused a number of Elkhart men to lose their seniority to make room for the Niles men. Among them was Rudy Bladel. He was laid off for a time, and was reduced in status when he was finally called back to work.

It seemed a cruel blow to a man whose entire lifetime had been dedicated to the Iron Horse. Bladel had no wife, no girlfriend, no hobbies, and no outside interests other than railroading.

"His first love and his last love has always been railroading," said his half-brother, a Chicago businessman who provided some insights into Bladel's background.

Rudy was born into a railroad family in Chicago on December 8, 1932. His father, Holgar, worked for the Chicago, Rock Island & Pacific Railroad Co.

Young Rudy grew up on the city's South Side, where he attended Chicago Vocational High School, taking automotive shop courses. After graduating in 1951 he went to work for his father's line, the Rock Island, as a fireman. "That's when you tossed coal in one end and got steam out the other," he liked to recall, in discussing his introduction to the job.

Bladel joined the Army when the Korean War broke out, and served as a military engineer, "hostling" locomotives around a South Korean rail yard, sometimes while under enemy fire.

After the war he returned to the Rock Island where he worked his way up through the seniority ranks before being bumped, laid off and demoted in the Niles-Elkhart job merger. By the time he was fired in 1971 for the Sayne shooting he had logged nineteen good years with various rail lines.

Although the Sayne case had been all but forgotten over the years, being marked "closed" after Bladel was sentenced to prison, it suddenly commanded Sergeant Keck's undivided attention.

Keck studied the Sayne file. Except for the fact that the intended victim lived, the pattern was identical to the other two Elkhart rail yard murders and the two Hammond slayings.

In Hammond there had been a witness who told police he spotted a man near the scene. "I couldn't see what he looked like in the darkness, but he walked like a gorilla, you know, a farmer-type walk, like behind a plow, looking at the ground," he related.

"That's Rudy," Keck told himself, in reading over the file. Bladel walked with an unusual gait due to a leg injury suffered in a motorcycle accident shortly after he returned from Korea.

The Hammond witness also recalled hearing a motorcycle leaving the scene.

Keck and the other detectives then went over the Marshall case, in which there were also several witnesses. Again, they could not put a face on the body they saw in the dark, but they put a walk on the man, and described his build. It fit Rudy Bladel.

"So we've got our pattern," Keck said. "Let's make it a point to find out everything we can about Bladel."

Sayne, the only surviving gunshot victim, remembered Bladel as a morose, brooding fireman who sat looking straight ahead, rhythmically slapping his knees with his hands to the clickety-click of the rails when the two men crewed together.

"No words were ever exchanged between us," Sayne said. "He would sit there on the left side of the cab talking to himself and playing pat-a-cakes with his knees."

Fawley, the Elkhart engineer who, as a union "griever" handled Bladel's futile attempt to win back his job after the Sayne affair, recalled, "Rudy dabbled in a lot of experimental things, particularly the idea of steam engines for automobiles. He thought steam engines were the coming thing in cars, and he said so long before the fuel shortages."

Fellow workers agreed that nobody really "knew" the powerfully built, bespectacled Bladel. He had no friends, nor did he seem to want any. While other crewmen shot the breeze or played cards as they waited for assignments, Bladel would disappear until train time. If anyone bothered to ask where he'd been, Bladel would reply, "I took a long walk. Walking is my way to pass the waiting time." During Rudy's long walks, fellow railroaders frequently saw him talking to himself.

Investigators determined that Bladel was living alone in a trailer in neighboring Blue Island, Illinois, at the time Bottorff and Overstreet were shot to death on August 3, 1963. Furthermore, he owned a motorcycle at the time.

In January 1978 police put Bladel under around-the-clock surveillance. He didn't know it, but undercover cops were on his tail when he drove over to South Bend and purchased a shiny, new .357 Magnum. Since it is a violation of federal law for a convicted felon to own a weapon, the Bureau of Alcohol, Tobacco and Firearms was notified of the transaction. On January 6, acting in consort with local police, U.S. Treasury agents arrested him for illegal possession of a firearm.

Bladel was convicted and sentenced to one to five years in the federal penitentiary at Sandstone, Minnesota. He was released on November 16, 1978—just six weeks before the bloody Jackson depot massacre.

Keck had already determined that there had been no shootings during the two periods Bladel had spent behind bars. The detective requested a resumption of full-time surveillance of the suspect, but was told that neither police nor Conrail security had available manpower.

Bladel, meanwhile, was becoming known and feared by railroaders throughout northern Indiana and southern Michigan, already uneasy over the shooting of four of their brother trainmen without apparent reason.

"He stalks the tracks. When you drive your train under a bridge you look up, and there's Rudy, staring down at you from the overpass," was a typical complaint.

On the night of the triple slaying in the Jackson depot, Sergeant Keck was having New Year's Eve dinner with his family at home, miles away in Elkhart. When an officer brought him news of the murders his first words were, "Find out where Rudy Bladel is!"

Jackson County Prosecutor Edward Grant, who was at home preparing for a New Year's Eve dinner party when police notified him of the shootings, experienced a similar reaction. "The first thought that crosses my mind," he said, "is Rudy Bladel."

Police immediately set out to locate Bladel, and they didn't have to look far. He was right there, in Jackson. He had spent the night in a local hotel, and had hurriedly checked out before sunrise on New Year's Day. When Jackson police spotted him at 7:00 A.M. he was walking as briskly as his bum leg could carry him toward the Greyhound Bus station to buy a return ticket to Elkhart.

In his pocket was a clipping from the morning newspaper, which reported that police were seeking him for questioning in the triple homicide. He was also carrying a map of Jackson.

"I figured I don't know what's going on here, but I figured I'd better get the heck out of here," he explained when police asked what he was doing in town. "My motorbike broke down while I was on the way to Detroit to look for work. I needed the map to find a repair shop."

"Why didn't you consult the Yellow Pages?"

"I'm a walker," he said, in explaining why he didn't let his fingers do the walking. "I can walk ten miles without thinking about it."

Bladel was questioned about the latest slayings, but authorities were forced to release him after forty-eight hours for lack of evidence. Witnesses who reported seeing a large, shadowy figure bundled in heavy clothes moving across the tracks at the time of the shooting never saw the man's face in the dark, and couldn't identify Bladel as the suspect.

Furthermore, the murder weapon could not be found. Scuba divers scoured the bottom of the Grand River behind the railway station, and helicopters were brought in to check out nearby rooftops—but no gun. Detectives even consulted psychics, without success. So long, Rudy. Take a hike!

Nearly three months after Bladel was reluctantly set free, a shotgun, broken down into two parts, was found under brush in the melting snow in Jackson's Cascade Falls Park. Ejection marks on spent shotgun shells found at the scene of the murders matched test slugs fired, in a police laboratory, from the recovered weapon.

Through the serial number on the shotgun police were able to trace the weapon to its point of purchase. On New Year's Eve, 1976—exactly two years to the day before the Jackson killings—the gun had been sold by an Elkhart gun dealer to none other than Rudy Bladel. The meticulous sales clerk had even recorded the buyer's driver's license and Social Security numbers.

"That's enough for me," Prosecutor Grant declared. "I'm charging Bladel with three counts of murder."

Bladel was arrested by Conrail police that same afternoon—March 22, 1979—while riding his bicycle in Elkhart, and turned over to Michigan authorities.

When Jackson Police Lieutenant Ronald Lowe confronted the suspect with the shotgun and other evidence showing that fiber particles on his clothing and from his suitcase matched those found in the breech of the weapon,

Bladel blurted out, "You've got me. What do you want to know?"

He then told Lowe and Sergeant Richard Wheeler that he checked into the Adams hotel on the day of the killings, carrying the 12-gauge Remington shotgun in his suitcase.

"I left the hotel about 6:15 P.M.," he related. "I went down to the platform, set the suitcase down, walked in the door at the right and shot the man sitting by the door [Robert Blake]. Then I shot the man at the picnic table [William Gulak]. I shot each man twice. Then the other man [Charles Lee Burton] came to the door and I went out and shot him. I walked out and shot him in the head."

Mission completed, Bladel said he broke down the shotgun, put the murder weapon back into the suitcase, and returned to the hotel.

"Would you be willing to put this in writing?" Lowe asked.

"I'm going to plead guilty anyway. I might as well," Bladel shrugged.

He then prepared a brief statement in his own handwriting, in which he said: "On Dec. 31, 1978, I walked into the hot room at the Jackson depot and shot three men to death. I then went back to my hotel room and got rid of the gun. The reason I shot the men is that the railroad took my job and other Elkhart men's jobs."

At his trial that summer, however, Bladel recanted his explicit confession. "The police were yelling at me, so I told them what they wanted to hear," he testified. "They got me all confused and confumbled."

His reason for being in Jackson, he said, was to claim his disabled motorbike. After learning that his fingerprints were found in the Jackson depot on the day of the killings, he explained, "I went there to use the trainmen's washroom."

As for the shotgun that fired the fatal blasts, yes, it was his, he admitted. But, Bladel added, he had sold it to a stranger in an Elkhart restaurant several weeks before the killings for $100.

He was cross-examined by Prosecutor Grant:

Q. Did you have some grievance against the railroad company?

A. In the past, yes. They gave our jobs away. The Niles men took our jobs and laid us off.

Q. And it caused you to lose quite a bit of time?

A. Right, 524 days.

Q. Did you do different things to harass the railroad?

A. Like what, for instance?

Q. Would you go around and stare at railroad employees and just stand by the trains and stare at trainmen and firemen, to make them feel uncomfortable?

A. I've stood at different places, just all kinds of places. I am sitting here and looking at you. Is this harassment?

The jury found Bladel guilty of all three Jackson murders, and on August 29, 1979, he was sentenced to three concurrent life terms and packed off to the Michigan State Prison.

That is not the end of the story, however. In 1985 the Michigan Supreme Court reversed the convictions after ruling that Bladel's signed confession should not have been used against him since it was obtained by police before he could talk to his court-appointed lawyer, even though he might have waived the right to have his lawyer present. The U.S. Supreme Court affirmed the Michigan decision, and on April 1, 1986, Bladel was returned to the Jackson County Jail to await a new trial.

In a jailhouse telephone interview with the authors, Bladel, then fifty-three, a highly articulate man whose military record lists an IQ of 145, insisted:

"This whole thing is because the railroad gave my job away. I can't tell you everything. The thing is going back to trial. I can say what the reason is, and that is: They took my job.

"The union has a right to make a contract with a carrier. Then they give our jobs away. If they keep giving jobs away, there is no end to this thing. All I want to do is redeem my own job. The original contract goes back to 1959. It's been a long fight. This is twenty-seven years old.

"All I'm interested in is securing my own job for myself. I am not interesting in taking anything from anybody. I am trying to stop anybody from taking anything from me."

Bladel was asked point blank: "The police say that you, and you alone, are responsible for the ambush murders of seven of your fellow railroaders. What do you say?"

"I will have no statement on that," he answered.

"The man had one objective in life as far as I can tell, and that was to kill Michigan trainmen," said Jackson Police Sergeant Wheeler, one of many lawmen who have catalogued Bladel's activities. "Bladel knew the reputation he had among railroad men and he played on that. He would go up around the rail yards in Battle Creek, Kalamazoo, and other towns just to stir them up. We know that for a fact."

It is also a fact that with Bladel's arrest the killings stopped. One of the law officers who repeatedly interrogated Bladel in custody was Sergeant Keck.

"We tried every way in the world to get to him, to try and bring out why he did what he did," Keck said. "When we talked about the families of the victims, his only answer was, 'They [the murder victims] should have thought of that.'"

In July 1986 a Circuit Court jury in Detroit awarded the widows of the slain railroad men damages totaling $8.9 million. With interest, the award against Conrail, for negligence for failing to provide adequate protection for the victims, would exceed $12 million.

Although Hammond Detectives Baron and Murray have since retired from police work, their findings in the Bladel case were made a part of the court record in the Detroit civil matter, identifying Bladel as a likely serial killer.

Baron told of sitting down with Bladel two years earlier in the Michigan State Prison, before the Jackson murder conviction was set aside. "I asked him for his help in clearing up our Hammond murder case," he related. "I said, 'Look, Rudy, you are doing life. What have you got to lose?'"

He said Bladel merely folded his beefy hands across his ample stomach and grinned, "You're a cop. Prove I did it."

EPILOGUE

Bladel's retrial for the triple murders in the Jackson rail depot was moved to Kalamazoo on June 16, 1987. His earlier confession could not be used, but Prosecutors Grant and Jerry Schrotenboer called detectives who testified that they had positively placed Bladel at the scene of the slayings of Burton, Gulak, and Black. Bladel's lawyer tried to show that the three trainmen had been killed in a robbery attempt.

After hearing four days of testimony, the jury deliberated less than two hours before finding Bladel guilty on all counts. Conviction for Murder One in the state of Michigan carries a mandatory life sentence.

He is currently serving three concurrent life terms in Michigan's Kinross Correctional Center, a minimum security prison near Sault Sainte Marie. If he is ever released, he still faces charges in connection with the murders of Roy Bottorff and Paul Overstreet in Hammond, and John Marshall and James McCrory in separate shootings in Elkhart.

CHAPTER 11

██████████████████████████████████████

THE UNFAITHFUL BRIDE OF SANIBEL

It's been more than a dozen years now since a guest at the Casa Ybel resort on Sanibel Island, off the gulf coast of Florida, looked out of his window and saw something on the sandy beach that was not in keeping with the historic cay's lure and charm.

Mornings on picturesque Sanibel are awaited by almost everyone. For sun worshipers, it is a time to tan and relax; for the fishermen, to prepare for a fresh catch; and for tourists, to walk barefoot along the sandy beach in search of myriad-colored sea shells of many sizes that wash ashore with the tide.

But it was not sea shells that Chris Hoover saw as he drew open the drapes to greet the sun at 9:30 on the morning of March 6, 1979. From his vantage point it first appeared that a large fish had washed ashore, or a dead alligator, perhaps, at the water's edge.

He focused in on the object as his eyes became accustomed to the bright sunlight. Then he dialed the front desk and exclaimed, "There's a lady's body on the beach! Somebody had better call the police."

Officer Richard Noon, the first lawman on the scene, quickly assessed the situation. The woman, naked except for a yellow belt, was lying on her back in ankle-deep water, parallel to the shoreline. She had dark hair, and creamy, white skin.

"She's partly decomposed. Must have washed in with the tide before sunup," he observed.

"That's a diver's belt around her waist," noted Sergeant William Trefny, who had joined the patrolman. "No bathing suit or anything. What do you make of it, Dick?"

"I don't know what to make of it right now. Too early for that," Noon replied.

The fifty-one-year-old sergeant was a former Greenwich, Connecticut, police lieutenant who had retired after twenty-two years of service. But a life of relaxation and inactivity was not to his taste, and when Sanibel formed its own police department in 1975 he became the island's first patrol officer. Trefny was promoted to sergeant five months later, and in 1987 he would be named chief.

On this Tuesday morning in 1979, however, he found himself confronted with the type of crime he had not experienced since leaving Connecticut—a possible homicide.

"We leave her right where she is until the medical examiner gets here," he advised Noon. They did not have long to wait. It was only a matter of minutes before the Lee County Emergency Medical Service helicopter appeared on the horizon after a quick flight from Fort Myers, just across San Carlos Bay.

The chopper touched down on the beach under the watchful eyes of Sanibel Police Chief John P. Butler, who had joined Trefny and Noon, along with auxiliary policeman Ben Pickens.

Butler briefed Dr. Wallace Graves, the medical examiner, and Salvador Medina, his pathologist, on what little was known about the body lying there in the surf. She was a well-developed young woman, whose pale, white skin bore numerous cuts or breaks.

"Superficial postmortem erosions," Dr. Graves commented. "Probably caused by fish and crab bites."

With the doctor's help police fashioned a makeshift breakwater of plywood around the body, to protect it from the surf while they set about the task of taking photographs and making measurements before it was removed from the water.

Trefny noted that the yellow diver's belt around the dead woman's waist bore no brand name. It contained four lead weights. "Looks like somebody put this thing on her to keep her down," he mused.

Little more could be accomplished at the scene, since the sandy beach obviously was not where the woman had died, and curiosity seekers were beginning to gather. Dr. Graves ordered the body placed aboard the helicopter, and taken to the Lee Memorial Hospital in Fort Myers for an autopsy. The cause of death, as well as the victim's identity, were yet to be determined.

During the postmortem examination the medical examiner determined that the woman was a brunette about twenty years old, five-feet-five-inches tall, weighed 120 pounds, and had worn size 7 shoes. From the condition of the body he estimated that she had been in the water from one to six weeks. Upon conclusion of the autopsy at 4:00 P.M. he confirmed that the woman's death had been a homicide.

"It appears that she was bludgeoned to death," Dr. Graves told Sergeant Ray Rhodes, who had been placed in charge of the investigation by Chief Butler. "She had been struck multiple blows to the head and face. Her jaw is broken. Both her arms are also broken."

The medical examiner removed bone samples and sent them to the University of Florida at Gainesville, requesting that they be examined by the department of anthropology to help determine the age of the victim, and other pertinent information.

From the woman's left hand Dr. Graves removed a white gold ring, set in what appeared to be two diamonds and an emerald. He turned the ring, along with the weighted diver's belt, over to Sergeant Rhodes. The belt, which had been tightened snugly around the woman's waist, was just over twenty-five inches in length and weighted with fifteen pounds of lead—two six-pound and two one-and-a-half pound weights.

The sergeant took the ring to Fort Myers gemologist Jerry Franklin. "Right now this seems to be the only clue to the woman's identity," he told the jeweler. "I'd like to know everything you can tell me about it."

After examining the ring, Franklin told the officer, "It's 14-karat gold, of the type favored by women mostly between the ages of eighteen and thirty. I'd estimate that it cost whoever bought it around $175. This one shows very little wear. It's relatively new."

But in placing the ring under an examining lens, Franklin made another discovery. "Look here, sergeant. There's clear indentation. This ring appears to have been struck with great force of some kind."

Dr. Graves had found trauma wounds on the victim's head and face. Marks on the ring could have been made when she put up her hands to defend herself from the fatal blows. There were no initials on the inside of the band, however, or anything else to indicate to whom the ring might have belonged.

The murder victim was still a Jane Doe, and until police could establish her identity they would have no easy time in determining her killer. How can you track down a murderer when you don't know who has been killed?

Chief Butler, taking an active part in the investigation, was busy checking with other law enforcement agencies to determine whether anyone matching the young woman's description had been reported missing. He also contacted every resort, motel, and restaurant on Sanibel Island, asking whether a young woman with dark brown hair might be unaccounted for.

That evening the chief advised Sergeant Rhodes that a twenty-two-year-old Fort Myers woman, Denise Campos, had called Sanibel police with a suggestion as to whom the murder victim might have been. "I saw the story on television, and I was thinking. I have this nineteen-year-old friend,

Shirley Rhodes. She works as a waitress, but I haven't seen or heard from her in about six weeks," she explained.

Sergeant Rhodes picked up Officer Noon, and they drove back over the Sanibel causeway to Fort Myers to talk to the possible witness. The sergeant had never heard of Shirley Rhodes, despite the similarity in names.

"Shirley lived with her husband, Alan, over on Cypress Drive," Campos told the two Sanibel officers. "Alan and Shirley were married last July. I stopped by to see Shirley on January 29. She wasn't home, but Alan was, and he told me Shirley was missing. I'm worried about her, sergeant. It's not like her to be gone like this and not tell me."

"Was anyone with you when you went to Shirley's house looking for her?"

"My husband," she replied. "Alan came out and said, 'Shirley and me have split.'"

"Did he give any kind of reason for he and his wife splitting up?"

"He said he discovered his wife in bed with a man and a woman when he came home from work unexpectedly during the afternoon of January 25. Alan worked down at one of the boatyards."

She added that Alan Rhodes had told her it was not the first time he had found his wife in bed with other people. "He told me, 'I've caught her three times before,'" she related.

Campos added that Shirley, herself, had once confided in her about such sexual encounters. "She told me, 'Alan caught me in a menage a trois situation three or four times.' Shirley said she was having marital problems due to sexual dissatisfaction."

"And this was January 25 that Alan said he caught her in bed with two other people?"

"Yes. He said the next day Shirley was gone."

Campos described Shirley Rhodes, who had been reared in a small Maryland town, halfway between Baltimore and Washington, D.C., as bearing a striking resemblance to "a nineteen-year-old Shirley Temple."

"Tell me more about Alan Rhodes. Can you describe him for me?" asked the sergeant, somewhat amused that he and a possible murder suspect shared the same last name.

"Yes. He's twenty-four years old, has dark brown hair like Shirley, and he has a mustache," she answered. "I'd say he weighs about 145 pounds and is five-feet-eight-inches tall. He's a boat mechanic, and he taught Shirley how to scuba dive."

Sergeant Rhodes then showed Mrs. Campos the ring that had been removed from the dead woman's finger, and asked, "Does this look familiar to you?"

"Yes, that's Shirley's ring," she gasped.

Police now had a tentative identification, and Butler assigned Sergeant Don Case to see what he could find out about Shirley and Alan Rhodes.

On the following afternoon, March 7, Case went to the Aquatronics shop on Periwinkle Way on Sanibel Island, where he had determined that Alan Rhodes once worked. He talked to Greg and Dianne Potts, owners of Aquatronics, and their mechanic, twenty-year-old Jan Gower, who lived on the property.

"Alan Rhodes? Yeah he worked here two years ago for a month or so," Potts told the sergeant. "Wait a minute. I'll dig out his W-4 form." The tax form showed Rhodes had been employed by Aquatronics from August 5 to September 23, 1977. Case made a copy of the form, which contained Alan Rhodes signature.

"He said he was originally from New York City," Potts offered. "He quit here because he wanted to attend a diving and underwater welding school in California, he told us."

"What kind of a fellow is he?" Case inquired.

"Ah, he was a loner, I'd say. Moody. But a neat and orderly worker," Potts replied. "He went to Bowman's Beach with his girlfriend to swim nude quite a bit. Thin, dark-haired girl, about five-foot-five, five-foot-six-inches tall. He finally married her."

The Potts and Gower said they had not seen Rhodes around in several months.

Later that afternoon Case called at the office of a local physician who had treated Shirley Rhodes for a skin allergy. The doctor's records provided her date of birth, May 23, 1959, and her maiden name, Shirley Pond. There was no record of her blood type, however.

Shortly after 5:00 P.M. Case talked to Mr. and Mrs. Mac Hamby, owners of the Tarpon Bay Marina. "I'm trying to get a line on a Shirley Pond, or Shirley Rhodes—that was her married name. I understand she used to work around here," he explained.

"Shirley? Yeah, she worked for Dorothy Edmondson in the Red Pelican shop," Hamby said. "Her husband worked for us too, as a mechanic, but I had to fire him for stealing."

Mrs. Hamby told the detective that Shirley had been friendly with her seventeen-year-old step-daughter, Jennifer Mitchell. Jennifer was presently visiting relatives in Atlanta, but Case was able to talk to Jennifer's sixteen-year-old sister, Becky. "Alan Rhodes smoked pot while working for my folks," she related. "He told me he found a lot of pot on the beach."

The next stop was the Red Pelican shop, which was situated on marina property. "Shirley is a very nice girl, and she was a good worker," Dorothy Edmondson stated. "She'd had an abortion about two years ago, but that was before she came to work for me."

"Have you seen her recently?" Case asked.

"The last time I saw Shirley was around January 15 or 16. She came over to the Red Pelican on a red motorcycle Alan had given her."

She, too, gave the detective a description of Shirley Rhodes which, like the others, matched that of the murder victim. Sanibel police contacted authorities in Laurel, Maryland, where Shirley Pond Rhodes had formerly lived, and asked for help in locating her family.

Shortly before 9:30 that evening Patrol Officer Betty Beir received a telephone call from Detective Daniel Statkus in Prince George's County, Maryland. "We've located the young lady's parents, Mr. and Mrs. Clayton Pond," he reported. "They told us they haven't heard from Shirley in several months now, and they're a little worried something might have happened to her.

"Shirley was in the habit of calling her parents on the telephone at least once a month, usually on the twenty-fifth, according to her mother. She said Shirley called them on Christmas Day and on January 25, but they haven't heard anything since. Leastwise, not in person."

Statkus explained that the parents told him that about two weeks after the last time they had heard from their daughter, her husband, Alan Rhodes, telephoned them to report that Shirley had left him, and he did not know where she was. When the Ponds asked their son-in-law whether he had checked with any of Shirley's friends, he told them, "I don't know any of them."

The last time that they had heard from their daughter, Mrs. Pond told Statkus, Shirley posed a hypothetical question about what one would think of a man beating up on his wife because he had caught her "fooling around" with another man. "The way Shirley phrased the question, it was like she was talking about a friend, but I had the feeling she was talking about herself," Mrs. Pond told the detective.

Shirley and Alan were still newlyweds, who hadn't been married a year, according to the Ponds. They said the couple moved to Florida, where Alan taught his bride to scuba dive, immediately after their marriage on July 15, 1978. They described Alan as a young man who possessed "an exceptionally short fuse." On one occasion his violent temper cost him his job at a marina, after he almost killed a customer in a fight over a disagreement about a motor he had repaired.

They said their daughter had been attending Edison Community College in Florida, but was not enrolled for the December quarter. In answer to a routine question as to whether Shirley had ever been in trouble with the law, they said she had a juvenile arrest record for possession of marijuana and trespassing, but had never been fingerprinted.

While there were no prints of Shirley Pond on record, Statkus was able to obtain a copy of her dental x-rays, and the couple's wedding photograph. He forwarded them to Sanibel Island police by air.

Meanwhile Sergeant Rhodes and Lee County Sheriff's Sergeant Rayfield Newton were doing their best to find the elusive Alan Rhodes, to see what he had to say about his wife's disappearance. They were unable to locate him at his Fort Myers apartment on Cypress Drive, but they did talk to his landlord, Pierce Tinsley.

"Haven't seen him around all day, but his rent's paid up until April 1. He paid me one month in advance on March 2," the landlord commented. "The wife and I did notice something funny last night, though. We though it unusual that his van was backed into the driveway, rather than pulled in front forward as it normally is."

With the van backed into the drive, the side loading door would have been next to the house—convenient for packing. The van was no longer there when police arrived, but a red Honda motorcycle was parked alongside the duplex apartment building. The detectives ran a make on the license number, which was registered in the name of Alan J. Rhodes.

"Sorry I can't help you officers more," Tinsley apologized. "You might try the young man's parents. Maybe they know where he is. They're just over in Cape Coral."

From the couple's apartment Sergeants Rhodes and Newton went to Perkins Steak and Cake House on U.S. Highway 41, where they learned that Shirley Rhodes had worked as a waitress. Records showed that her last day on the job was Saturday, January 27. She had been scheduled to work Sunday, the twenty-eighth, but her husband telephoned and said she would not be in. Her $70 paycheck for 45.7 hours of waiting on tables was still waiting to be picked up.

Back at Sanibel Sergeant Rhodes picked up Officer Noon, and they drove over to Cape Coral to talk to the missing man's parents, Lawrence and Helen Rhodes, but were stonewalled. Mrs. Rhodes talked to the sergeant by phone, but refused to allow him to come to her home. "My husband's out of town, and I will not accept any visitors until he returns," she declared.

"But Mrs. Rhodes, we are attempting to identify the body of a young woman who could be your daughter-in-law," the sergeant protested.

"What do you want me to do about it?" she snapped.

"Well, if you won't help us, perhaps you can tell us where Alan might be, so we can talk to him."

"I have no idea as to the whereabouts of my son."

On the following morning, March 8, Sergeant Rhodes alerted Dr. Graves that the missing woman's dental records were on the way from Maryland, and should arrive around noon. He also briefed Assistant State Attorney Rad Sturgis on the case. "Okay, sergeant. If and when the body is positively identified as that of Shirley Rhodes, we'll get a search warrant for the couple's apartment," he advised.

As the lunch hour approached, Sergeant Rhodes and Officer Noon met Sergeant Tom Wallace in the medical examiner's office, to await the delivery of Shirley Pond's dental records from Paige Field, the Lee County airport. When the x-rays arrived Dr. Graves huddled over them with Dr. Gerald Laboda, a dentist and oral surgeon. "No question about it," Laboda said, after comparing the charts with x-rays of the dead woman's skull. "These are one and the same."

Two and one half days after her body was found bobbing in the surf off the Casa Ybel resort, police had positively established that the murder victim was indeed Shirley Pond Rhodes.

Meanwhile, as word of the identification was broadcast on radio and local television, Sanibel police received a call from a woman who said she had worked with Shirley as a waitress in a Fort Myers restaurant. "I think she was fooling around," the woman said. "You know, I think she was having an affair with a man who worked with us. He was fired last week. But awhile back her husband came to the restaurant looking for her, and he was very upset."

While the search for Rhodes continued police learned that he had failed to show up for work at the local boatyard on Tuesday, the day his wife's body was found. A friend of the missing man, Chris Wood, told them that Rhodes had stopped by his home in Cape Coral the previous night.

"Alan came by and asked me to hold his personal diving gear for safekeeping. He told me he was leaving town for awhile," Wood said. The gear he left behind included scuba masks, air tanks, and swim fins.

Police went over the equipment with Wood, and determined that Rhodes' yellow diving belt was not among the items. That was undoubtedly the weighted belt found tightened around the dead woman's waist in an unsuccessful effort to keep her body at the bottom of the Gulf of Mexico.

Sergeant Rhodes, Noon, and Wallace then proceeded to the sheriff's office, where a search warrant was drawn up for the couple's apartment at 1741 Cypress Drive, in the Pine Manor subdivision of Fort Myers. While waiting for the document to be finalized, Sergeant Rhodes learned that the missing man's 1972 Ford van had been located. Alan Rhodes had sold it to a man who identified himself as Daniel Richmond.

Contacted by phone, Richmond agreed to bring the van over to the sheriff's office. He pulled in at 5:30 P.M., and signed a release permitting Deputy Sheriff Sam Johnson to search the vehicle.

Johnson conducted a luminol test of the van, using ultraviolet light to detect blood stains. The light picked up several stained areas on the carpeting, as well as on a pair of boots that Rhodes had left in the vehicle when he sold it.

As soon as the search warrant was properly filled out, Sergeants Wallace and Rhodes drove to the home of Circuit Judge Wallace Pack, who signed the document authorizing a search of the apartment on Cypress Drive. Police returned to the white stucco building, where they were admitted by Tinsley, the owner of the duplex.

Beginning at 6:30 P.M., Sergeants Wallace and Rhodes, and Deputy Johnson, spent the next five hours going over every inch of the apartment.

What appeared to be drops of dried blood were found on bedroom walls, living room walls, under the dining room table, on kitchen cabinets, and on the kitchen floor. A number of stains were found along metal stripping which secured a carpet to the tile floor in the kitchen.

Human hair attached to skin tissues was also found in the living room, and in the bristles of a scrub brush. The brush apparently had been used to wash down the apartment after what must have been a gory bludgeoning.

The search team also collected wedding pictures of the couple, two books relating to sexual problems, five butcher knives, a meat cleaver, and various pictures of Alan and Shirley Rhodes in happier times. The fleeing husband had apparently taken little more than what he could carry when he left. The evidence was presented to Prosecutor Sturgis, who authorized the filing of formal murder charges against Alan Rhodes, the missing husband, on March 9.

Police theorized from the evidence that Rhodes killed his unfaithful wife in the apartment, most likely with the meat cleaver. He then wrapped the weighted diver's belt around her waist, placed her naked body in his van which had been backed up close to the door, and drove to a local beach.

He then put the body in a small boat, cruised to what he thought would be a safe distance offshore, and disposed of his handiwork at sea, never realizing it would come back to haunt him on the beach at historic Sanibel Island.

An announcement from the prosecutor's office, citing the cooperation between various law enforcement agencies, said that "after extensive investigation" by the medical examiner's office, the Lee County Sheriff's Department and Sanibel police, an arrest warrant had been issued charging Alan Jeffrey Rhodes with his bride's murder.

Only one problem: Alan had flown the coop. "Media coverage of the discovery of the body permitted the suspect to flee the area prior to any questioning," Sergeant Rhodes explained. Of course, one could hardly blame the media for its interest. Murder doesn't happen every day on Sanibel Island.

Sergeant Rhodes, along with Rayfield Newton from the sheriff's office, paid a return visit to the suspect's parents' home at Cape Coral. The fugitive's fifty-six-year-old father, Lawrence Rhodes, had returned from his trip and cooperated fully with the investigators.

"We lived in Brooklyn, New York, before moving down here to Florida," the elder Rhodes explained. "The last I saw of Alan was March 6. He came by and asked to borrow some money. I gave him $300. He and Shirley were having difficulties with their marriage. My son is a reliable husband and worker. But he told me he had caught her in bed with another man."

That was the apparent motive police were looking for. But as to where Rhodes had been able to go on the borrowed $300, plus what he got for the sale of the van, they have been unable to determine to this day.

In December 1979, nine months after Shirley Rhodes' body washed ashore, her father, Clayton Pond, offered a $1,000 reward for information about the whereabouts of his missing son-in-law. There have been no takers, and the reward remains unclaimed.

EPILOGUE

Fugitive murder suspect Alan Rhodes has been on the run and out of sight for more than a dozen years, but he has not been forgotten by Sanibel Island police or the Lee County CrimeStoppers. Over the years Captain Dennis Duffala of the Lee County Sheriff's Police, active in the citizen-run Southwest Florida CrimeStop Program, Inc., has kept the case alive through every public relations means at his disposal, from radio broadcasts to TV spot commercials.

At the urging of the CrimeStop program, the Federal Bureau of Investigation joined the manhunt on a nationwide scale, seeking Rhodes for unlawful flight to avoid prosecution for his wife's murder.

Alan Rhodes would be thirty-six years old at this writing. He remains at large, and the $1,000 reward posted by the slain woman's father, along with an additional $1,000 put up by CrimeStop, is still waiting to be collected. Sanibel Island police hope that someone who reads this story might recognize the suspect's photo and contact authorities. The Southwest Florida CrimeStop number is (813) 332-5555.

CHAPTER 12

<hr>

THE MYSTERY OF STARVED ROCK

One would hardly know it, hiking lazily through the winter wonderland of glistening snow and frozen waterfalls of St. Louis Canyon, but Starved Rock State Park in downstate Illinois harbors two grisly stories within its 2,600 sprawling acres of pristine beauty.

How Starved Rock got its name is one of those stories. It is a legend, the nature of which historians do not dispute.

In the 1760s, as fighting broke out among Indians living near the towering sandstone column, a desperate band of Illiniwek took refuge atop the formation from attacking Ottawa-Potawatomi tribes.

The Illiniwek had precious little food to begin with, and obtained water by lowering baskets into the Illinois River 130 feet below. The enemy, camped at the foot of the rock, caught on and literally cut off that source of life by severing vines holding the baskets.

After that there was no need to attack. There was no escape for the Indians on the rock, who slowly starved to death.

The more modern story is the horrifying tale of three well-to-do matrons from one of Chicago's more exclusive suburbs, who went there in March 1960 as a tonic for the winter blahs. It turned out to be a one-way trip.

All three were wives of local business executives, all were mothers, and all were prominent for their own civic involvement in the landmark western suburb of Riverside.

Frances Murphy, forty-seven, and Mildred Lindquist, fifty, hatched the idea of a mid-week getaway vacation while chatting after the Sunday service at Riverside Presbyterian Church, where all three of the women were active. "You deserve a vacation too, Lillian," they told fifty-year-old Lillian Oetting, who had spent the long winter months ministering to a sick husband. "Why don't you come with us?"

The fatal die was cast. The three women went grocery shopping and filled their refrigerators to make sure their families would be provided for over the next few days. Then, on Monday morning, March 14, they headed for the state park on the banks of the Illinois River just below Ottawa. They arrived after a two-hour drive and checked in at the rustic Starved Rock Lodge overlooking the snow-covered park.

Esther Eickoff, the desk clerk, assigned them to adjoining rooms, 109 for Mrs. Oetting, with Mrs. Lindquist and Mrs. Murphy in 110. After freshening up they had lunch in the spacious dining room. Then they put on their hiking shoes, made sure they had film in their cameras, and set off for a 1.2-mile walk into St. Louis Canyon, a geological formation that constituted one of the park's feature attractions.

Mrs. Oetting, whose husband, George, suffered from a heart ailment, had promised to phone him that evening to make sure all was well on the home front. When he did not hear from her Oetting telephoned the lodge, but got no answer when the operator rang his wife's room. Oetting, an Illinois Bell Telephone Company executive, tried contacting Lillian again on Tuesday, but with no success.

Later that day a postal card arrived at the lodge, addressed to the three women. Esther Eickoff, the desk clerk, put it into a pigeon hole for one of the rooms the trio occupied.

Meanwhile, after several more puzzling attempts to get through to his wife both Tuesday night and Wednesday morning, Oetting called his brother, Herman, in the neighboring suburb of Berwyn. "Herm, I can't seem to reach Lil down at Starved Rock Lodge, and I'm getting a little edgy," he said. "I wonder if you'd give it a try. Maybe you'll have better luck."

Herman Oetting did give it a try, several times, but he was unable to get an answer when he called his sister-in-law's room. He then called the lodge office and asked an employee to check the parking lot to make sure the women's car was there.

The lodge worker, not feeling overly cooperative, told him, "If you're interested in doing that, you probably ought to talk to the sheriff in Ottawa—but you should make the decision, not me." A frustrated Herman Oetting relayed the message to his brother. George then called Frances Murphy's husband, Robert, an official of Borg-Warner Corporation, and expressed his concern for their wives.

Murphy put in a call to his wife at the lodge, with the same negative results. He then called Robert Lindquist, a vice president of Harris Trust and Savings Bank. Lindquist had not heard from the women either.

The influential husbands were not without resources, and if the people at the lodge were not willing to help them, they knew how to rattle a few cages. Murphy phoned Virgil Peterson, operating director of the Chicago Crime Commission, who was a friend of all three men and their wives. "That's what we seem to be up against, Virg," he said, after filling him in on the details. "What do you think we ought to do?"

"Bob, I'll put in a call to Bill Morris, the State Police superintendent," Peterson told the worried husband. "While I'm doing that, you phone Sheriff Ray Eutsey in Ottawa— that's E-U-T-S-E-Y. Tell him that the girls haven't been heard from since they checked in at the lodge. Tell him you talked to me. He'll get the ball rolling."

The calls from Chicago spurred downstate authorities into action. After verifying that the three matrons were not in the lodge, and that their beds had not been slept in, the sheriff's men embarked on a massive search of the state park.

The hunt ended Wednesday almost as soon as it began. Fanning out from the lodge, one search party made its way into St. Louis Canyon, where its members spotted ominous red splotches on a large rock protruding from the snow at the mouth of a cave. The searchers were hardly prepared for the grotesque scene that awaited them as they cautiously poked the beams of their flashlights into the dim cavern.

Lillian Oetting, Frances Murphy, and Mildred Lindquist were lying on the bloodstained floor of the cave. Their skirts had been pulled up around their necks and they had been stripped naked from the waist down. All three had been bludgeoned to death. Mrs. Murphy's and Mrs. Oetting's wrists were bound with twine.

After evidentiary photos were taken, the battered corpses were removed to nearby Ottawa, where two pathologists for the La Salle County coroner's office, Doctors Albert Schweitzer and John E. Maloney, performed autopsies. The postmortem examinations disclosed that all three women had died of skull fractures and brain damage suffered in a savage beating. Traces of blood found in Mrs. Murphy's lungs indicated she had inhaled it after being beaten, meaning she did not die instantly.

The time of the deaths was set at about 2:30 or 3:00 P.M. Monday, shortly after the trio had embarked on their nature hike.

The pathologists were unable to determine immediately whether the victims had been raped, although they suspected the worst.

"While we must leave open the fact that the victims might have been violated, we should also consider that the murders could have been disguised as a sex killing," cautioned State's Attorney Harland Warren, who joined State Police Superintendent Morris and Sheriff Eutsey in the homicide investigation. "For all we know, their clothing could have been disarranged deliberately to throw us off the track."

"I think we should be looking for a psychopath," Sheriff Eutsey asserted. "I would stake my reputation that these murders were committed by a parolee or an escapee from a mental institution. I don't think anyone else is capable of this type of murder."

The possible murder weapon, a bloody tree limb, three feet long and four inches thick, was found on the hard-packed snow near the entrance of the cave.

A search of the victims' rooms turned up Mrs. Murphy's purse, which she had left at the lodge. In the purse police found a farewell note from her twelve-year-old daughter, Mary. Scrawled in childish hand on a page from a spiral notebook, it read:

> Farwell!
> Mom
> Hope you have a nice trip.

Below the message the child had drawn caricatures of three women identified as Three Musketeers, labeled "Mrs Otting [sic], Mrs Lindquist, and You the Best Mom in the whole world." At the bottom was a poem:

> A camping they will go
> A camping they will go
> Hi Ho the dario
> A camping they will go

The initial phase of the homicide investigation involved interviewing the 62 employees of the park and lodge where the women had registered shortly before their fatal walk in the wilderness. That produced yet another mystery.

One of the first employees questioned, Esther Eickoff, the desk clerk, recalled that one of the Riverside women had received a postcard on Tuesday. "I clearly remember placing it in one of their boxes, but I can't recall whether it was 109 or 110," she related. "The card was gone when I checked the boxes afterward. I just assumed one of the ladies had picked it up."

This would have been impossible, since all three women were already dead by the time the missive was delivered. Question: Who took the postcard out of the pigeonhole, and why? It would certainly appear that someone at the lodge had gone to great lengths to make it seem that the women were still around the day after they had been murdered.

Investigators subsequently determined that the card had been sent by a friend of the women from Riverside, saying she wished she could be enjoying their vacation with them.

On Saturday two polygraph examiners from State Police Headquarters in Springfield, Thomas Howerton and William Abernathy, set up their lie detecting apparatus in the Hotel Creedon in Ottawa, where authorities began administering lie tests under the direction of Superintendent Morris.

The first suspect to go on the lie box was a bakery truck driver, who had been seen near the entrance of the canyon on Monday. Investigators had found twine, similar to the cord used to bind the wrists of two of the murder victims, in his delivery van.

Others given lie tests included a salesman who said he had seen three women talking to two men in a blue and white Chevrolet near the park entrance on Monday afternoon; a busboy from the lodge who had been fired for drunkenness; the operator of an area bait shop who had warned one of his employees not to talk to police who were canvassing the area; and a young stable hand who was missing from his home near the park on Monday, and did not return until Wednesday, after the bodies were found.

All of those questioned throughout the weekend passed the lie tests, showing they knew nothing about the triple murder which had stunned the quiet downstate community of 18,000.

There continued to be no shortage of suspects, however. One Monday, one week after the women disappeared, state police and La Salle County authorities, along with investigators from Cook County, found themselves in an all-out search for a La Salle area man described as "a physically powerful and vicious sexual degenerate." The town of La Salle was just down the road from Ottawa.

Police became interested in the man after a pair of twenty-nine-year-old Chicago burglars named William Ceiley and William Blaha, who said they here his accomplices, told authorities he had hidden some guns in a canyon in Starved Rock Park. The fact that he had been described as a vicious and powerful sexual degenerate, coupled with the Starved Rock connection, suddenly made him a prime suspect.

Ceiley and Blaha were taken under heavy guard to Starved Rock by aides to Paul D. Newey, chief investigator for the Cook County State's Attorney. The two burglars were chauffeured around the park by State's Attorney's Investigators Robert Schroeder, Emil Demko, and Sidney Moaz, until the thieves yelled "Stop!" at a point about half a mile from the main entrance. "Okay, this is where we parked once, and the guy got out of the car and walked to his weapons cave," they told Newey's men. "He came back fifteen or twenty minutes later with nine stolen guns."

The spot was just one-half mile from the cave in which the three women had been bludgeoned to death. Could there be a connection?

Meanwhile, Police Chief James Callahan of nearby La Salle located a witness who said he had seen the suspect, an accused burglar free on bond, driving a blue pickup truck on the day the women were murdered. A second witness told Callahan he had seen a blue pickup speed out of the park's south gate around four o'clock that same afternoon, followed by a gray station wagon.

The description of the second car tallied with a report by a La Salle auto salesman, who had told detectives he was driving past the end of the park near St. Louis Canyon on State Highway 178 earlier on the afternoon of the slayings, and saw three women talking to a man who was standing alongside a gray Plymouth station wagon. The salesman described the man as in his mid twenties, about five-feet-eight-inches tall, 165 pounds, and having wavy or kinky reddish-brown hair.

"He was wearing a yellow-gray fingertip coat and blue pants, maybe blue jeans," the witness recalled. "The man was gesturing, as though pointing the way into the canyon."

These stories gave credence to the tale told by the two burglars. The search for the La Salle man intensified.

"There is no doubt in my mind that this witness saw the three murder victims," State Police Lieutenant Emil Toffant, who was Morris' top homicide investigator, opined. "He described their clothing, the fact that one had a pair of opera glasses on a strap around her neck, and another had a camera on a shoulder strap."

In checking out the guest list at the lodge, other investigators for Chief Morris found a clergyman, now in Brookings, South Dakota, who had made 8 mm movies and color slides of St. Louis Canyon the previous Monday afternoon. At the request of Illinois authorities the Reverend A.W. Helfin, pastor of the Open Bible Church of Des Moines, was questioned by Police Chief James J. Connelly of Brookings, where he had gone to preach.

"I walked a few rods into the canyon about 2:00 P.M., but decided not to go all the way to the cave because the terrain was too rugged," Helfin told Connelly. The minister turned his films over to authorities to be developed. "You'll find they contain pictures of many individuals—possibly the women who were murdered and their killer or killers—and several automobiles," he suggested.

The ever-widening manhunt was joined by John F. Schaich, supervisor of the Illinois State Crime Laboratory, who huddled with Chief Morris, Sheriff Eutsey, and Prosecutor Warren in the state's attorney's office.

Schaich was shown the cord that had bound the wrists of Frances Murphy and Lillian Oetting. "This is twenty-strand twine, of the type used for tying parcels, freezer packages, and meat in butcher shops," he said. A similar piece of twenty-strand twine found near the mouth of the murder cave had been tied in a granny—a mistied square knot—to a piece of ten-strand twine.

"One important factor here is that the twine from the wrists of the two victims appears to have been cut. One segment appears to have been severed with a sharp knife, and the other segment appears to have been sawed and then pulled apart," the crime lab expert noted.

"This could mean that the women had been tied together at one time and then their bonds cut apart."

After his meeting with Schaich, State's Attorney Warren contacted Dr. Meyer Kruglik, chief psychiatrist at Stateville Penitentiary. "Doc, we need your help," the prosecutor told him. "Do you think you could compile a prototype of the type of man or men who might have murdered these three women at Starved Rock? It would help to give us an idea of what kind of man we're looking for."

After reviewing the evidence, Dr. Kruglik reported back, "I cannot visualize the prototype with any degree of certainty, because my analysis was made only from pictures of the victims and a factual account of the crime. But the tying of the twine, and the severing of it, indicates the crime could be the work of a sadist who got sex satisfaction out of that act without actually molesting the women after killing them."

Police meanwhile had developed the film in the victims' cameras, with startling results. A picture snapped by Mrs. Oetting appeared to have been taken moments before she and her companions were slain. It contained the blurred figure of a man—possibly the killer himself—in the background!

"I believe we have a picture of the killer," Sheriff Eutsey exclaimed, showing reporters a four-foot-square enlargement of the 35-millimeter camera film. "I believe Mrs. Oetting saw a man appear in the background and snapped his picture, but because she was nervous, she got a triple exposure in trying to roll the film. The picture shows something hanging from the right hand of the man. I believe it may be the club he picked up there and used to kill the women with."

Sheriff's Deputy William Dummett pointed out that the picture, a multiple exposure, depicted the figure of a man standing on the floor of St. Louis Canyon about fifteen feet from the cave where the women's bodies were found.

The man appeared to be in his twenties, about five-feet-eight-inches tall, weighing 160 to 165 pounds. He wore blue trousers tucked into his boots, and a parka-type jacket or fingertip coat with a hood.

The description of the man in the blurred photo matched that of the area suspect authorities had been seeking. The search for the suspect intensified. Then it blew sky high when two *Chicago Tribune* reporters, Tom Powers and Sandy Smith, located him right under the noses of police, and determined that he had been miles away at the time of the murders.

The husky, twenty-three-year-old suspect was cleared after undergoing a lie test which confirmed that he had no knowledge of the killings. "I might have done a lot of things in my life, but I could not kill three women as old as my mother," he asserted. "I should be locked up if I'm as bad as the police say I am. This is idiotic. It's goofy. It's like a cartoon run backwards and it doesn't make sense."

The next bizarre turn in the gory case came when investigators discovered that the killer might possibly have used the victims' rooms at the lodge to tidy up after bludgeoning the women to death.

A maid, Nellie Falletti, revealed that when she entered the rooms on March 15, the day after the women disappeared, she found two damp towels on the bathroom floor, a ring of greasy dirt in the bathtub, and a bar of wet soap.

"I went into the rooms to make the beds, but found they had not been slept in, except the spread on the bed in 110 had been turned down and an impression in the pillow indicated someone had rested there," she said. "I picked up the damp towels, cleaned the tub, and removed the soap without giving the matter any thought at that time."

Lillian Oetting's key could not be accounted for. The killer could have used it to get into the rooms.

"It has not been found near the cave where the women were murdered. If it is not there, hidden under the snow, then it must have been taken by the killer," Superintendent Morris suggested.

Investigators put together a timetable for the victims, from the minute they arrived at the lodge at 12:28 P.M. on March 14. The schedule ruled out the possibility that any of them might have had time to use the bathtub. They checked in, went to their rooms, had lunch, changed into their hiking clothes, and were seen leaving the lodge all within an hour's time.

"If we had only known about the maid's story the day the bodies were discovered, we might have recovered the damp towels and subjected them to a microscopic examination," Lt. Toffant observed with dismay. "The crime lab guys could have taken the drain from the tub and determined whether the killer had washed blood from his body after the slayings."

Another blow to the investigation came when state crime lab specialists told Morris that the bloody tree limb found near the murder scene could not have been the instrument of death. They determined that the blood covered limb was so rotten in some places it undoubtedly would have cracked on impact if it had been used to bludgeon the women.

Sheriff Eutsey now pinned his hopes of solving the triple homicide on the fuzzy picture found in Mrs. Oetting's camera. He sent the triple exposure to the Eastman Kodak Company in Rochester, New York, to be examined by photo interpretation experts.

Clutching at straws now, investigators also traveled to Iowa City, where they hoped to question a twenty-nine-year-old truck driver in the Veterans Administration Hospital. The trucker had been found unconscious from an overdose of barbiturates in a Rock Falls, Illinois, motel the day after the women's bodies were found. He was eliminated as a suspect, however, after his work record showed he could not have been anywhere near Starved Rock on the day of the murders.

As of March 24, five men who had been considered "good suspects" had been cleared by lie tests or ironclad alibis, but police still weren't running out of candidates. That evening Morris revealed that two new suspects had come under police scrutiny. One was a twenty-three-year-old motorist arrested in Macomb as he drove around town stark naked, trying to entice women into his car. The other was a twenty-seven-year-old mental patient who had escaped from Chicago State Hospital. He was described as having red hair and freckles.

While state police checked out one suspect after another, Sheriff Eutsey continued to maintain that the key to identifying the killer was the fuzzy photograph found in the Oetting camera. His theory was not shared by others, however, as it became increasingly clear that various investigative agencies were hardly working together in attempting to solve the triple homicide.

The "red-haired man" theory gained impetus as state police investigators turned up five more witnesses who said they had seen a man matching that description near the state park prior to the murders. On several occasions the red-haired man acted as a guide, and volunteered to take pictures of women with a camera he carried slung around his neck.

"If this man is the killer, these witnesses came close to violent death themselves," Lieutenant Toffant told Chief Morris.

The report that the suspect carried a camera led authorities to speculate that, if he was indeed the killer, he might have photographed his victims after beating them to death and stripping their bodies of clothing from the waist down. And the fact that he offered to act as a guide would seem to indicate he was a "local" who knew his way around.

The long-awaited movie film from the Des Moines minister, which South Dakota police had mailed to Sheriff Eutsey, turned up damaged in a dead-letter box at the Chicago Post Office.

The sheriff dispatched a deputy to claim the film and take it to Aurora for developing. He then hopped a plane for Rapid City, South Dakota, to have a chat with the traveling preacher to see whether he could shed any light on the murders. Chief Deputy Dummett, Assistant State's Attorney John Wolslegel, and Stephen Kindig, a polygraph expert, accompanied the sheriff on the flight.

While the sheriff was chasing down leads in South Dakota, state police in Chicago came up with two more possible suspects, a burly man with a long police record who lived in the neighborhood of the slain women, and a thirty-eight-year-old ex-convict in Terre Haute, Indiana. And the search continued for the elusive redhead.

To the surprise of almost everyone involved in the investigation, final results of the autopsies performed by the two pathologists showed no evidence that the three women had been raped. Apparently their killer was a voyeur who got his jollies by pulling off his victims' clothing from the waist down and enjoying the view.

Back in South Dakota the Rev. Aubrey Heflin agreed to return to Ottawa with Sheriff Eutsey to help analyze the home movies he had taken. The first thing authorities did when he arrived at Chicago's Midway Airport on Sunday, March 27, was to have him submit to a "routine" lie detector test, which verified that he had no personal involvement in the slayings.

A screen was then set up for the long, anticipated preview of the reverend's movies. Disappointingly, they turned out to be nothing more than amateurish panoramas of the scenic parkland.

The next day a section of leather strap and a buckle, apparently torn from a camera carried by one of the women, was found on a trail 100 yards down from the cave. This indicated that the women encountered their killer on the trail, where he attacked them before forcing them into the cave and clubbing them to death. A broken piece of a woman's comb was also found along the trail.

Two days later Sheriff Eutsey and Deputy Dummett were airborne again, this time for Rochester to go over the shadowy triple exposure found in Lillian Oetting's camera with Eastman Kodak experts. State police scoffed at the sheriff's mission as a search for an elusive will-o'-the-wisp.

The Chicago press, which was doing its best to keep the story alive with daily page one headlines, reported: PARK MURDER PICTURE CLEW PROVES A DUD.

Robbery suddenly loomed as the motive for killings after a state police inventory of the victims' belongings revealed that two rings generally worn by Lillian Oetting were missing—and presumably stolen by the killer. "This puts an entirely new light on the crime," Lieutenant Toffant said hopefully. "The questioning of all suspects up to now was developed on the basis that the murders had a sex motivation. We will start all over again and re-question everyone, in the light of this new evidence."

Investigators were also dispatched to area pawn shops, where they hoped the missing jewelry might turn up.

The robbery theory went down the drain on April 15, when a sheriff's detective found the missing rings in the dead woman's left-hand glove, which she had stuffed into her coat pocket before she was slain. Apparently she suspected the worst when she and her companions came face-to-face with a stranger on the trail.

The clothing of all three women had been returned to the La Salle County sheriff's office by the state crime lab, which presumably had gone over everything with a fine-tooth comb. Score one for Sheriff Eutsey's side.

While overlooking the rings, the crime lab did discover several bloody fingerprints on the victims' clothing, apparently left by the killer.

This led to the largest mass fingerprinting task ever undertaken by Illinois State Police, as Morris ordered fingerprint checks of some 500 employees of the state park and concessionaires doing business with the park.

The embarrassing ring incident caused Joseph Bibb, Illinois Director of Public Safety, to call for legislation to combine the state crime lab with the state police. "The crime lab certainly goofed and muffed its examination of evidence in this case," he declared. The controversy led to the resignation of James Christensen, superintendent of the Illinois Bureau of Criminal Identification, which operated the lab.

Sheriff Eutsey, no longer wanting anything to do with the state laboratory, sent several strands of hair, found clutched in Lillian Oetting's hand, to the Michigan State Police Crime Laboratory in East Lansing for examination. The bloody tree limb was also sent to an independent crime lab, which determined— contrary to what the state lab had found—that it could, indeed, have been the murder weapon.

As spring moved into summer, and summer into fall, it seemed that every transient who had the misfortune of passing through north-central Illinois found himself strapped to the lie box; every owner of a gray car was questioned; and every criminal suspect arrested for almost anything, anywhere in the state, was quizzed about the murders.

It seemed to be a never-ending quest. State Police Sergeant William T. Hall, who would later become police chief of Springfield, Illinois, put in thirty-two days and nights on the case before he got a day off.

By mid-October investigators had zeroed in on yet another possible suspect, Chester Otto "Rocky" Weger, a husky, twenty-one-year-old dishwasher at Starved Rock Lodge. Weger, who earned his nickname as a light-heavyweight boxer in the Marine Corps, was married and the father of two small children.

It had taken probers a long time to get around to him, but when they did he made a poor showing on a series of lie tests.

State police, working with Prosecutor Warren, placed young Weger under surveillance after lengths of string, identical to the twine used to bind the wrists of the murdered women, were found in a tool shed used by the suspect. A buckskin jacket, worn by Weger and marked with dark stains, was sent to the state crime laboratory for blood testing.

The ne'er-do-well dishwasher seemed to revel in the attention. At times he came out of his house to chat with detectives posted in their cars parked outside. On one occasion he playfully pointed his .22 caliber rifle at Detective Dennis Jaskoviak, who was participating in the around-the-clock stakeout, and then flashed the lawman a friendly smile.

Weger had first come to the attention of investigators early in the case because of cuts and abrasions on his face, and because he had been working at the lodge on the day the three Riverside matrons checked in. He initially passed a lie test in which he said he had cut himself while shaving.

State police subsequently found pieces of a love letter to a girlfriend, which the married Weger had written on the day of the murders, torn up and scattered along a trail leading to St. Louis Canyon. The torn love letter, which state police detectives working under Lieutenant Toffant and Sergeant Michael Frankovich painstakingly pieced together, definitely placed Weger on the trail on the day of the murders.

Then Detectives Elmer Nelson and Robert Murphy discovered the twine in the shed, and noted that some of it was tied in knots similar to those used to bind the victims.

Discreetly checking into Weger's background, detectives learned that he had raped a seventeen-year-old girl in the fall of 1959 at nearby Matheissen State Park, after binding the girl and her teen-aged boyfriend with twine. During the attack, the girl later told police, Weger kept a .22 caliber bullet clenched between his teeth to remind her she would be shot if she ever told anyone what he had done.

Weger was arrested for the attack, but subsequently freed on a legal technicality when lax prosecutors failed to bring him to trial within the prescribed length of time.

When state crime lab technicians reported back that the stains on Weger's buckskin jacket were animal blood, the dogged state detectives—dissatisfied with the analysis—sent the jacket to Mount Sinai Hospital in Chicago for a more thorough examination. Contrary to the state lab report, chemists at Mount Sinai determined that the stains were human blood, of the same type as the murder victims.

Prosecutor Warren, a candidate for reelection, used the information state police had developed to carry out his own investigation, with the aid of sheriff's deputies. Then, on November 17, he unexpectedly ordered Weger's arrest without informing the state investigators.

Seeking to minimize the damage, Sheriff Eutsey called a press conference to announce that Weger had confessed the slayings to veteran Illinois State Police Sergeant Frankovich. According to the sheriff, the motive for the slayings was robbery, after which Weger killed the women "because I got scared."

The handcuffed suspect accompanied lawmen to the scene the following morning, where he coldly reenacted the triple murder. After encountering the trio on the trail, he said, he bound their hands and feet with twine he routinely carried in his pocket to amuse his children, ages one and three. He was marching the women from the canyon when Frances Murphy unexpectedly freed herself.

"She came running after me. I didn't know how she got loose. The first thing she did was hit me with a pair of binoculars on the back of the head. I bent down and picked up a club, the limb of a tree. The club was sticking out from under a log. All the time she was hitting me. I turned around and struck her with the club," he related.

"She was looking at me when I went to swing. I think I caught her in the back of the neck. She tried to duck. When she fell, she closed her eyes and was out. I carried her back to the cave. Mrs. Lindquist tried to kick me. Then the other two women got up. One of the women tried to scratch me. I had laid down the club. I picked it up and hit them so they couldn't identify me. I kept striking them. They laid back.

"Just then the other woman [Frances Murphy] came to. I thought I had killed her first. I thought she was dead. She got up and hit me with the binoculars. That's when they broke and cut my chin. I grabbed them away from her and hit her with the club and she fell. I hit her. She fell back. And I beat her till I killed her."

Weger said he then dragged all three bodies into the cave, where he disarranged their underclothing to make it appear the crime had been the work of a "sex fiend."

After he was returned to jail Weger repudiated his confession. He asserted that the story was coerced from him by the ambitious prosecutor's aides, who told him, "Chester, you're going to ride the thunderbolt, sure as hell, if you don't cooperate with us." The "thunderbolt" was the electric chair, which Illinois at that time used as a means of disposing of convicted murderers.

Weger went on trial for Lillian Oetting's murder in late January of 1961 before Judge Leonard Hoffman in the La Salle County Courthouse in Ottawa. "I didn't kill anybody," he insisted, testifying in his own defense.

The trial dragged on for more than a month. On March 3, Weger's twenty-second birthday, the jury found him guilty. The jurors denied the prosecutor's demand to put him aboard that "thunderbolt," however, and fixed his punishment at life imprisonment.

Weger was never prosecuted for the murders of Frances Murphy and Mildred Lindquist. The state decided further prosecution would be unnecessary, since he was already under lock and key.

After Weger was packed off to prison, several of the jurors expressed dismay on learning that, under Illinois law, he would be eligible for parole in twenty years. "We thought 'life' meant 'life,' and he would spend the rest of his life in the penitentiary," they said.

Weger, who turned fifty-two in March 1991, is serving his time in the Graham Correctional Center at Hillsboro, Illinois. Every bid he has made for parole since he became eligible has been rejected—but he never stops trying.

EPILOGUE

Some good actually came of the Starved Rock murder case, which at the time was ranked as Illinois' "Crime of the Century." The bungling State Crime Laboratory, then no better equipped than a high school chemistry lab, was abolished by the legislature. In its place Illinois today has what ranks among the finest state crime laboratory systems in the country, along with a proven record of cooperation between law enforcement agencies.

CHAPTER 13

FEEDING GRANNY TO THE DOG

On Christmas Eve 1983 Elaine Witte, a seventy-four-year-old widow from the tiny northern Indiana town of Trail Creek, telephoned her longtime friend and neighbor, Ruth Kessell. "Ruth, I've just been so darned busy I haven't had a chance to get over and see you," she apologized. "So, I just had to call and wish you a Merry Christmas."

"Well, Merry Christmas to you, too, Elaine. So nice of you to call. Perhaps we can get together over the holidays."

"Oh, I'd love to, Ruth. We'll do it. I'll call you as soon as I get some of my family commitments out of the way."

That was the last Ruth, or anyone else for that matter, ever heard of Grandma Witte. Except for the family dog, who had her for lunch.

Not all of her, to be sure. Parts of Elaine Witte's body were ground up in a garbage disposal. Some of her was stuffed into a trash compactor. Her head was microwaved. And the rest was distributed evenly about the countryside, all the way to San Diego.

Virtually everyone in Trail Creek, a retirement community just west of Michigan City, knew Grandma Witte. She had worked for many years for the Indiana Bell Telephone Company, and was president of the local chapter of the

Pioneers, a group of phone company retirees. Their annual Christmas party, which she helped organize, had been a glorious success.

Her forty-three-year-old son, Paul, operated a kennel and bred Siberian huskies. He lived with his wife and two school-age boys in nearby Beverly Shores, where he also served as a volunteer firefighter.

Tragedy struck the family on September 1, 1981, when Paul Witte was shot dead as he napped on the sofa in his home at 159 Beverly Drive. His fifteen-year-old son, Eric, tearfully told police he was examining a small handgun as he walked across the room, and the weapon went off when he tripped on the carpet. The bullet struck his sleeping father in the head.

After a routine police investigation the death was ruled accidental. Eric's mother, Marie, his twelve-year-old brother, John, and their maternal grandmother, fifty-five-year-old Margaret O'Donnell, all corroborated the boy's account of the unfortunate incident.

Shortly after Paul's death, Elaine Witte, who lived alone, took her son's widow and the two boys into her home on Johnson Drive. It would help relieve the heartache of losing her only son to have her two grandsons—his own flesh and blood—under her roof.

With her home once again filled with the sounds of boyish laughter, Grandma Witte continued her involvement in community activities. Unlike many women approaching the three-quarters-of-a-century mark, she was never a stay-at-home.

After the Christmas Eve call to Ruth Kessell, her neighbor waited for Mrs. Witte's promised visit, but it never came. On New Year's Day, 1984, she telephoned Elaine Witte to wish her a Happy New Year.

"She's down with the flu and can't come to the phone," she was advised. "We'll tell her you called." When the neighbor called back a week later she was told, "Oh, she's just fine. She's gone off on a long trip."

"Well, please tell her to call me when she gets back," Mrs. Kessell said. After she hung up the phone she thought it strange that her friend of more than thirty years would not have told her she was going away.

With the approach of spring Mrs. Kessell and other neighbors noticed that Grandma Witte's carefully maintained yard was turning into an unkempt tangle of weeds. "That just isn't like Elaine at all, to let the yard go that way," observed Betty Lloyd, who lived right next door. Other friends also thought it unusual that the normally active woman hadn't been seen around of late.

Two teen-aged girls from across the street asked young John—who liked to be called Butch—about his grandmother as they walked to school one day. "Oh, Grandma's off on a vacation," he told them. But whenever they made future inquiries, he always named a different place where his grandmother was supposed to be. If the truth were known, bits and pieces of her were probably at every place he mentioned.

The older grandson, Eric, had turned eighteen, meanwhile, and joined the Navy. He took his recruit training at Great Lakes Naval Training Center north of Chicago, and frequently brought sailor buddies home by the carload when he was on weekend pass.

By late May, when nobody including her closest friends had heard a word from Elaine Witte, a group of Telephone Pioneers went down to the police station and told Village Marshal Michael Chastain they were worried about her.

Marie Voisinet, who had once worked with Mrs. Witte, told the marshal, "That's all people were talking about at our last meeting of the Pioneers. Nobody has seen nor heard from Elaine since the Christmas party, and we agreed that someone should call this to the attention of the authorities.

"I called the house myself to see if she was coming to our April luncheon, but her daughter-in-law, Marie, told me Elaine was on a trip for a year. She said she had gone to California, and was then going to visit other places she hadn't seen.

"I thought it strange that she had not mentioned any-thing about the trip to me or any of her close friends. And she hasn't called or written to any of us, not even a postcard. The other girls called at Elaine's house and were given the same story. Since they hadn't seen her around, they thought she might be in a nursing home, or something."

Marshal Chastain, a lawman for the past nine years, knew Elaine Witte well, as did just about everybody else in Trail Creek, population 2,600. He went to the home at 320 Johnson Road and personally inquired about her. "She's not the type of person to go off somewhere without telling someone," he explained when the daughter-in-law came to the door.

"Well, she told us, didn't she?" responded Hilma Marie, who preferred to go by her middle name. When Chastain tried to pin her down, both she and young Butch gave vague and contradictory answers.

Puzzled, Chastain embarked on a quiet investigation of his own. He determined that Elaine Witte's bank account had been systematically drained of more than $9,000 since the first of the year. Moreover, her Social Security checks, which had been mailed to her home regularly on the third of each month, had been cashed right on schedule.

Another old friend of Mrs. Witte, Ed Weidenman, a former neighbor who had since moved to Westville, another small town outside of Michigan City, also suspected that all was not well. He drove over to Trail Creek to make a personal call on her, but was met by young John at the gate. "Grandma isn't here," he told the visitor.

"Well, where is she?" Weidenman persisted.

"Oh, she's off following her other grandson, Eric, around in the Navy," explained Marie, who came out of the house to help terminate the inquiry.

The brief conversation only heightened Weidenman's suspicions. His next stop was the Indiana State Police post at Lowell. "I think Mrs. Witte is dead and buried," he told Captain Anthony Vicari, commander of the post, and Detective Sergeant James Wallace. "I think you ought to check out that house see what happened."

To his surprise, the two lawmen already knew about the missing grandmother. "We've been working on this matter with the village marshal," Vicari explained. "But we just can't barge in there on supposition."

In July, as the two police agencies pressed their investigation, Marie Witte showed the first signs of concern over questions being asked about her mother-in-law. She abruptly closed up the two-story frame home, took her fifteen-year-old son, and moved away, leaving no forwarding address. Authorities suspected she might have headed for California to join Eric, who was now stationed with the Navy in San Diego.

Deputy Sergeant Arlen Boyd of the state police, meanwhile, determined that endorsements on all of Elaine Witte's Social Security checks since January had been forgeries. Since these were United States Treasury checks, this enabled federal authorities to join the investigation.

In early November Secret Service agents located Hilma Marie Witte in San Diego, where she was living with her two sons in a mobile home on San Ysidro Boulevard. Agents determined that nineteen-year-old Eric had rented space No. 62 in the trailer park on July 28, and was joined by his mother and younger brother several days later.

The federal investigators also learned that the young sailor had rented a post office box in Chula Vista under the name of E. Witte. Moreover, in checking area banks, the agents discovered that on October 17 Mrs. Witte and her older son had opened a checking account at the Pacific Commerce Bank of Chula Vista under the names of Elaine Witte, Hilma Mari (sic) Witte, and Eric Witte.

Over the next two days, Marie Witte deposited Social Security checks made out to Elaine Witte, and began writing checks on the account.

Indiana authorities were notified, and Trail Creek Officer Eugene "Skip" Pierce and State Police Detective Boyd flew out to San Diego, arriving on Wednesday, November 7.

As the Indiana lawmen huddled with Secret Service agents to plot their next move, bank officials tipped off federal investigators that Marie Witte and Eric had just come in to deposit two more of Elaine Witte's Social Security checks, totaling $667. The sheriff's office was notified, and the mother and son were taken into custody as they left the bank.

Assistant U.S. Attorney Phillip L. Halpern, a top aide to U.S. Attorney Peter Nunez, ordered the two charged with forgery and conspiracy. The question now became: What ever happened to Elaine Witte?

Boyd and Pierce went out to the trailer park, where they found fifteen-year-old Butch awaiting his mother's return. Astonished, and no doubt impressed that the two Indiana lawmen had tracked him all the way to Southern California, the youngster blurted out the whole sordid story of what had befallen Grandma Witte.

"I killed my grandma," he told the startled lawmen. He explained that he was carrying out his mother's orders while the elderly woman slept in a second-floor bedroom of the home she had opened to her son's widowed wife and children.

The instrument of death was a medieval crossbow!

Now it was the Indiana investigators' turn to be astonished as the ninth-grader calmly and unemotionally described in grisly detail how his grandmother had come to an end—and, worse yet, what happened to her afterward.

The family-style execution was carried out shortly after Christmas. Elaine Witte had sealed her own fate when she discovered that her daughter-in-law and older grandson, Eric, had been looting her bank account.

"You will have to kill Grandma," the youth said his mother told him.

He said she explained that, being a juvenile, he would almost certainly escape punishment if the deed was ever discovered. Marie Witte went to great pains, however, to make sure that no one would ever be the wiser.

There would be no loud shot that might attract the attention of neighbors. She also ruled out drugs, and pushing the old lady out the window. No, after thinking it all out Marie offered her young son three alternative means of putting granny out of the way: Strangulation, suffocation with a pillow, or the wooden crossbow.

"She said it was up to me," the boy told Boyd and Pierce. He said he did not find the first two suggestions to his liking, since they would have involved bodily contact with his grandmother. So he opted for the crossbow.

He climbed the stairs, slowly and silently stalking his prey, took careful aim at the seventy-four-year-old woman asleep in her bed and squeezed the trigger, zinging an arrow into her breast.

Elaine Witte uttered a short gasp, and went limp. After the two boys and their mother made sure she was dead, they carried her downstairs where her body was cut into pieces as the trio munched on McDonald's hamburgers. They used a chain saw, knives, and a chisel to dismantle the victim.

The smaller parts of his grandmother were fed into a garbage disposal unit, the boy related. Other remains were placed into a trash compactor, a deep fat fryer, a microwave oven, and muriatic acid. Residue from the grisly operation was mixed with dirt, in bags, and scattered about.

What could not be gotten rid of on the spot was placed in a freezer for future disposition. Occasionally a treat was given to the family pooch.

Throughout the spring and summer, as pesky neighbors kept asking about the missing Mrs. Witte, bits and pieces of her were being distributed about the countryside, young John told the incredulous officers. He said his mother's new boyfriend, Douglas Menkel, a twenty-two-year-old sailor friend of her son's, assisted in the operation.

"When you killed your grandmother, how did that make you feel?" the boy was asked.

"I felt neutral," he shrugged. "I really didn't care one way or the other."

"What about the weapon—the crossbow?"

"We burned it," he answered matter-of-factly.

After local authorities began getting nosy, the youth added, his mother decided it would be wise to pull up stakes and head west. The frozen remnants of granny were packed along with the rest of the family belongings. They set out for California in two vehicles, a Chevrolet and a Winnebago motor home—with what was left of granny in the cooler. Once the tiny caravan arrived at San Diego, the last pieces of Elaine Witte were committed to the Otay sanitary landfill site.

With the last macabre bits of evidence out of the way, Marie Witte and her boys figured they could sit back and enjoy life in sunny California, as long as Grandma's Social Security checks kept rolling in. They had not reckoned on the Indiana Bell Pioneers and Elaine Witte's other curious neighbors.

Pierce and Boyd relayed the youngster's incredible story back to Indiana, where Judge Arthur Keppen in Michigan City issued warrants for the suspects' arrests. Marie and her youngest son were charged with murder. Eric and his sailor friend, Menkel, were charged with being accessories after the fact, and assisting a criminal. LaPorte County Prosecuting Attorney Walter Chapala assigned his chief deputy, William Herrbach, to prepare the state's case against the suspects.

While Marie Witte and her boys were being held in California, a nationwide search was launched for her boyfriend, Menkel. It did not last long. He was found in the Great Lakes Naval brig, where he'd been locked up for desertion.

Young John agreed to waive extradition, and he was returned to Indiana where Judge Keppen ruled he would be tried as an adult. Menkel was turned over to civilian authorities, and held in the LaPorte County jail in lieu of $50,000 bond. He agreed to cooperate with authorities, and told Marshal Chastain that he had ground up the victim's teeth, and helped to dispose of other parts of her body in a trash compactor.

Back in California, to make sure the other two suspects weren't going anywhere pending extradition proceedings, a federal grand jury indicted Marie Witte and Eric on charges of forgery and conspiracy in connection with cashing the murdered woman's Social Security checks.

Word of Grandma Witte's ghastly fate shocked neighbors in Trail Creek, and brought the news media to the tiny community in droves. Newspaper reporters and television crews were soon tramping across lawns, ringing doorbells, and asking questions about Grandma Witte and her family.

"Butch was weird," a fifteen-year-old schoolmate recalled. "He told me once that he was going to make me fall down on the ground with his powers, and then drew a circle around himself on the ground," she added. "When his father was shot the family moved in with his grandma, and Butch talked to us about it. He acted as if it didn't bother him at all."

The young coed was not the only person whose thoughts had turned back to 1981 when Paul Witte was "accidentally" shot by his other teen-aged son. Town Marshal Richard Landis of Beverly Shores felt that the unusual death of the gunshot victim's elderly mother called for a fresh look at the three-year-old case.

"There were doubts at the time. It was questionable. It kind of makes you wonder, now," he told Indiana State Police.

Detective Sergeant James Wallace agreed. After conferring with Porter County Prosecutor Daniel Berning, he decided to reopen the case. "Although at this time we have nothing to indicate that Paul Witte's death was anything other than accidental, we do plan to take a much closer look at that case in light of current events," he advised Landis.

The Wittes, a close-knit family, had operated the Wind-O-Lakes kennels prior to the father's death. A native of northwest Indiana, Paul Witte had settled in Beverly Shores in the late 1950s after serving in the Navy. A pipefitter by trade, he had worked for United States Steel before opening the kennel, where he bred Siberian huskies.

Paul had met Hilma Marie in a Florida nudist camp, where they were married in 1964. The sixteen-year-old bride wore a veil, and nothing else. It was Marie's second marriage.

A year earlier, she had married a U.S. Coast Guardsman in the same nudist camp. Not surprisingly, that marriage didn't last.

Paul and his older son, Eric, used to hitch up the huskies for dogsled races and wilderness camping trips in northern Michigan. One winter the father and son spent an entire month in the bush near Manistee on the eastern shore of Lake Michigan.

After her husband's untimely death at the age of forty-three, Marie closed the kennel. It was more than she and the boys could handle on their own. For a time she worked in the ticket office of the South Shore Railroad, but later took disability leave.

Grandma Elaine Witte, in the meantime, suddenly found herself living alone and starved for company. After her husband, Leonard, a railroad man, died in 1967, her sister, Mildred Moran, moved in with her. Mildred died in 1981, however, the same year a bullet in the head ended the life of Elaine's sleeping son. That was when Grandma Witte invited Paul's widow and the two boys to move in with her, and Marie started intercepting her elderly mother-in-law's Social Security checks.

As the renewed investigation into Paul Witte's death continued, California authorities went ahead and prosecuted his widow and eldest son for cashing a total of $1,135 worth of his late mother's Social Security checks. On April 8, 1985, Marie Witte was sentenced to ten years in federal prison on those charges. Eric, who was convicted with his mother, was handed a four-year prison term.

Back in Indiana the youngest son, Butch, found himself looking at the death penalty if convicted of his grandmother's murder. The idea of being zapped by a couple thousand volts of electricity was enough to convince him that cooperation at this point in his life was more important than family loyalty.

He not only told authorities everything they wanted to know about Grandma Witte's death, but revealed that the fatal shooting of his sleeping father had been no accident, either.

His father's death was orchestrated by his mother, and carried out by his brother, Eric. Furthermore, his maternal grandmother, Margaret O'Donnell, was also in on the plot, he told investigators.

Mrs. O'Donnell, fifty-nine, admitted her role in her son-in-law's slaying after learning that her grandson had spilled the beans. She told Prosecutor Berning the same story he had heard from the boy—that Marie Witte was the mastermind behind the death plot.

Mrs. O'Donnell told the prosecutor that her daughter had induced her to poison her son-in-law "over a period of several weeks" in the late summer of 1981, by mixing quantities of the drug, Valium, with his food. When that failed to show results the women laced the unsuspecting husband's lunch with rat poison.

When that, too, failed to have an effect on the robust outdoorsman, Marie resorted to the gun, with Eric, who was fifteen years old at the time, designated as the triggerman, she related.

Mrs. O'Donnell was booked on a charge of attempted murder in connection with Paul Witte's death, and lodged in the Porter County jail in Valparaiso in lieu of $25,000 bond.

Prosecutors Herrbach of LaPorte County and Berning, of adjoining Porter, agreed to bring Eric and Marie Witte back from California to face murder charges in Michigan City for the slaying of Elaine Witte, and in Valparaiso for the death of her son, Paul.

Young Butch, who turned sixteen while in custody, agreed to testify against the others in exchange for leniency. On Friday, May 24, 1985, he pleaded guilty to a charge of voluntary manslaughter in the crossbow death of his grandmother, and was sentenced to twenty years in prison.

Eric also testified against his mother. He was sentenced to five years in prison for his role in helping to dispose of the elderly woman's body. He even left parts of her at the Great Lakes Naval base, he admitted.

In November 1985, Marie Witte, then thirty-eight, was convicted of murder and conspiracy to commit murder, in the scheme over forged Social Security checks that ended in Grandma Witte's death.

Judge Donald D. Martin in LaPorte Superior Court sentenced her to ninety years in prison—sixty years for murder and thirty years for conspiracy, to be served consecutively. "All these aggravating circumstances pale to insignificance when compared to the primary one—that you not only destroyed Elaine Witte, you destroyed your younger son," the judge remonstrated.

A month later, in Valparaiso, a jury found Marie guilty of murder and attempted murder in the shooting death of her husband, even though it was her son, Eric, who pulled the trigger at her behest. She was sentenced to 50 more years, bringing the total of prison years hanging over her head to 140.

Her two sons were not prosecuted further.

"The boys, they pretty much did what their mother wanted them to do," Deputy Prosecutor Scott Duerring explained.

EPILOGUE

There was one more bizarre twist to the incredible case. In July 1986, while serving the first of her 140 years in the Indiana Women's Prison at Indianapolis, Hilma Marie Witte received a proposal of marriage from Donald Laisure, Jr., an eccentric Texas billionaire.

Laisure, who had been married at least thirty-six times, according to press clippings, had only recently shed his latest bride, Susan Atkins, a follower of imprisoned cult slayer Charles Manson, whom he married while she was in a California prison.

Introducing himself as an oil billionaire who "sometimes intervenes in cases where people may have been railroaded," Laisure addressed Mrs. Witte as "dream girl" and "delectable you." He asked her to write back and "seal it with a kiss." Hilma Marie turned the letter over to her lawyer, Scott King, who read it and said, "This is goofy."

CHAPTER 14

THE TELL-TALE CISTERN IN MISSOURI

At around 7:30 on the night of October 20, 1983, sheriff's police came upon a late-model Cadillac Coupe de Ville which had run into the ditch along Central School Road in St. Charles County, about thirty miles west of St. Louis. Sharon Williams, a forty-four-year-old airline ticket agent, was still alive, but unconscious, when ambulance attendants pulled her from the wreckage.

Taken to St. Joseph Health Center, she was diagnosed as clinically dead from massive head injuries, and placed on a life-support system. On the following day her husband, James H. Williams, Sr., an electrical contractor, mercifully consented to let her doctors pull the plug.

Two months later a popular St. Louis area singer, forty-year-old Walter Scott, disappeared while preparing to leave for a New Year's Eve engagement at the Pocono Playboy Club in Hershey, Pennsylvania. He was last seen December 27, when he left his suburban home on a bitter cold night to pick up a battery for his wife's car. The dark green 1978 Lincoln was found abandoned the following day at Lambert Field.

It would be nearly four years before authorities fully realized that they had a double homicide on their hands, thanks to a small-town sheriff with a highly suspicious mind.

There was something about Sharon Williams' death that didn't sit right with Sheriff Edward J. Uebinger from the very start.

For one thing, police at the accident scene detected a strong odor of gasoline on the victim. But an examination of the wrecked 1982 Cadillac indicated there was no fuel leakage or rupture resulting from the crash. The sheriff was also puzzled over her injuries. Her face, chest, and the front of her body bore no visible damage, such as might have been expected in an accident involving impact at the front end of the car.

Furthermore, Deputy Edward Copeland noted in his accident report that the injured woman was found on the passenger side of the car, not the driver's side. Also, the seat had been pushed all the way back, a position that would have made driving awkward for the slightly built female.

Curiously, although Sharon and James Williams had been married for twenty-five years, the husband had failed to attend his wife's wake in Marion, Illinois, where she had grown up, and was returned for burial. Sheriff's investigators questioned "Big Jim" Williams, a giant of a man standing six-feet-seven-inches tall and weighing 250 pounds, but he was not overly cooperative.

Suspicions. There were a lot of them surrounding the case of the Cadillac in the ditch, but you can't arrest someone simply because you don't like the lay of the land.

Sheriff Uebinger's suspicions were rekindled, however, after the popular singer, Walter Scott, vanished on the way to pick up a battery for his wife's car. In investigating the disappearance, police discovered that James Williams had been conducting a year-long affair with Scott's thirty-seven-year-old wife, Jo Ann.

"Could there possibly be a connection between Sharon Williams' accident and this singer's disappearing act?" Uebinger asked his investigators. "If so, romance is the link we're after, and it just might be the motive for murder. I know the doc ruled that the lady died in the crash, but I'd like to take a closer look at that so-called accident, now that we know her husband was seeing this other guy's wife on the side."

The "closer look" only enhanced the curious lawman's nagging suspicions.

Investigators learned there was a $100,000 insurance policy on Sharon Williams' life, and her newly widowed husband was the sole beneficiary.

In questioning members of the dead woman's family, deputies learned that Sharon never operated a motor vehicle without wearing a seatbelt—yet her seatbelt was not fastened on the night her car went into the ditch. Furthermore, they said she could not have driven the Cadillac with the seat pushed all the way back, because she was not tall enough to reach the pedals. Only her six-foot-seven-inch husband could drive the Caddy with the seat in that position, and she always had to readjust it forward when she used it.

Family members also recalled that the couple had been having domestic problems, and had quarreled violently the night before the car went off the road.

Scott's wife, Jo Ann Notheis, who did not use her husband's professional name, acknowledged that she and Williams had been seeing one another for at least a year. She said she had asked Scott for a divorce, but he refused. She refused to discuss her husband's disappearance further, and hired an attorney.

Despite the lack of cooperation from the two central figures, sheriff's investigators learned that Williams, an avid kegler, bowled every Tuesday night with his company-sponsored team. On the Tuesday evening that Walter Scott disappeared, however, he reportedly "forgot" his bowling night.

The singer's parents, Walter and Catherine Notheis, who lived in the St. Louis suburb of Affton, were suspicious from day one that Williams might have been involved in their son's disappearance.

"On the morning after Walter vanished we stopped by his home to talk to Jo Ann, and here was this big man sitting at the kitchen table with her," Mrs. Notheis told investigators. "She told us, 'This is my friend, Jim Williams.'"

"And that's not all," Walter Notheis added. "This fellow had Walter's attache case out with his jewelry in it, and he was looking at it with a magnifying glass. He'd look at one piece and say, 'This is good,' and then he'd look at another piece and he'd say, 'This one isn't,' right in front of us."

While this was going on, Jo Ann went to the phone and began calling clubs where Scott had been scheduled to perform during the holiday season, and canceled her husband's engagements.

"How do you know he's not going to return?" Catherine Notheis asked her daughter-in-law.

"I've got a feeling," she responded. "I know he's not coming back."

At that point Williams brazenly suggested that he would like to use the singer's travel trailer in his contracting business. "Don't bury him yet!" the missing man's mother declared incredulously.

Then, for no apparent reason, Williams began telling the missing man's parents about his wife's fatal car accident two months earlier. "It was right out of the blue," Mrs. Notheis recalled. "He didn't seem upset. It was like he was talking about a casual acquaintance."

Convinced that Scott had been conveniently disposed of, Sheriff Uebinger ordered an all-out search for his body.

It had been extremely cold the night Scott disappeared, six degrees below zero, with a wind chill factor of sixty below. The record cold snap lasted twelve bone-chilling days. "This weather has left the ground hard as a rock," the sheriff noted. "Too hard to dig a grave to bury anyone. If this man is dead—and I think he is—his body has got to be hidden in a container of some kind."

Police scoured the area, checking every dumpster, barrel, packing crate, and empty oil drum. They uncovered a lot of unwanted junk, but no dead body. On the remote possibility that Scott might have simply gotten fed up and walked out on his wife, they dug deeply into his background to try to determine where he would have gone.

Nationally known in entertainment circles, Scott was probably best remembered for the recording of his pop hit, "The Cheater," in 1965 while he was lead singer with Bob Kuban and the In Men. Police talked to Kuban, who told them that Scott had left the group to form his own band. When not on the road, he performed regularly at the St. Louis Playboy Club and the Hoffman House.

"I've known Walt since 1962, when he auditioned with the band while we were playing at the Jackson Park tennis courts in Berkeley. He became our lead singer almost immediately," Kuban recalled. "His range was tremendous. There weren't a lot of white singers who had that kind of range. When we first recorded 'The Cheater' it scored high on all the soul stations. They thought we were a soul group."

A year after "The Cheater" climbed to the Top 10 on pop charts, Scott left the In Men to form an English-style group which he called The Guys. He rejoined Kuban's band in 1969, but broke away again and went off on his own.

"He thought he was on the verge of moving into the national spotlight. We all have dreams in this business—and that's just part of the business," Kuban added. "We've remained close, and we were planning a twentieth anniversary reunion for the In Men at the Fox Theatre next June 23.

"Walt started rehearsing with the band about two months ago, in preparation for the show this summer. It was amazing. We hadn't been together for years, and it was like we had played together just the night before."

Kuban said the band had also hoped to record an album with Scott, and possibly embark on a nationwide tour. "He was excited. He felt this was the rebirth of what we had twenty years ago. I think he felt this was his big chance. He felt if he didn't do it now, he might not have a second chance. I'm sure he dreamed of someday having a No. 1 record, being another Kenny Rogers or a Neil Diamond. He had all the talent. He wanted a life better than a six-nights-a-week gig."

Kuban's portrayal of Scott hardly sounded like that of a man bent on dropping from sight intentionally.

On the night he disappeared Scott was preparing to leave for the Playboy club engagement in Pennsylvania. He could not have gone there, however, since his airline ticket was still at the house, his wife told investigators.

While Scott's career seemed to be on the upbeat, as related by Kuban, his domestic life had been playing the blues, his parents revealed. While his wife, Jo Ann, was being romanced by Williams, Scott had been stepping out with a showgirl from his act.

"When my husband and I got together with Walter and Jo Ann at Christmas, she remarked, 'I don't know why he even bothered to come home,'" Mrs. Notheis recalled.

"What's the problem?" the mother-in-law inquired.

"It's the same old stuff," Jo Ann replied.

The couple, who had been married for fourteen years, had twelve-year-old twins, Melinda Ann, known as "Mindy," and Bryan Christopher. Scott also had two children by a previous marriage.

"Even if he and Jo Ann weren't hitting it off anymore, Walter wouldn't just up and abandon his children," his parents insisted.

The search for the missing singer led nowhere, however, so the sheriff's investigators turned their attention to Williams, who lost no time in openly taking over as Jo Ann's regular boyfriend after her husband vanished and his own wife died in the auto accident.

They learned that he had worked as an electrical inspector for St. Charles County, but resigned and went into business for himself after being questioned about his work ethics. He subsequently met the attractive Jo Ann Notheis while doing electrical work in her home.

Police came up with little more, however, and the twin investigations into Sharon Williams' questionable death and Walter Scott's mysterious disappearance eventually bogged down. With the passage of time, the busy detectives were forced to focus their attention on more pressing matters.

The missing singer's parents, Walter and Catherine Notheis, refused to give up, however. They spent several thousand dollars enlisting the aid of private investigators, but to no avail. The elderly couple spent two weeks in Pennsylvania, where Scott was to have performed shortly before he disappeared, searching for clues to his whereabouts. In 1985, two years after their son vanished, they spent two days in Champaign, Illinois, looking at faces, after a longtime friend of their son's thought he had seen a man jogging who looked like Scott.

Some two years after Scott disappeared, Jo Ann filed for divorce, charging him with abandonment, and throwing in emotional abuse and adultery for good measure.

Since Scott obviously was not around to contest the action, the divorce was granted. In April 1986, Jo Ann married "Big Jim" Williams. The widowed Williams had been living in a split-level home on Gutermuth Road near the town of St. Peters, a few miles west of St. Charles. After the nuptials he moved in with Jo Ann and the fifteen-year-old twins. One of Williams' sons then moved into the house on Gutermuth, that Williams once shared with his late wife, Sharon.

The thing that prevented authorities from doing anything about what they were convinced was a homicide, was the lack of a corpus delecti. There was no evidence of a body, hence, no proof that Scott was really dead. As for Sharon Williams, the medical examiner had officially ruled her death accidental. It was so obvious to him that he hadn't bothered to order an autopsy.

It was a totally unrelated incident that gave Sheriff Uebinger an idea that would bring all the loose ends together.

Though he held a political office Uebinger, who had been sheriff of St. Charles County since 1981, was a professional lawman through and through. He had served as a sheriff's detective for five years before being elected to the top office. He was a graduate of the FBI National Academy training course for police officers, and held a master's degree in public policy administration from the University of Missouri.

The event that would help him solve the Williams-Scott mystery came in the fall of 1986 when a madman named Mike Wayne Jackson painted his face silver and embarked on a three-state rampage of abduction and murder from Indiana to Missouri.

At the height of the manhunt for the crazed killer a wrecked 1984 Ford LTD was found crashed into a utility pole at the St. Peters exit ramp of Interstate Highway 70 in St. Charles County. The driver, forty-seven-year-old Earl D. Finn of nearby O'Fallon, was dead at the wheel.

The incident had all the earmarks of a fatal automobile crash, and in another day would have gone down as such. However an autopsy by Dr. Mary Case, the county's new medical examiner, disclosed that Finn had been killed by a shotgun blast, a victim of Jackson's rampage.

Dr. Case, an eminent forensic and neuropathologist, had been St. Charles County medical examiner since 1986, replacing a less-qualified physician—the doctor who had buried Sharon Williams without performing an autopsy.

The new medical examiner's discovery of murder in what had appeared to have been an auto accident convinced Uebinger of the wisdom of having a properly trained professional in that office. After the killer was brought to bay and the hubbub of the Jackson incident died down, the sheriff went to Dr. Case with a proposition: Would she examine the police file on the death of Sharon Williams?

"My officers and I have some reservations about this death," Uebinger explained. "Her injuries were not indicative, at least to us, of those that might be sustained in that type of automobile accident."

Dr. Case, who taught a course in blunt force trauma at St. Louis University Medical Center, where she had served as an associate professor of pathology for ten years, agreed to take a look at the three-year-old file. It did not take her long to confirm the sheriff's suspicions.

"In looking over the medical records of Sharon Williams' death, I am convinced that it would have been quite unlikely that she died in a traffic accident," she told Sheriff Uebinger.

"The impact injuries were caused to the back of the head with a blunt instrument. These are injuries that could have come from something like a lead pipe."

It was Halloween—October 31—when Dr. Case, more curious than ever now, drafted a letter to State's Attorney Charles Garnati of Williamson County, Illinois, asking for legal assistance in obtaining a court order to exhume the body of Sharon Williams.

The medical examiner's communique pointed out the possibility of foul play in the Missouri woman's death, and cited the necessity to personally examine the body that had been buried at Marion, to confirm or dispel such a suspicion.

Getting cooperation from the downstate Illinois prosecutor in a homicide investigation seemed a foregone conclusion. Instead, the three-year-old case, which had suddenly picked up a new head of steam, appeared headed for certain derailment.

After waiting three days for a reply from Garnati, and hearing nothing, Dr. Case telephoned the Illinois prosecutor at his office in Marion and explained the urgency of her request. "This involves a murder investigation," she emphasized. The medical examiner was somewhat taken aback by what the voice on the other end of the phone said in reply.

"I just can't believe this," Dr. Case reported back to Sheriff Uebinger. "He told me he did not want to become involved. He said this was no concern of his."

"I'm not surprised," the sheriff mused. "I've been trying to get through to that state's attorney myself, and had no luck at all. I called his office in Marion and he refused to talk to me. I told his secretary that my call concerned an investigation of two possible murders. The secretary said she'd get back to me, and when she did, she told me her boss was busy."

The rebuffed sheriff and the medical examiner brought the matter to the attention of Daniel G. Pelikan, the St. Charles County counselor.

"I can't believe this guy's attitude," the sheriff complained. "Good Lord! Crime has no boundaries. He has a duty to the citizens of Williamson County; but he also has a duty to uphold the Constitution of the United States. We are not getting any cooperation from him at all."

Pelikan, a St. Louis lawyer who, as counselor for St. Charles handled all civil matters in the county, agreed to do what he could. Since he was licensed to practice law in Illinois, as well as Missouri, he felt he'd have better luck approaching Garnati on his own level. He asked the Illinois prosecutor's help in getting an exhumation order for Sharon Williams' body, but—like the sheriff and the medical examiner—got nothing but a cold shoulder.

"He told me he didn't have the time," Pelikan explained incredulously. "I'm going to file a petition myself with the Williamson County Circuit Court." Several days later he got back to Sheriff Uebinger and Dr. Case.

"My worst fears have been confirmed," the lawyer said, shaking his head from side to side in disbelief. "The Williamson County judge requested that I give notice of the petition to Sharon Williams' next of kin, her husband. The judge said he, himself, would not allow the exhumation on his own."

"My God! Williams is our chief suspect," Uebinger declared.

"I know, I know," Pelikan agreed. "We cannot notify James Williams of our intentions for fear of jeopardizing your investigation."

"Give me a little more time on this, Dan. I think I might be able to come up with some kind of an alternative," Uebinger told Pelikan.

Going over files that had been accumulated in the traffic case, the sheriff determined that the dead woman's mother, Alice Almaroad, still lived in Marion, Illinois. With the help of his detectives, he was able to locate her.

He and Dr. Case then told Mrs. Almaroad their suspicions surrounding her daughter's death.

"But we can't prove a thing without exhuming her body

so Dr. Case here can perform an examination," Uebinger explained. "Mrs. Almaroad, I know this must be awfully painful for you, but would you give us permission to exhume your daughter's body?"

"Sheriff, I always knew something was wrong. I always felt like there was a piece of the puzzle missing," she answered without hesitation. "Maybe this will solve it. You bring me the necessary papers, and I'll sign them."

Mrs. Almaroad explained that her son-in-law, James Williams, had been raised by grandparents in Vincennes, Indiana. After the old folks died he came to live with his mother and step-father in Marion, where he met his future wife.

"Sharon and Jim were in high school together," she said. "They were married for twenty-five years, and it was a good marriage until toward the end. The last time I visited them in St. Charles, Sharon would try to get lovey and hug him, and I could see Jim's resentment. My daughter visited me about a month before her death and asked if I thought her husband was stepping out on her. I didn't know what to say. She dearly loved him."

With Pelikan's help, the sheriff obtained the required papers, and Sharon Williams' body was removed from her grave in the Marion cemetery on Wednesday, April 1, 1987, by Larry Hughes, the same mortician who had committed her there more than three years earlier.

The body was placed in Hughes' hearse and driven back to St. Louis for the long-overdue postmortem examination. It did not take Dr. Case long to determine that the sheriff's efforts had not been in vain. "This woman did not die in any car crash," she said. "She was beaten to death with a blunt instrument."

The persistent sheriff now had one murder on his hands, for sure, but he was not ready to make his move. There was still the matter of Walter Scott, the singer, who dropped from sight while the conveniently widowed Williams was dating his wife, Jo Ann.

The case now took another curious twist. Williams, the No. 1 suspect in his wife's death, had a twenty-seven-year-old son, James, Jr., who was the spitting image of his daddy—six-feet-eight-inches of brute strength, weighing in at 280 pounds. The sheriff discovered he was being held in the Monroe County Jail in Key West, Florida, on a whole raft of charges.

Young Williams had been arrested in Key West for auto theft and armed robbery, and was the subject of fugitive warrants from Illinois and West Palm Beach, Florida. He'd been convicted for assaulting a police officer in Marion, Illinois, and a felony charge was pending against him in Benton, just north of Marion, for possession of marijuana.

"Take a plane down to Key West and talk to this boy," Sheriff Uebinger suggested, calling two of his top investigators into his office. "He's got a lot hanging over his head. He might be willing to cooperate at this point in hopes of getting a little leniency. Take a copy of Dr. Case's autopsy along, just in case."

Uebinger's deputies interviewed young Williams in the Key West jail on April 7. The sheriff's hunch paid off.

Williams said he had known about his father's dalliance with Scott's wife, Jo Ann, for about a year. Just before his mother died in the auto accident, he recalled, his father had offered him $500 to run Scott out of town.

"What do you mean, he offered you $500 to run his girlfriend's husband out of town? Just exactly what did your father say to you?"

"He just asked me what I knew about Walter Scott," the hulking twenty-seven-year-old told the sheriff's detectives. "I said I knew a little about him, and he said, 'You can make $500 to get him run out of town.'"

The deputies then showed Williams a copy of the autopsy report on his mother, indicating that she had been beaten to death. "God," he said, letting out a deep breath. "I never was convinced that she was killed in the crash, but I never thought my dad had anything to do with it. I never suspected anything like that."

Cautiously hinting that his father was, indeed, a suspect in his mother's death, the sheriff's investigators gradually worked the conversation around to Scott, the missing singer.

"Now, supposing that your father knew something about that case, where do you think he might hide a body in December?"

"Check the river."

"The river was frozen."

Young Williams thought for a moment, as though running a scenario through his head. Then the jailed man had an inspiration.

"He's in the cistern!" he asserted.

"Cistern? What cistern?"

Williams explained that there had been a water-filled cistern behind his father's home in St. Peters. Shortly before Scott disappeared the cistern had been covered over by a brick barbeque grill. But Williams recalled that when he visited his father's home in July 1984—the summer after the entertainer vanished—the barbecue grill had been replaced by a large wooden planter.

"There's no way you could tell that there was a well under there," he explained. "There were only a few people who knew about it—me, my brother, my mom, my dad, and my granny."

The sheriff's investigators then arranged for Williams to telephone his father from the Key West jail. During the chat, which would be tape recorded, he agreed to bring up the subject of Scott's disappearance. As he and his father talked, the younger man mentioned the $500 his father had once offered him to run Scott out of town. "Oh, yeah, I remember saying something like that, but I wasn't serious," his father said.

Before the sheriff's men headed back to Missouri with the recorded conversation, they gave young Williams $20 to get whatever he needed from the jail commissary. "If we find that cistern, and there's a body in it, we'll make sure the Florida people here know about your cooperation with our investigation," they told him.

Arriving back in St. Charles the jubilant detectives couldn't wait to tell Uebinger, "Sheriff, we think we've found your 'container.'"

The sheriff obtained a search warrant for the Williams homestead, now vacant, and his men started with the yard. Around the rear of the house they came upon a large, octagonal planter. When the heavy container was shoved aside it revealed the opening to the old cistern.

Deputies lifted the lid and directed the beams of their flashlights into the dank chamber. There was something down there. Walter Scott was floating face down in the stagnant water. His hands and knees were bound with rope, and he was still wearing the jogging clothes he had put on that cold winter night more than three years earlier to run an errand for his wife.

Dr. Case suddenly found herself performing a second autopsy in the investigation, in which the pieces of the puzzle were rapidly falling into place. She determined that Scott had been shot once, in the left shoulder. "The projectile severed a major artery," she told Uebinger.

In addition to discovering Scott's body, the sheriff's men fished three spent .410-gauge shotgun shells, a Missouri driver's license, two Playboy Club cards, and a Visa charge card, out of the cistern.

Sheriff Uebinger finally had his two murder victims, and with the help of Dr. Case, was able to show how each had died.

On Saturday, April 11, 1987—just ten days after the body of Sharon Williams was exhumed from her grave in Illinois, her forty-eight-year-old husband, James H. Williams, Sr., was charged with beating her to death. He was also charged with the fatal shooting of his wife's first husband, Walter Scott. Jo Ann Williams was located the following day at the home of a friend in Florissant, Missouri, where she was arrested for first-degree murder in the death of her husband.

Williams' lawyer, Michael A. Turken, sought to get his client released on bond pending trial, arguing that the evidence against "Big Jim" was purely circumstantial.

A. John DeVouton, the county's assistant prosecuting attorney, agreed that the evidence was circumstantial, indeed. "But essentially sitting on a body for three years in his cistern is a strong presumption of murder," he asserted. "We're looking at two capital murder charges. We think there is enough evidence to secure a conviction and the death penalty."

EPILOGUE

Incredibly, more than four years after Williams and his new wife were arrested for murder they still had not been brought to trial. Both were released on bond as the case bogged down repeatedly by legal maneuvering, motions, and countermotions. Defense lawyers argued that search warrants that resulted in the discovery of Scott's body in the well were illegal, and that the exhumation of Sharon Williams' body was also illegal.

Prosecuting Attorney William Hannah, who held office during much of the delays, was trounced when he ran for reelection in November 1990. His successor, Tim Braun, subsequently contended that it would be a conflict of interest for him to prosecute the case, because as a former public defender he had contact with defense witnesses in the matter.

One of Braun's first acts after taking over as prosecutor in 1991 was to petition the St. Charles County Circuit Court to ask the Missouri attorney general to appoint a special prosecutor. Meanwhile the two defendants must be considered innocent of all charges unless determined otherwise in a court of law.

CHAPTER 15

THE SILVER FACE OF DEATH

The murder rampage that eventually provided St. Charles County authorities with the key to unraveling the Sharon Williams and Walter Scott puzzles is a story that bears repeating, because it offers a questionable commentary on the do-gooders, social workers, psychiatrists, and bureaucrats who might have prevented the tragedy if they had only taken the time to listen to a very sick individual's pathetic cries for help.

But with the dawning of September 22, 1986, whatever had been brewing inside Mike Wayne Jackson had reached the boiling point, and there was no safety valve.

The former mental patient from Indianapolis started the new work week by painting his face and dark, flowing beard a brilliant silver. Then he tucked a pistol into his belt, loaded his homemade shotgun for business, and went out on a killing spree.

For a long time members of Jackson's family, including his terrified mother, had been trying to convince authorities that the man needed help, but nobody would listen. As of 8:18 A.M. Monday, the listening time was over.

The silver-faced Jackson, a forty-year-old career criminal with a glaring record of more than thirty arrests for rape, robbery, auto theft, and assault with intent to kill, stepped calmly out the front door of his home at 1730 East Pleasant Run Parkway, leveled his shotgun at the well-dressed stranger coming up the front walk, and pulled the trigger.

The blast scored a full-frontal hit on thirty-nine-year-old Thomas Gahl, a federal probation officer, who was calling on Jackson to obtain a routine urine sample, in order to make sure he was taking his medication, and was free of illicit drugs. The unsuspecting Gahl became the first federal probation officer killed in the line of duty since the founding of the Parole and Probation Service in 1927.

As the government agent lay sprawled on the sidewalk in an ever-widening pool of blood, Jackson—gun in hand— stepped over the body and headed for the market.

At 8:33 A.M. he arrived at J.B.'s Market on South Meridan Street. Leveling the shotgun at the forty-five-year-old operator, James Hall, he demanded, "Give me your money." When the bewildered Hall didn't move fast enough to please him, Jackson shot him in the throat, killing him instantly. Victim No. 2.

Jackson then turned the shotgun on Russell VanOsdol, a bakery driver who had been delivering bread to the store, and ordered him to drive him to Indianapolis International Airport. VanOsdol was not about to argue. At the airport Jackson freed his captive, robbed Mark McLean at the Airport Holiday Inn of an undetermined amount of money, and drove off in McLean's red Isuzu truck.

Back in Indianapolis Jackson abandoned the truck in the 7200 block of North Carlson Avenue, where he accosted twenty-seven-year-old Jody Smith as she was taking out the garbage. He commandeered the woman's Ford Escort, and her along with it. Concealing a handgun beneath a red bandanna, Jackson forced her to drive to a service station in the 2500 block of High School Road. There he filled the Escort with gas, slid into the driver's seat, and sped off without paying.

Armed with two weapons and a full tank of gas, Jackson headed out of town with the terrified woman at his side. "You try to get away and I'll kill you," he warned.

Frightened as she was, Smith kept her wits about her and waited for her chance. At 10:15 A.M., as Jackson slowed down to pass through the small community of Frankfort, about thirty miles north of Indianapolis, she hit the right door handle and rolled out of the moving car, bouncing onto the pavement with such force that she broke one of her ankles. Not wanting to attract undue attention, Jackson kept going, leaving the injured woman in the road.

A crowd quickly gathered. Someone called an ambulance, and she was taken to Frankfort Hospital, where she poured out her story to local police.

By the time he'd reached the edge of town Jackson realized the woman would put authorities on his trail, and he was an easy mark driving her Escort. Pulling off to the side of the road, he went looking for a new set of wheels.

Deborah Smith was in her mobile home, tending her young son, Jason, when Jackson burst in, brandishing his shotgun. He forced Mrs. Smith and the child into the woman's beige 1982 Mercury Marquis, where he pointed a gun at the young mother and ordered, "Drive." It was an ironic coincidence that two of Jackson's hostages in a row were women named Smith.

About five miles down the road Jackson instructed the woman, "Pull over here, and get out of the car. The kid, too." He then robbed her of a small amount of cash and jewelry and drove off, leaving her and the child unharmed. The Mercury was next seen in Carroll County, about seventy miles from Indianapolis, heading in the direction of Chicago.

By that time Indiana State Police had radioed a description of Jackson to all local departments and to neighboring states: White male, five-feet-ten-inches tall, 195 pounds, brown hair, hazel eyes, and full beard. Last seen wearing a dark-colored felt hat with a narrow brim, a dark blue or black trench coat. Face and beard painted silver.

One might think that a distinctive silver-bearded face would not be hard to spot, especially in broad daylight, but the wily Jackson managed to elude the dragnet that authorities had set out for him. Possibly taking to the side roads somewhere between Indianapolis and Chicago, he looped back and headed southwest toward St. Louis. He made it all the way across Illinois without incident.

The next reported sighting came at 6:00 P.M. when a wild-eyed gunman with his face painted silver pulled up to the Galleria in the St. Louis suburb of Richmond Heights, and robbed Cynthia Mosley at gunpoint. Leaping back into the Mercury, he then headed west on Interstate Highway 70.

About forty-five minutes later a silver 1984 Ford LTD was found crashed against a utility pole at the I-70 exit ramp to St. Peters. There were no witnesses to the accident. The driver, forty-seven-year-old Earl D. Finn of nearby O'Fallon, who had been alone in the car, was dead of bloody head injuries. The body was removed to a local funeral parlor, where it did not take the county's new medical examiner, Dr. Mary Case, long to determine that Finn had not died as a result of the crash. Death was due to a lethal shotgun blast to the head.

Jackson, meanwhile, had pulled off the interstate at O'Fallon, some thirty miles west of St. Louis, and was trying to get rid of the beige Mercury he had stolen in Indiana. Looking around, he spotted forty-one-year-old Cheryl Kline getting into her 1985 Ford Escort in the IGA Food Store parking lot. Brushing the astonished woman aside with his shotgun, the silver-faced stranger jumped into her tan station wagon and drove off.

It was just a few minutes before 7:00 P.M. when the woman scurried back into the food store and telephoned police to report the theft. On running a "make" on the beige Mercury with Indiana license plates the thief had left behind, O'Fallon police discovered that Jackson's latest victim had been lucky to lose only her car. Indiana State Police advised Missouri authorities that the fugitive was wanted for the shotgun slayings of a federal probation officer and a grocer, and for leaving the scene of the accident in which one of his hostages had broken her ankle.

At the same time, O'Fallon police got word of the fatal shooting a few miles back on the interstate. From all indications, another motorist had pulled alongside and shot Finn in the head through the rolled down driver's side window, while both cars were heading west at a high rate of speed. The LTD, with Finn dead at the wheel, veered off the exit ramp and plowed into the lamp pole.

"The victim's silver Ford LTD kind of looked like a police officer's car," St. Peters Police Chief Elwyn Chapman advised O'Fallon lawmen. "We've got a theory that Jackson thought Finn was a police officer and shot him on the fly."

Back in O'Fallon things were happening fast. Jackson headed north through the community of 7,000 in the stolen Escort from the supermarket. He drove only a short distance, however, before abandoning the car. His plan was to have police looking for a tan Escort, while he was off in a different vehicle.

Ernest Younggren, seventy-two, was talking to his twenty-nine-year-old daughter, Linda Scherer, in the Ridgeway Court parking lot on the north side of town when the silver-faced man approached at 7:16 P.M. Brandishing the shotgun, he took the keys to the woman's 1985 Buick and motioned for her to get into the car. Instead, she turned and ran for her life, leaving Jackson holding her keys. Befuddled, he jumped into the Buick and drove off.

At 7:23 P.M. the woman's husband, Robin Scherer, was driving toward his father-in-law's home when he noticed his wife's car approaching from the opposite direction at a high rate of speed. Seeing the silver-faced stranger behind the wheel, Scherer executed a fast U-turn and took off after the Buick. The fleeing Jackson let go with two shotgun blasts, which blew out the windshield of the pursuing car. Scherer was unhurt, but wisely decided to drop out of the chase.

The confused ex-mental patient was now trying to find his way back to the expressway. At 7:36 P.M., as he drove past the Casalon Apartments in the central part of town, he spotted Rick Darcy, a twenty-six-year-old real estate agent, waxing his Cadillac in front of the building. It was an opportune time to change cars and throw off the pursuit.

Ditching the Scherer Buick, Jackson advanced toward Darcy with the shotgun drawn, shouting, "I'll kill you! I'll kill you!" Ordering the startled Darcy into the car, Jackson slid behind the wheel, turned the key in the ignition, and peeled rubber. With the frightened realtor giving directions, he got back onto the interstate and headed west a short distance, before leaving the "I" once again for the less-traveled side roads.

Jackson drove the partly waxed Caddy aimlessly along back roads until dark. At nine o'clock he stopped and ordered his passenger to get out. He then robbed Darcy of $20, told him, "Get into the trunk," and slammed the lid shut on him.

Jackson, alone in the front seat, continued weaving his way westward until he came to Wright City, about twenty miles from O'Fallon. Figuring it was safe by then to return to the highway, he got back onto the interstate, aiming to continue on toward Kansas City, with Darcy still locked in the trunk with the spare tire.

Law enforcement agencies were looking for the silver-faced killer across the state, however, and Wright City Police Chief Bill Burgess and Officer Roland Clemonds spotted him when he stopped for gas along I-70 at 9:25 P.M. As they cautiously approached the suspect Jackson opened fire with his shotgun without warning.

"He didn't say a word," Clemonds said afterward. "He just came up with a shotgun and—Boom! I returned the fire and he started to drive away, and I fired a second shot. He didn't seem mad. He just stopped the car and fired."

Jackson's second volley grazed Clemonds in the fore-head. Though wounded, both he and Chief Burgess continued shooting as Jackson sped off in the Cadillac. With bullets zinging around him, Jackson lost control of the car and crashed into a fence in the median strip. He leaped from the wreckage and fled on foot as the dazed Darcy stumbled out of the trunk—which had popped open on impact—badly shaken but otherwise unhurt.

More than 100 lawmen from surrounding communities, along with teams of FBI agents, assisted by helicopters and canine units, converged on the area around Wright City, population 1,200, to flush out the silver-faced fugitive. They searched throughout the night, without success.

Leaving a bloody trail of three dead, one wounded, five hostages, including one with a broken ankle, seven stolen cars, another wrecked, and a ninth damaged by shotgun blasts, and five robberies—the wild-eyed man with the garishly painted face and beard had made good his escape.

It was September 23, his forty-first birthday.

In the wake of Jackson's day-long rampage of murder and mayhem, followed by his spectacular escape from the wrecked Cadillac in a hail of bullets, there were no more shootings, no more hostages known to have been taken, and no more automobiles reported stolen. This meant that he was most likely holed up somewhere nearby.

As teams of local lawmen and federal agents conducted a house-to-house search of Wright City and the surrounding area, authorities put together a profile of the wanted man in an effort to determine just what made him tick, and what his next move might be. Much of the information was supplied by two men who knew Jackson well, Charles Peterson, special agent in charge of the Indianapolis office of the Treasury Department's Bureau of Alcohol, Tobacco and Firearms, and C. Joseph Russell, assistant United State's attorney, and a member of the President's Task Force on Organized Crime and Drug Enforcement in Indianapolis.

Mike Wayne Jackson—the press erroneously identified him as Michael—was born September 23, 1945, in Pontotoc, a small town just outside of Tupelo, Mississippi. His first arrest, when he was in the ninth grade, was for the armed robbery of a taxi driver. In 1963, at the age of eighteen, he was arrested on charges of rape, kidnap, and entering to commit a felony, but not convicted.

He was married at nineteen. He and his wife, Carolyn, lived with his parents for a time, then with her parents, as his violent life continued.

He was arrested for premeditated assault and battery with intent to do great bodily harm, charges that were later dropped. But in 1965 he was fined $350 and sentenced to six months in jail for auto theft. In 1969, after intermittent arrests for assault, battery, and stealing cars, he was convicted in Indiana for forgery and theft, and sentenced to prison for two to fourteen years.

Jackson was not out long when, in 1972, he was again convicted in Indiana, this time for burglary, and given a prison term of one to five years. In 1977 he was convicted of rape in Tennessee, and sentenced to ten years in the state penitentiary there.

During Jackson's periods of incarceration his wife divorced him. After he was released from prison they were remarried, and had two children. As his life of violence continued, she divorced him a second time. During a ten-year period he saw his family only three times.

On at least two occasions in 1983 and 1984 members of Jackson's family tried desperately to have him committed to mental institutions in Mississippi because of attacks by him. Once, his seventy-three-year-old mother had to be hospitalized for broken ribs after he kicked her down a flight of stairs. Another time, his brother was stabbed after Jackson made threats against the lives of his sisters.

His mother had him arrested twice in Mississippi on a charge of "lunacy," and he was twice committed to the Whitfield State Hospital. Both times psychiatrists at the state institution placed him on drug treatment programs and released him within a few weeks.

"They put him in Whitfield twice down here and my sister tried to tell them peckerwoods down there, 'You people need to be working on our system,'" Jackson's uncle, Cecil Poynter, complained after his nephew was released. "But no one would listen."

Jackson's distraught mother then wrote to authorities begging that her troubled son "be committed permanently to an institution where he can be helped mentally and physically." As before, her pleas fell on disinterested ears.

Ironically, it was a minor shoplifting charge that eventually led to Jackson's murder spree, and put his name on the FBI's list of "most wanted" criminals.

On March 1, 1985, Indianapolis police were called to the Marsh Supermarket on East Washington Street, where a security guard had detained Jackson for attempting to leave the store without paying for several magazines. "I was going to pay for them. It was just absentmindedness on my part," Jackson insisted.

But the security officer didn't believe him, and after police arrived things began to get serious. A routine "wants and warrants" computer check revealed that Jackson was wanted on three outstanding warrants for failing to appear in court on traffic charges.

At the time of his shoplifting arrest Jackson had been back in Indianapolis only a few days. He had driven up in his pickup truck from his mother's home in Mississippi, after a violent quarrel in which she complained to police that he had abused her.

In searching the pickup truck police found a homemade 12-gauge shotgun fashioned from a length of pipe, and four Molotov cocktails. The firebombs, made from large plastic soft drink bottles, contained wicks and were ready for use. Jackson explained that he had made the shotgun for self defense. He refused to discuss the firebombs.

While he was being held in jail on the shoplifting charge, police test-fired the shotgun and found it worked like the real McCoy. They also learned that Jackson had been involved in a running feud with another Indianapolis man, and had apparently planned on using firebombs to settle things.

Jackson was indicted by a federal grand jury for firearms violations, since a convicted felon is not permitted to carry a gun. In reviewing the suspect's arrest record and history of mental problems, Russell, the federal prosecutor assigned to the case, obtained a court order to have Jackson examined by psychiatrists at the U.S. Medical Center for Federal Prisoners at Springfield, Missouri.

The psychiatric report indicated that Jackson was paranoid and schizophrenic, with pronounced antisocial behavior. The shrinks declared, however, that he was competent to stand trial.

While under lock and key in the Marion County Jail in Indianapolis, Jackson, who impressed jailers as a dead-bang Charles Manson look-alike, was repeatedly cited for rules infractions. On one occasion he was caught with a homemade knife, or "wire shank," as inmates called it. Another time he fought with a cellmate over a cigarette butt, and in another instance he set his cell ablaze. He was finally placed in isolation, for the protection of other prisoners.

With time weighing heavily on his hands, and no one to quarrel with, Jackson took pen in hand and another facet of this strange man—the letter-writing side—became evident. "He liked to write letters and he prided himself on them," said one of his lawyers, David Mernitz. "He wanted to be a writer, and so his outlet was writing letters."

No one, it seemed, was too high and mighty to receive a missive from Mike Jackson. He dispatched a threatening letter to President Ronald Reagan, bearing the return address of "Ted Kennedy, Marion County Jail."

To someone addressed only as "Sissy" he begged her to visit him and wrote, "I love you, Sissy. Like it or not." Despite his meager ninth-grade education, his flowing script was easy to read. The envelope addressed to Sissy was decorated with drawings of birds, and trees, and children playing in the sunshine.

Some of the letters were downright extortion notes. One demanded $25,000 from an uncle in Mississippi. Another, to an Indianapolis lawyer not even connected with his case, demanded a $25,000 contribution to Jackson's "defense fund." When the lawyer ignored the request, Jackson wrote a follow-up letter threatening to get even.

Jackson was also busy preparing his own court motions, consisting of rambling documents alleging that a giant conspiracy existed against him. He accused police of threatening to kill him, and claimed to have knowledge of others whom they had killed. In one such document Jackson wrote:

"Citizens have even been killed by federal officers, authorities, here in Indianapolis (and elsewhere which I'll get into soon, but at a later date) for no other reason then just to kill . . . innocent people and/or citizens charged (but not found guilty and may not be guilty as I'll state soon at a later date when all are charged in a class-action suit) that they (federal officers) have killed (murdered without provocation) and threatened to kill me and conspire to kill me."

Jackson announced that he intended to call a number of television and movie personalities, including Robert Redford, Vanna White, and Loni Anderson, as defense witnesses when he went to trial on the weapons charge. Mernitz and his other court-appointed lawyer, Brian Touhy, eventually convinced him that it would be best to accept a government plea bargain and plead guilty.

On September 20, 1985, three days short of his fortieth birthday, he pled guilty to two counts of possession of incendiary devices, in exchange for the government dropping remaining charges.

Federal prosecutors asked for a maximum sentence of ten years on each of the two counts, but a lenient judge imposed a sentence of only one year. With credit for seven months already spent in the Marion County Jail awaiting trial, he had only five months to go.

While finishing out his term Jackson threatened several jailers, after which a panel of three psychiatrists determined he was "suffering from a significant mental disease or defect and is considered dangerous to others."

Based on Jackson's violent behavior, U.S. Attorney Robert G. Ulrich asked for a federal court order to keep the prisoner in custody until his condition improved, ignoring his scheduled February 14 release date.

Before a federal judge could act on the request, however, Jackson was placed on the drugs Navane and Cogentin, which resulted in a marked improvement in his behavior. A new panel of psychiatrists determined that the medication had placed his mental illness "in remission," and he was no longer a danger to anyone.

He was released on three years probation on April 24, with the stipulation that he be placed in a halfway house in Indianapolis, and remain under the supervision of a federal parole officer. Things started going bad right from the start, however, with Jackson having a hard time finding any halfway house that would put up with his idiosyncrasies.

He was finally settled into the home on Pleasant Run Parkway. Probation Officer Thomas Gahl had been on Jackson's case only two days that September Monday morning when he strolled up the front walk, intending to ask for a urine sample to make sure his charge had been taking his prescribed medication, when Jackson turned the shotgun on him.

Now, one day later and 250 miles away, Jackson was out there somewhere, armed to the teeth. The question was: Where?

"We think he's still in the area because there have been no reports of stolen vehicles," said Missouri Highway Patrol Captain John Ford. "We've got nothing, but everyone is still out and that will continue until he's caught, or it's determined that he's out of the area. Our fear is that he has someone hostage in a house."

Residents of the community were warned to stay inside with their doors locked. Police wearing military fatigues and flak jackets, armed with automatic weapons, canvassed neighborhoods, stopped cars, and even searched passing freight trains.

The county-wide manhunt was a cooperative venture between the Highway Patrol, under Captain Ford and Lieutenant Dale Buschmann, working out of Kirkwood; the Warren County Sheriff's office; the tiny Wright City police force; and the FBI. Three SWAT teams were rushed into the area, from FBI field offices in St. Louis, Kansas City, and Knoxville, Tennessee.

Despite the army of hunters, Jackson, who had vowed he would not be taken alive, eluded them all for eleven tension-filled days, through daylight and heat, darkness and rain.

"There's still no sign that he's left the area," said Ford. "His mode of operations is to move, take hostages, and kill people. He'd done none of that that we know of since the first Monday. We're trying to keep the pressure on him. We're trying to flush him out. If he's found an empty house and a good food supply, he might be living a fairly normal lifestyle. But if he's just out in those woods, he's hurting. He's wet, tired, and hungry. He's got to come out sooner or later."

But he didn't. The Tennessee SWAT team flew in a professional tracker, J. R. Buchanan, from the Great Smoky Mountains National Park. He would be the one who would ultimately bring an end to Mike Jackson's odyssey of bloodshed.

On Tuesday, September 30, Missouri Trooper Don Frey and a St. Louis FBI agent had checked out an abandoned farm house about a mile from the interstate, where Jackson was last sighted. It was their fifth visit to the dilapidated frame house since the manhunt began. They figured that the wily fugitive might try to hunker down in a place that had already been searched, thinking that no one would come back.

The search parties had already determined that Jackson had used an abandoned camper trailer located about two miles from the interstate. Silver-tinted whiskers found in a water pan indicated that he had shaved off his beard there.

The old farmhouse was in a line between the abandoned camper and the highway, and Jackson must have noticed it in passing. Frey and his FBI companion saw nothing out of the ordinary, however—a few sticks of rickety furniture, scattered rubbish, and a weathered overcoat hanging on a peg in the hallway.

Two days later, on the afternoon of October 2, the state trooper and FBI man returned to make another check. As in their previous inspections, they found nothing to indicate anyone had been there of late. They were about to leave when Frey grabbed the FBI man by the arm and exclaimed, "Wait a minute. Something's changed."

"What do you see, Don?"

"It's what I don't see," the trooper replied. "That old overcoat that was hanging in the hall the other day? Take a look. The peg is empty."

The two lawmen reported the oddity on their return to the command post, where Buchanan, the sixty-year-old mountain man, was waiting. A professional tracker for more than thirty years, he had learned the trade from his uncle, Jerry Hearon, and his granddaddy, Tom Hearon, both creatures of the Tennessee hill country.

The previous afternoon Jackson had come upon a set of footprints made by a man wearing tennis shoes—as Jackson had been reported. He followed the trail until the prints played out on a blacktop road. "I figure they're two or three days old," he told posse members.

When Trooper Frey and the FBI agent came in with their story, Buchanan was raring to have a look at the place before darkness fell. "I work strictly by sight," he drawled. "Found lots of lost people in my time. We can't waste no time, though. Another good rain will wash away any tracks."

The FBI man and Frey, along with two SWAT team sharpshooters, drove Buchanan back to the farmhouse. The ramshackle building stood less than three-quarters of a mile from the blacktop where the tennis shoe prints had petered out. The search party arrived shortly before dusk.

They checked the house from top to bottom, but it was as empty as before. "Here they are again!" Buchanan exclaimed, pointing to a path leading away from the back of the house. "These are the same footprints. But I'd say these are probably less than an hour old!"

The lawmen walked apprehensively alongside as the keen-eyed tracker followed the tennis shoe prints, step by step, for a distance of about seventy-five yards to a point where the wet, muddy tracks led to an abandoned barn.

With the FBI man at his side, Buchanan cautiously entered the deserted outbuilding. Taking in the lay of the land, they observed several empty animal stalls, an exposed center loft, and two higher side lofts. As Buchanan and the federal man edged quietly toward a ladder to check out the lofts, a muffled shotgun blast shattered the silence about ten feet overhead.

The FBI man leaped backward out the door as Buchanan dived for cover in one of the stalls. "What the hell was that? Anybody hurt?" barked an anxious voice over the tracker's hand-held radio. "Naw, I'm OK. I'm gonna need someone to create a diversion so I can get the hell out of here," Buchanan radioed back.

The SWAT men outside fired their weapons in the direction of the hayloft as the pinned-down tracker sprinted to safety. "The son-of-a-bitch is in there all right, that's for dang sure," he panted, brushing the dirt off his clothes.

The lawmen radioed for reinforcements, and within minutes the barn was surrounded. A helicopter hovered directly overhead, illuminating the farmyard with its powerful floodlights.

At 11:30 P.M., after lobbing tear gas into the old barn, the posse stormed the building. Using iron grappling hooks to pull down mildewed bales of hay, they discovered Jackson's bloodstained body in the north loft.

Keeping his vow not to be taken alive, he had apparently ended his own troubled life. A 12-gauge shotgun, its barrel and stock sawed off, was at his side, along with a jug of water and some soybeans. He was wearing the old overcoat from the farmhouse, its pockets bulging with shotgun shells. The grotesque silver paint had been scrubbed from his face.

EPILOGUE

Mike Jackson's mother, Modine Embry, wept quietly when word filtered down to her in Mississippi that the long campaign to get someone to pay attention to her emotionally disturbed son was finally over. By the time folks took proper notice, of course, four people were dead—Thomas Gahl, the federal parole officer; James Hall, the grocer; Earl Finn, the hapless motorist; and Jackson himself. "Something should have been done when Mike was in those institutions," she said, dabbing her eyes with a handkerchief. "He told the doctors and me that he couldn't cope."

CHAPTER 16

THE NAKED AND THE DEAD

If Tommy Pitera's neighbors in New York City had any idea what was going on in the house of horrors next door, chances are they might have packed their bags and skedaddled for safer surroundings.

Had they been equipped with X-ray vision, that enabled them to see through the walls, they might have observed the thirty-five-year-old martial arts expert huddled naked in the bathtub—but he wasn't lathering his armpits or washing between his toes. And that wasn't bath water swirling down the open drain, it was human blood.

According to the United State's Attorney for the Eastern District of New York, Pitera is one of the Mafia's most prolific hitmen, with as many as thirty kills to his credit. And whenever he went about cleaning up after one of his business deals he liked to strip for action, literally—buck-assed naked.

Affidavits filed in U.S. District Court in New York in June 1990 describe how Pitera disposed of his victims:

After someone was unfortunate enough to have gotten in the way of one of Pitera's bullets, he would undress the dead body and lay it out in the nearest bathtub. Then he would peel down to his birthday suit, so as not to soil his expensive silk raiment, climb into the tub, straddle the body, and turn on the faucet.

267

With the water running to keep down the resultant mess, Pitera would first disembowel his victim, and then take a sharp knife and hacksaw to what was left, reducing the dead body to little pieces—convenient for carrying.

After being thoroughly washed off, the bits and pieces of flesh and bone would be wrapped in plastic bags and placed into suitcases, to be buried in a remote corner of a Staten Island bird sanctuary. And Pitera would wash himself off and get dressed.

"He enjoys killing," said one federal investigator. "He chops up the bodies, puts the torsos into suitcases, and buries the suitcases with help from four to eight younger thugs, or GITs—Gangsters In Training—as he calls them."

Victims not buried in the wildlife park may have been disposed of in such hard-to-get-at places as the bottom of the East River. Pitera, whom crime family higher-ups referred to as "The Wacko," was once overheard advising an admiring colleague, "As long as you got them, cut his lungs out so the body don't float. Cut his stomach, cut his stomach out, cut both lungs."

How government agents knew so much about Pitera's secret operations was no secret. From 1986 to 1990 they had been eavesdropping on his conversations everywhere he went. The feds had bugged his apartment, his girlfriend's, the apartments of friends, a nightclub he helped operate, and even his black 1983 Oldsmobile.

A typical conversation between two of Pitera's gang members, Thomas Carbone and Richard Leone, was recorded as the pair rode in the boss' Oldsmobile on August 3, 1988. In discussing how they intended to pull off an upcoming murder, Leone, a man with a limited vocabulary, was overhead telling Carbone:

"Let me look at, take it to the prior location, call Richie (Richard David), tell him to meet us, tell him to bring one of the fuckin' mufflers (silencers). We'll go in like we're gonna make a fuckin' deal with the guy, the guy will let the three of us in, and then we whack him." Leone made it clear he was not keen on working with David, but had no choice. He explained to Carbone, "I hate to involve the fuckin' guy 'cause he's a fuckin' pain in the ass . . . You know, he's got all the fuckin' silencers. I know, I know he won't let me use the silencers or lend them to me, 'cause they're not his, they're Tommy's."

As a result of conversations Pitera and his associates unwittingly shared with agents for the Drug Enforcement Administration and FBI, plus information supplied by confidential informants, Pitera was named in a federal indictment linking him to at least seven murders in 1986, 1987, and 1988. The government added, however, that he and members of his "crew" were believed responsible for "at least two dozen more."

"He is a very scary guy," one federal investigator explained. "He's considered a rogue soldier within the Bonanno crime family. Very tough guys were scared to death of him."

Indeed, investigators said Pitera got business, or murder contracts, from all five of New York City's crime families. They regarded "The Wacko" for the most part as a crazy killer, unpredictable and dangerous. Mobsters, themselves, avoided him like a dose of the clap for fear that he might turn on them.

Members or associates of his gang accused of involvement in murder, drug dealing, and various other crimes with Pitera were identified as Vincent "Baldy" Giattino, also known as "Kojak"; Richard David, a former New York City court officer and business partner of Pitera; Thomas Carbone, AKA Jerry Buccheri and "Uncle"; Anthony Flotte, AKA Tony Presto and Tony Diamonds; William "Billy" Bright; Frank Gangi; Lloyd Modell, AKA Lorenzo Modica; Frank Martini, alias Frankie Jupiter; Manny Maya; Michael Cassesse; Louis Mena; Angelo Favara; Judith Haimawitz; Ray Albertina; and Dennis Michael Harrigan.

The three-year federal investigation revealed that Pitera and David were the owners of a nightclub known as Overstreets/Lazers at 429 Eighty-sixth Street, in Brooklyn. According to DEA Agent James Hunt, "Pitera has used a bathtub at Overstreets/Lazers to dismember bodies of his murder victims on several occasions during the past three years."

One of the persons Pitera was accused of murdering and butchering was twenty-nine-year-old Phyllis Burdi, a close friend of his wife, Celeste. Government agents charged Pitera drugged, shot, and dismembered Burdi on November 27, 1987, because she was with Celeste when she took a fatal drug overdose two months earlier, and he blamed her for failing to save his wife's life.

According to an informant who told DEA agents he was personally involved in the crime, Frank Gangi brought the woman to an apartment in New York City. Pitera arrived a short time later with two other men. He then took Burdi into a bedroom and shot her. Pitera then dismembered her body in the bathtub, and disposed of the remains in the usual manner.

Other victims attributed to Pitera and his associates were listed as:

• Wilfred "Willie Boy" Johnson, a fifty-three-year-old ex-boxer, gambler, loanshark, and longtime associate of Gambino crime family boss John Gotti. He flipped (turned FBI informant) in 1966 and reportedly provided authorities with reams of underworld information under the code name "Wahoo." Willie Boy was cut down in a barrage of gunfire outside his Brooklyn home on August 29, 1988.

Johnson had provided testimony in 1973 that sent Gotti to jail for two years in connection with the death of a man suspected of killing a nephew of Carlos Gambino, then boss of the Gambino crime family.

According to Andrew J. Maloney, U.S. Attorney in Brooklyn, "Mr. Pitera believed he was doing a favor to John Gotti with the extermination of Willie Boy Johnson." He hoped the deed would enhance his standing with the Bonanno family.

• Richard Leone, a forty-four-year-old member of Pitera's crew, whose voice was recorded by bugs placed in

Pitera's Oldsmobile, disappeared on March 15, 1989, along with forty-seven-year-old Sol Stern, one of Leone's criminal associates. According to federal affidavits, Pitera, assisted by Bright and David, shot Leone to death because they feared he was an informant. Stern was fatally shot because of his association with Leone. Their bodies were then dismembered in the bathtub at Overstreets/Lazers.

• Talal Siksik, an Israeli living in New York, was fatally shot by Pitera in the victim's own apartment at 2807 Kings Highway, Brooklyn, in June 1987. His body was then dismembered in his own bathtub, and the parts were packed into a suitcase for burial. After Siksik was slain, Pitera commandeered the victim's furniture to enhance his own apartment. After all, it was of no further use to Siksik.

• Carlos Acosta and Fernando Aguilera, both Colombian nationals, were murdered by Pitera crew members in the garage of a Brooklyn apartment building at 1429 Shore Parkway on July 22, 1988.

According to a federal complaint, Pitera's men arranged to buy 30 kilograms of cocaine from Acosta and Aguilera, but shot them dead in lieu of paying cash on delivery. They then dutifully turned part of the cocaine over to the boss.

• Joseph Balzano was shot and killed by Pitera while riding in the front seat of Pitera's Oldsmobile on April 24, 1988, according to confidential informants. Pitera then drove to a gas station in Brooklyn and dumped the body in a nearby alley.

• Andrew Jakakis was murdered in the front seat of a silver Honda on May 16, 1988. After the slaying his body was dumped in a vacant lot in Brooklyn.

U.S. Attorney Maloney and Robert Bryden, regional director of the U.S. Drug Enforcement Administration, said Pitera regularly attended his victims' wakes, consoled their families, and took home their mass cards as souvenirs of his hits. In some cases, they said, he also kept pinky rings and other jewelry taken from his victims' bodies, and stashed them in a wall safe in his apartment.

The federal prosecutor said Pitera and his associates dealt in large quantities of cocaine, marijuana, and heroin, and often paid off dealers with bullets instead of the expected cash. "They took the cocaine from them and left the bodies behind," Maloney said.

After the indictments against Pitera and his fifteen associates were unsealed, he was arrested without incident on Sunday, June 3, 1990, as he drove along Atlantic Avenue in Brooklyn. He had just dropped off his girlfriend, Barbara Lambrose, to visit a friend. The others were taken into custody, one by one, on charges of racketeering and drug trafficking.

The perceptive Carbone was sure he knew how the feds had gotten onto him and his pals. "It was the telephone, right?" he said as the handcuffs were being slapped onto his wrists. "My wife, she just had to have a phone!"

A subsequent raid on Pitera's Brooklyn apartment at 2355 East Twelfth Street turned up a library of torture, dismemberment, and murder manuals, including how-to books bearing such titles as *The Hitman's Handbook, Torture, Interrogation and Execution, Mantrapping, Assassination, Theory and Practice, Getting Started in the Illicit Drug Business,* and *Kill or Be Killed.*

"It's certainly the largest collection I've ever seen," remarked DEA director Bryden, holding aloft a copy of *The Hitman's Handbook.*

The dog-eared copy of *Torture, Interrogation and Execution* by the Marquis de Robespierre, appeared to have been the most studied volume in Pitera's literary collection. "Ranging from the Rack and the Strappado of the Inquisition to the ancient Oriental methods such as the Death of a Thousand Cuts, to impalement introduced by the Turks, this work takes you clear down into modern times," the Marquis advised. "Read and be informed."

The "strappado" referred to was a painful torture device in which the victim was dropped and brought up short by a rope tied to his wrists behind his back. Pitera had also spent time in Japan where he studied means of committing murder. He was familiar with bacteria and poisons.

In addition to his library of death, police confiscated an arsenal of sixty automatic weapons, pistols, shotguns and assault rifles, Samurai swords, bayonets, and butchering knives.

Authorities also arrested Pitera's girlfriend, Barbara Lambrose, after DEA agents found three guns in her Bensonhurst apartment. They also raided the Sheepshead Bay apartment of his late wife, Celeste, where they found yet another firearm. Curiously, the apartment had been left exactly as it was on the day Celeste died, as if Pitera had expected her to return at any moment.

In the basement of the Just Us Lounge at 123 Avenue S, Brooklyn, in which Pitera also had an interest, authorities recovered a pick and shovel, which informants said had been used in the murder victim burial details. Another shovel, a spade with a red handle, was kept in the basement of Pitera's Ovington Avenue house.

Following Pitera's arrest and the raids on his apartment and hangouts, a team of thirty New York City homicide detectives and DEA agents headed for the William R. Davis Wildlife Refuge on the south shore of Staten Island on a grisly mission.

They were armed with a search warrant for "A plot of land from the service road beginning at Exit 8 on the West Shore Expressway [South Avenue Exit] and beginning at light pole number NS539M continuing down and around the service road to Gulf Avenue and then continuing to telephone pole number 1038 in Staten Island, New York [hereinafter referred to as the 'Burial Site']."

The warrant authorized investigators to search for "forensic evidence relating to murders only."

This would be the moment of truth. Were the endless natterings the agents had recorded on the court-approved eavesdropping devices in Pitera's haunts really true? Was the quiet bird sanctuary indeed a clandestine gangster burial ground?

The grim body hunt began in an isolated, wooded area near Exit 8 of the West Shore Expressway. At the onset the searchers scoured the surface with metal detectors and void machines, devices which locate hollow spaces in the ground, but came up with nothing. Failing at this they brought in trained dogs, and long steel rods.

The method they followed was to disturb the surface, and then let the dogs sniff around to see if they could detect an odor. If the dogs indicated they were on to something, the rods were used to poke down into the marshy soil.

On Friday, June 15, the first results were uncovered. After one of the metal rods jammed against something solid several feet below the surface, the search team dug up a battered suitcase containing human remains. Before the day was done a second suitcase had been unearthed, and disgorged parts of yet another murder victim.

Pitera's GITs had not done their job. Instead of laying the suitcases flat in the graves, as instructed, they had deposited them in an upright position, thus leaving the tops dangerously near the surface.

The next day, Saturday, parts of three more dismembered bodies were found in six plastic bags. The corpses found Saturday had all been decapitated, with the heads buried separately to hamper identification.

"We are still searching," DEA Agent Mark Hannon advised David Shapiro, an assistant U.S. attorney who was preparing the case against Pitera. "Once we came up with one body, it confirmed the information we had. Coming up with five bodies really solidifies the information. We will stay out here until we are sure there are no more bodies."

By the end of the week a sixth dismembered corpse had been uncovered in the makeshift Mafia graveyard. The last set of remains, enclosed in a body bag, appeared to have been in the ground for as long as ten years. All of the others appeared to have been interred within the previous two years.

The search continued for two months, before being halted in mid-August amid complaints from environmentalists that the macabre digging was destroying the pristine landscape.

"We got heads, we got arms, we got legs. You name it," one DEA agent asserted. "There's no question but that this was a dumping ground."

"We've never seen anything like this," added Bryden. "To my knowledge it's the largest Mafia graveyard ever found in New York."

Authorities now set about the grim task of identifying the putrefying remains.

One of the dismembered bodies was that of a female. Pathologists used medical records to identify the corpse as that of Phyllis Burdi, the friend of Pitera's wife, Celeste. She was reported missing in late 1987, shortly after Celeste died of the drug overdose.

Parts of other bodies dug up in the bird sanctuary were ultimately identified as those of Marek Krucharski, a thirty-year-old Polish boxer; Richard Leone, the crew member Pitera turned on; Leone's buddy, Sol Stern; and Tal Siksik, the Israeli who had sought safe haven in the United States.

The government now had enough corpus delicti to prove that murder had been committed, and enough information from informants and wiretaps to tie Pitera to the homicides. He was ordered held without bond under a twenty-three-hour-a-day lockup in the Metropolitan Correctional Center in Manhattan. He was allowed one hour each day for recreation.

A burly man with ice-blue eyes, he was not without a conscience, however—at least in his own contorted mind. In one conversation federal agents overhead as Pitera rode in his black Oldsmobile with a confederate, he stated his credo:

"Believe me . . . I never did something stupid. I never hurt anybody innocent, I never did it, all right? For me and you to be drinking, and then me all of a sudden take out a knife and stab you for no reason, I couldn't do it. For me to go and rip off an old lady's change, I couldn't do it. I don't care . . . I couldn't do it."

Tommy Pitera is obviously a man of principle.

EPILOGUE

As this book went to press Pitera was pacing the floor of his lonely cell in New York City's Metropolitan Correctional Center, with each day bringing him closer to a trial that could seal his fate. By mid-1991, seven of his fifteen co-defendants had pleaded guilty, and two more advised government prosecutors they were ready to make a deal. That would leave only Pitera and six others left to stand trial, with some of their ex-colleagues expected to testify against them in hopes of saving their own skins.

If Pitera is, indeed, responsible for thirty murders, as federal authorities contend, he still has a long way to go to achieve the lofty status of Indiana's Belle Gunness. More about Belle later.

CHAPTER 17

███████████████████████████

THE SOCK HEARD
'ROUND THE WORLD

Officers Edward McAuliffe and Robert Sargis had no idea
what they were about to get into as they cruised quietly along
Milwaukee Avenue on the city's Northwest Side that balmy
Tuesday afternoon of October 2, 1984.

What had started out on the opposite side of the Atlantic
as a romantic interlude in a luxurious Vienna apartment a
year and a half earlier, was about to end with a sock on the
jaw on a Chicago street corner. And the unsuspecting cops
would suddenly find themselves up to their badges in a sordid tale of sex, drugs, murder, and intrigue spanning three
continents.

"Hey, look over there, Ed," Sargis pointed, as the blue
and white squadrol moved into the 3300 block. "Couple of
jokers slugging it out on the sidewalk. Guess we'd better pull
over and preserve the peace."

As the two uniformed officers parked the squad and
waded into the fray, shouting "Break it up! Break it up!" one
of the combatants took off running down the street. The
other, who appeared to have gotten the worst of it, yelled
through a bloody lip, "Get him! He's a murderer!"

The fleeing suspect, a twenty-six-year-old Egyptian
named Ibrahiem Hamza Allam, was caught after a short foot

chase and brought back to the fight scene, just outside a lawyer's office. Since he appeared to have been the aggressor, he was placed in the squadrol and taken to Albany Park District Police Headquarters. The other man, thirty-two-year-old Faysal Allam, also an Egyptian, followed in his own car, dabbing at his bloody lip with a handkerchief.

It seemed the two men were related by marriage, which accounted for each having the same last name.

Ibrahiem and his eighteen-year-old wife, Dalia, who had arrived in Chicago only a week earlier, had gone to the attorney's office to see about a divorce. Ibrahiem planned to continue on to California alone, leaving his wife free to marry her cousin, Faysal, and return to Egypt. There appeared to have been a last-minute snag, however, and the present and future husbands were trying to iron it out with their fists while she waited in the lawyer's office.

As McAuliffe and Sargis were writing up the complaint charging Ibrahiem with battery, Lieutenant Donald Cain called Faysal aside and told him, "I'm curious. What did you mean when you told the officers that this other guy was a murderer?"

"Yeah, I'm a little curious about that, too," added Captain John Collins, the watch commander. "What exactly did you mean by that?"

"Well, before I go into detail, could we bring in my cousin, Dalia?" Faysal asked. "That's his wife. She is waiting outside in my car. She will be able to confirm everything I tell you."

"You speak pretty good English," the lieutenant observed.

"We are multilingual, all three of us," Faysal explained. "English, German, Spanish, and several other languages—as well as Egyptian, of course."

"Okay, bring the lady in and tell us your story," Collins said. "In English, if you please."

It was a most incredible narrative. As the dark-eyed Dalia nodded in agreement, Faysal told Cain and Collins that Ibrahiem had been marketing his young wife's body in

Vienna, Austria, for sex purposes, and had slain one of her wealthy customers. The couple then took the dead man's purse and car and fled to America, by way of Italy, Spain, Africa, Brazil, and the British West Indies—leaving a few more dead along the way.

"What Faysal tells you is true," the eighteen-year-old bride said, wringing her hands. Dalia was hardly the picture one might conjure up of an Egyptian woman hiding behind her veil, as she sat in the captain's office, with her dark hair hanging down over her slender shoulders. She was smartly attired in expensive designer jeans, a red knit sweater embroidered with pink and white elephants, and stylish deck shoes. Ibrahiem and Faysal, in casual sports clothes, both looked as if they had just stepped out of the bar at a swank polo club.

"You tell an amazing story, Mr. Allam," Collins said. "But how do we know it's for real? You could be making it up because the guy smacked you in the kisser. Maybe you just want to get even."

"Oh, it is true," Faysal insisted. "In my apartment there is a signed confession, in Ibrahiem's own handwriting. He admits to everything."

"This I've got to see," Cain said. "Would you mind if we sent an officer over to your place to pick it up?"

"Not at all. I want you to see it," Faysal responded.

The Egyptian gave Cain the address and keys to his apartment in Rogers Park, on Chicago's far North Side, and the lieutenant sent a team of detectives out to see what they could find. Cain also put in a call to Lieutenant John Minogue, commander of the Grand Crossing Area violent crimes unit. "I think you ought to come over here. We just might have something that will interest you," he suggested.

Minogue and two of his investigators, William Kaupert and Russell Weingart, were waiting when the district detectives returned with the some papers they had found in the Egyptian's apartment, and presented them to Cain with a wry smile.

"What the hell?" he remarked, wrinkling his brow as he ran his eyes over the handwritten pages. "Well, I have in my hand a document, of some kind, but I don't know what to make of it."

"It is written in German," Faysal explained. "As I told you, we are multilingual."

"That's just great," the Irish lieutenant erupted. "An Egyptian confession in German. Find me someone who speaks German—someone beside the defendant and his accuser here. What I want is an independent reading of this thing."

Detectives asked around the station, "Any Krauts here? We need someone who talks Kraut."

"What're ya gonna do—send out for some *Weiner schnitzel?*" someone guffawed.

"No, smart ass. Hamburger. The lieutenant's got some German writing that he wants someone to tell him what the hell it's all about."

None of the cops in the building knew any German. The dispatcher was about to put out a radio request when a young reporter from the City News Bureau volunteered, "I took German in college."

A detective ushered the "City Press kid" into the captain's office and told Cain, "Lieutenant—the scribe here knows German."

"Yeah?" the lieutenant beamed, shoving the papers at the reporter. "Read this to us, slowly. Who knows? You might have yourself a goddam scoop."

The reporter looked at the document. "Could I use a typewriter, lieutenant? I think it would be easier if I typed it out in English. Then you'd have a copy. Otherwise, if I just read word for word, a lot of the German phrases would come out ass-backward."

"Somebody get the man a typewriter," Cain directed.

The City News reporter laid the paper out on the desk in front of him and began to type, as Cain looked over his shoulder. The "translation" filled two pages, single-spaced. It was a story right out of the Arabian Nights—only a twentieth century version:

Ibrahiem Allam, an auto mechanic, had married Dalia in Egypt in 1982. He was twenty-four and she was sixteen. From there they traveled to Vienna, the city of Ibrahiem's birth, where they moved in with his elderly grandmother. Unable to find gainful employment, Ibrahiem went to work as a male prostitute to help pay the couple's room and board. He soon found he could earn more money by offering the exotic Dalia for sale than himself, and began placing "sex for sale" advertisements in adult journals circulating in the Austrian capital.

A wealthy Viennese merchant, Herbert Kavale, responded to one of the ads. Initially a voyeur, Kavale met the handsome Egyptian couple in a hotel room in the city's Prater District, on the north bank of the Danube, where he paid them generously to let him watch while they enjoyed sex with one another.

The encounter blossomed into a three-way friendship between the well-heeled Kavale and the young couple, with whom he had been visually intimate. "You can call me Harry," he told them.

At a second session, in late April or early May, in Kavale's luxury apartment, Ibrahiem discovered much to his chagrin that his name had been stricken from the playbill. "This time I would like to make love to Dalia, alone," Kavale explained.

It was his money, so Ibrahiem reluctantly agreed to take a walk as his bride and the rich man stripped for action. Strolling impatiently along Praterstrasse, however, the rebuffed husband entertained second thoughts about the arrangement. The more he envisioned what must have been transpiring between Dalia and her lover in Kavale's bedroom, the higher his Arabian temper began to rise.

Abruptly he wheeled about on his heel and ran all the way back to the apartment, only to find the door bolted from the inside. Banging furiously on the door, he finally got the attention of Kavale, who pulled on a robe and opened it to see what the commotion was about. Ibrahiem shoved the Austrian across the room and pushed him backward onto the bed, where moments before he had been making love to Dalia. She had gone to the bathroom to take a shower.

The angry Ibrahiem flung himself jealously atop the naked merchant, pressed his knees to Kavale's chest, and wrapped his fingers around his throat. The fury of the men wrestling on the bed brought Dalia out of the bathroom, clad only in a flimsy gown. According to Ibrahiem's "confession," he ordered his wife to fetch a cord, or a towel, with which to bind the struggling businessman.

Dalia handed her husband an electrical lamp cord, which he wound tightly around Kavale's neck until "the Austrian's face turned blue." As the merchant lay dead upon the very bed on which just minutes before he and the woman had been writhing in ecstasy, Ibrahiem and Dalia meticulously wiped down the apartment of fingerprints and prepared for a judicious retreat.

After availing themselves of what money Kavale kept on hand, they snatched the keys to his red 128 Fiat automobile, grabbed three pistols they found in the apartment, and pulled the door shut behind them as they left. Back at their own quarters, they packed their bags, bade grandmother a hasty good-bye, and were off to Italy that very night in the dead man's Fiat.

After crossing over into Italy, however, they read a newspaper account of the murder in Vienna, and feared that police might be on their trail. There was nothing to do but get rid of anything that might link them to the victim. Reluctantly, they abandoned the red Fiat by the side of the road, and threw Kavale's three weapons into the bushes.

With what money they had left they made their way to France, and rented a motorbike. They headed south toward the Spanish border on the bike, which was now stolen, since they had no intention of returning it. Their entry to Spain was blocked at the tiny country of Andorra, however, when border guards refused to let them pass with the motorbike because they had no ownership papers.

Undaunted, the young Egyptians backtracked, and struck up a friendship with a German couple their own age, who said they were on the way to Algiers. Ibrahiem and Dalia joined them, lashing the motorbike to the roof of the couple's white van. But the friendly foursome got no farther than the Spanish border where Ibrahiem and his bride were again blocked because they had no papers for the bike.

The quick-thinking Ibrahiem then struck a deal with the border guard. Although the Spaniard adamantly denied the couple entry without papers for the two-wheeled vehicle, he was not averse to purchasing the bike for his own use. With the high cost of petrol in Spain, economical motorbikes had become an extremely popular mode of transportation. According to Ibrahiem's so-called confession, money exchanged hands, the border patrolman wound up with the bike, and waved the white van on through without further delay.

Then a rather strange thing happened, according to the document being translated by the young City News reporter. Halfway across Spain, as the quartet proceeded southward toward El Costa del Sol, the Germans abruptly decided to return to the Fatherland.

Unaccountably, they sold the van, plus all their belongings, to the Egyptians, and hopped a flight back to West Germany.

Collins and Cain had heard a lot of stories in their years as Chicago police officers, and some were harder to swallow than others. "If you were on vacation, captain, would you suddenly up and sell everything you owned, including your car, to a couple of foreigners you had just met?" Cain asked.

Collins simply shook his head, but the lieutenant could read his thoughts. By their own admission, Ibrahiem and Dalia had already killed once and were on the lam. It was unlikely that they would hesitate to kill again, if it would aid in their flight. If the German couple existed at all, there was a good possibility they were slain for their van, and their bodies disposed of along some remote mountain road in the Pyrenees.

But on with the odyssey, as it unfolded in Ibrahiem's own handwriting:

From the southern coast of Spain he and Dalia booked passage across the Straight of Gibraltar to Morocco. For the next year or so they earned their keep by working as tour guides in Casablanca, Rabat, and Marrakech. Ibrahiem also ran a little whiskey between Spain and the northern coast of Africa.

Early in 1984 the Egyptians met a yachtsman who was sailing to Brazil for the pre-Lenten carnival. Ibrahiem and Dalia signed on as crew members, and cast off with him from Morocco. After crossing the strait to the Spanish port of Algeciras, in the shadow of the Rock of Gibraltar, the boat's owner changed his mind and decided to go no farther. This left Ibrahiem and Dalia no choice but to shoulder their luggage and fend for themselves.

With the same amazing good fortune that had earlier brought them together with the white van, they met a Dutch-born Canadian couple who owned a forty-four-foot sailboat, the "Reaithem." As luck would have it, the Canadians were looking for someone to help them sail down the African coast to the Canary Islands. In Ibrahiem and Dalia, they had found their crew.

Once they made landfall in the Canaries, however, the Dutch-Canadian couple had to fly back to Amsterdam on business. Incredibly, they left their $100,000 yacht in the hands of the Egyptians, who promised to keep an eye on it while they were gone. It was an expensive mistake, but it might have saved the couple's lives.

No sooner had the boat's owners flown back to Holland than Ibrahiem and Dalia assumed possession of the sleek motor-sailing vessel, and set out to recruit their own crew to resume their journey across the Atlantic. The object was to put as much distance as possible between them and the Viennese police, who were still looking for Kavale's killers.

It was truly amazing, by Ibrahiem's account, how opportunity seemed to follow the handsome Egyptian couple wherever they went. Their quest for a crew led them directly to Brigette and Bernard, a young French couple who were floating several feet off the ground. Heavily into Hashish and LSD, the mind-bending drug, they said they were looking for passage to the French island of Martinique, off the coast of Venezuela in the Caribbean.

Its new crew assembled, the "Reaithem" set sail at once for the Cape Verde Islands, their last port of call before heading across the choppy Atlantic. As darkness enveloped the boat toward the end of the second day, Ibrahiem and Dalia retired to the captain's quarters below deck, while Bernard took the helm for the night watch. Brigette was curled up on her bunk in the forward cabin.

At around eleven o'clock Ibrahiem was jarred awake by the onslaught of a sudden squall that battered the forty-four-foot vessel about like a toy. Gingerly inching his way topside to see if Bernard needed a hand, he discovered there was nobody at the wheel. Figuring that Bernard had abandoned his post, Ibrahiem angrily went to the couple's cabin to order the Frenchman back on deck. He was not there, however. Nor was Brigette. The cabin was empty.

A thorough search of the boat revealed that Brigette and Bernard were no longer on board. Undoubtedly Brigette had gone above deck to keep Bernard company, and both were washed overboard by the raging storm.

This posed a dilemma for the two survivors, Ibrahiem wrote. Fearing that he and Dalia might be falsely accused of killing the French couple, they took the couple's cash and VISA credit card—good almost anywhere in the world—and pitched the rest of their belongings over the side.

Taking turns at the wheel, they brought the "Reaithem" in to port at Cape Verde alone—an amazing bit of seamanship. After mending the sails and repairing the storm-damaged hull, they painted out the boat's name and rechristened it "Shaharazad."

During the layover the ever-friendly Egyptians fell in with another French couple, who owned a boat called the "Mostache." As they got to know one-another, the four of them decided it would be a great adventure to sail both boats across the Atlantic to Brazil. Ibrahiem and Dalia, the less-experienced sailors, would follow the "Mostache" with the "Shaharazad."

Toward the end of the seventeen-day crossing the Egyptians lost sight of their companion boat, and had to go it alone. Relying on their compass, and hailing passing ships for directions, they made it to Capadillo on the northern coast of Brazil.

After mooring the "Shaharazad" at a local yacht club, they fished out Bernard's and Brigette's stolen credit card and went on a shopping spree. They then laid in new supplies, weighed anchor, and proceeded up the coast to Cayenne, in French Guiana.

They tied up at Cayenne, where Ibrahiem found work as an auto mechanic, while he and Dalia lived aboard the boat. French police became suspicious, however, about the attractive foreign couple who could afford a $100,000 yacht while the breadwinner worked as a lowly mechanic.

Possibly, Ibrahiem wrote, authorities had somehow heard about the missing French couple, or perhaps by now the "Reaithem" had been reported stolen.

A French *agent de police* followed the couple into the interior, where they had gone prospecting for gold, and questioned them about their activities. That was all it took to activate the panic button. Giving the French cop the slip the Egyptians raced back to Cayenne, where they hoisted the sail and put out to sea.

The wind took the "Shaharazad" to Trinadad, where they spent the next several months island-hopping in the Caribbean. They lived off Bernard's and Brigette's credit card, with VISA unwittingly sending the bills to the missing couple's last known address.

The good life ended when Ibrahiem inadvertently ran the "Shaharazad" aground on a tiny island near Grenada. The best they could get for the damaged boat was $11,000 from a salvager in Curacao. Before leaving the "Shaharazad" behind they took photographs of the boat, as a remembrance of their great transatlantic adventure. Dalia showed Chicago police the pictures, as proof of their incredible story.

From Curacao the Egyptians booked steamship passage to the Windward Islands of St. Vincent and St. Lucia, and up to St. Kitts, in the Leeward Islands off Puerto Rico. At St. Kitts they took a plane to Miami, but were denied permission to remain the United States because they lacked proper visas. No problem. Still armed with Bernard's VISA card, they hopped a plane from Miami to Mexico City.

The Egyptians had no intention of remaining in Mexico. They stayed there only long enough to regroup for their next assault on the U.S.A.

Using the credit card, they purchased sporty jogging outfits in Mexico City. Then they traveled by bus and rented car up Highway 101 to Matamoros, across the Rio Grande from Brownsville, Texas. Donning their new sweat suits, they looked like a typical pair of suntanned health enthusiasts as they literally jogged into the United States by running across a Brownsville golf course.

Once in Texas they lost no time in telephoning their cousin, Faysal, in Chicago. Unaware of the murder and intrigue that had brought Ibrahiem and Dalia to the United States, he gleefully hopped into his car and drove down to Brownsville to meet them. The trio arrived back in Chicago on September 27, and settled in Faysal's North Side apartment.

Strangling lovers, sailing the stormy Atlantic, existing on stolen credit cards, keeping one step ahead of the police—this was hardly Dalia's idea of wedded bliss. "I want to dissolve this marriage, but I am afraid Ibrahiem will implicate me in the murder in Vienna," she confided to Faysal. "Let me talk to my cousin," Faysal told her.

He somehow talked Ibrahiem into writing the confession, which absolved Dalia of any part in the actual slaying. The handwritten document was given to Dalia, who hid it in Faysal's apartment.

It was well-past the end of their working day by the time Detectives Kaupert and Weingart had digested the bizarre tale of murder and foreign intrigue. It would take some time to check it out. Rather than wait until the next day, they turned the case over to investigators Cindy Pontoriero and Lawrence Poli, who had just come on duty on the middle-watch.

Pontoriero put in a call to the State Department in Washington, D.C., and outlined the facts of the case. The State Department contacted the Austrian Embassy and briefed an English-speaking member of the legation on Ibrahiem's "confession." "This sounds crazy. Give us a little time to check with Vienna, and we'll get back to you." Austrian officials reported back to the State Department a short time later, and Washington relayed the information to Chicago police. A man named Herbert Kavale had indeed been murdered in his Vienna apartment, and the killer or killers had never been apprehended.

Detectives Poli and Pontoriero then called in Assistant Cook County State's Attorney Susan Fleming, who took a detailed statement from Ibrahiem. While this was being done, Dalia confided to Pontoriero, "I am going to marry my cousin, Faysal, and we are going to return to Egypt and live a happy, normal life."

Under questioning by Pontoriero, she calmly went over the series of events, from the murder in Vienna to the couple's arrival in America in their jogging togs. "It was when we went to talk to the lawyer about a divorce that Faysal and Ibrahiem had the fight," she explained. "Ibrahiem has been very despondent about what happened in Vienna, and he was tired of running away. After the divorce he thought he could start over again in California."

The bizarre case had so many ramifications and international facets that Chicago authorities were uncertain as to the proper procedure to follow. They called on the office of U.S. Attorney Dan K. Webb for advice.

The "duty assistant" in the U.S. Attorney's downtown Chicago office that day was Dean J. Polales, a University of Chicago law school graduate who had joined Webb's staff in July 1983. As duty assistant assigned to the criminal receiving and appellate division, all criminal matters requiring federal action were brought to his attention.

Polales went directly to the Northwest Side police headquarters where the Egyptians were being detained. After a complete briefing by Poli, Pontoriero, and prosecutor Fleming, he notified Webb and the Justice Department in Washington. The Justice Department then advised Austrian authorities through Interpol, the International Police Assistance Agency, that two suspects were in custody in Chicago in connection with the Vienna homicide a year and a half earlier.

Polales personally signed a federal complaint before U.S. Magistrate Carl Sussman charging Ibrahiem and Dalia Allam with murder. He acted in anticipation of a formal request to extradite the couple to Austria.

The official document, signed by a magistrate in Vienna and charging both Ibrahiem and Dalia with the slaying of the Austrian businessman, was hand delivered to the State Department by an Austrian government representative on October 4. It began:

"The Austrian Embassy presents its compliments to the Department of State and has the honor to submit herewith a formal request for the provisional arrest of Mr. Ibrahiem Hamza Allam and Mrs. Dalia Allam for suspicion of murder . . ."

The two waived extradition, and Sussman ordered them held without bond in the Metropolitan Correctional Center pending their return to Vienna to stand trial. It had been, without a doubt, one of the most bizarre cases Chicago police ever found themselves involved in.

While waiting for the deportation papers to be processed, they learned that Herbert Kavale was not the first person whose life Ibrahiem Allam had snuffed out. Interpol advised Police Sergeant Joseph Salvo that Ibrahiem had murdered his previous father-in-law in 1977 by burying him alive, while living in Germany.

Ibrahiem, always on the lookout for easy money, claimed his first wife had paid him to do away with her father. She divorced him while serving sixteen years in a German prison for her role in her father's death. Ibrahiem, who was released from prison after serving four and a half years, traveled to Egypt and found a new wife.

With the completion of the necessary paperwork, U.S. Marshal Peter J. Wilkes took custody of the couple to personally escort them back to Vienna. Accompanied by Inspector James McLaughlin of the U.S. Marshal's Northern Illinois office, and Deputy Marshal Leanne Sobol, the party boarded a jetliner at Chicago's O'Hare International Airport on Sunday, October 7. They changed planes in New York for the transatlantic flight to Vienna, arriving at ten o'clock the next morning.

The Chicagoans were met at Vienna's Schwechat Airport by a squad of Austrian police, headed by Chief Homicide Detective Alois Fiala. "We are surprised, and pleased, at the quick response of your government to our extradition request," he declared. It was the first time anyone could recall that American lawmen had surrendered a prisoner to Viennese police.

The suspects were taken directly to Vienna's Criminal Division headquarters. Fiala and Wilkes rode with the couple in the lead car, with Austrian drug agent Heribert Stocker at the wheel. During the twenty-five-minute trip along the Rennweg Simmeringer Hauptstrasse, Ibrahiem—now switching to fluent German—repeated his murder confession to Fiala.

Satisfied that they had the right suspects, Vienna authorities ordered Ibrahiem and Dalia held for trial. The penalty for murder, under Austrian law, is twenty years in prison.

Upon returning to Chicago Wilkes, who thought American involvement in the case was over, received an unexpected telephone call from the Royal Canadian Mounted Police. Sergeant Kenneth Rehman was on the line from Victoria, British Columbia. "We've just learned of the Egyptian couple's arrest from Interpol, and we're trying to track down a boat named "Reaithem," which they made off with," he explained. "The rightful owners have been looking for it ever since they left Amsterdam. They have since retired here in Canada, which is how we got our feet in the case."

Wilkes told the sergeant what he knew about the missing boat, and the Mounties, who had been trying to find the "Reaithem" switched their search to the "Shaharazad." By that time, of course, the well-traveled craft could have been sailing under yet another name, and could be anywhere.

The incredible case of the "sock heard around the world" was over, as far as Chicago police were concerned. Patrolmen McAuliffe and Sargis, who had stopped to break up a street-corner fistfight, had inadvertently solved a slaying on another continent.

EPILOGUE

Ibrahiem Hamza Allam was tried in Vienna for his role in the slaying of the well-to-do merchant, Herbert Kavale. Ibrahiem was convicted of murder and sentenced to twenty years in prison. Charges against Dalia, of being an accessory to murder, were dropped.

There remain some nagging questions in the case that authorities fear might never be answered:

Did the unidentified German couple who "sold" their van and personal belongings to the Egyptians in Spain *really* return to their homeland?

And did the unfortunate French couple, Brigette and Bernard, *really* fall overboard in a storm?

Only Ibrahiem and Dalia know for sure.

CHAPTER 18

████████████████████████████████████

THE SECRET OF BELLE'S BARNYARD

Belle Gunness was no raving beauty. Her picture attests to that. But she was no underachiever, by any means. Belle made a fortune in insurance. She didn't sell it, mind you, she collected it—on one late husband after another. Then she switched to rich boyfriends, to cut down on the paperwork. Were she alive today she would discover her name inscribed in the *Guiness Book of World Records* as the most prolific murderess of modern times.

By some accounts, at least forty-two starry-eyed suitors called to court the widow Gunness at her isolated farm outside LaPorte, Indiana, but only one ever lived to tell about it. Lucky for George Anderson, he was a light sleeper. Other accounts place the number of Belle's hapless victims at as many as 180 men, women, and babies.

At any rate, no one appeared any the wiser until the early morning hours of Tuesday, April 28, 1908, when a raging fire burned Belle's cozy farmhouse to the ground, leaving the charred corpses of a woman and three children in the ashes.

It rated only a small story in the Chicago papers the following day. An article under the headline, FOUR DIE IN FIRE; SUITOR IS IN TOILS, told how the wealthy widow and her three children had perished in the flames:

The blackened forms of the little ones were found huddled about that of the mother, as if they had sought her protection as the flames engulfed them. Late this afternoon the bodies of Mrs. Gunness and her three children, Myrtle, aged 11; Lucy, aged 9; and Philip, aged 5, were removed from the smoldering ruins.

The story went on to relate that only the previous afternoon the middle-aged widow, expressing fear for her own life, had brought valuable papers into town and placed them in a safety deposit vault. She was quoted as telling her lawyer, M. E. Leliter, that she was frightened of her ex-handyman, Ray Lamphere, who had become infatuated with her. "I'm afraid he's going to kill me and burn the house," she told Leliter.

As soon as Sheriff Albert Smutzer got wind of Belle's chat with the lawyer, he hauled Lamphere off to jail for questioning.

An April 30 newspaper account of the arrest, beneath a photo of the loving Mrs. Gunness and the three tots, was a testimonial to turn-of-the-century interrogation methods:

> Ray Lamphere, arrested last night in connection with the destruction of the country home of Mrs. Belle Gunness, a well-to-do widow, which resulted in her death and that of her three children, was today subjected to two sweatings by Prosecutor Smith and Sheriff Smutzer, but maintained that he did not set fire to the house.

The article also disclosed that a will, executed by Mrs. Gunness just twelve hours before her death, left her estate to the three children or, in the event of their deaths, to the Norwegian Orphans' Home in Chicago.

Then came the first of many startling revelations in the grisly case: Coroner Charles Mack, in examining the charred remains of the victims, discovered that the dead woman had no head. A newspaper item of May 1 picked up the story:

> Where is the head of Mrs. Belle Gunness? Today a score of men dug among the ruins in a vain search for the head. If it

cannot be found, credence will be given to the theory that a murderer stole into her room in the dark, decapitated her, and then set fire to the house so that the flames might cover up the evidence of his deed.

The unknown author of those lines could not have been more wrong. For, as fate would have it, Asle Helgelein was on the way. Helgelein, a Norwegian from Mansfield, South Dakota, had been worried for some time about his brother, Andrew, who had disappeared after drawing $3,000 out of a bank in Aberdeen—a small fortune in those days. The last anyone had seen of him, he was boarding a train for Indiana, to answer a matrimonial advertisement placed by none other than Belle Gunness in a Scandinavian language newspaper.

When he answered the ad, Belle wrote back to him in Norwegian: "I'll make a cream pudding. Do not say anything about coming here. Sell all you can get CASH for. Make yourself free from Dakota. I have a sister, who lives in Chicago, I also have a brother, who lives in Norway. He is a contractor in Trondheim. Now my dearest friend come soon."

When Asle Helgelein heard nothing more from his brother after he boarded the train for Indiana, he wrote to the widow Gunness asking if Andrew had arrived. "He has returned to Norway," she advised him by return mail.

Asle refused to believe it. Andrew had never said anything about going back to Norway. Beside, he would never take off like that without notifying his family of his plans. Then Asle picked up his newspaper and read about the fire at the Gunness farm. He hopped the next train for Indiana to see for himself what was going on.

As soon as he got to LaPorte he told Sheriff Smutzer about his missing brother, and convinced the lawman that, as long as his men were digging through the fire ruins for Belle's missing head, it wouldn't hurt to dig around in the adjoining farmyard as well.

"Come to think of it, there are some soft spots in the widow's chicken yard," the sheriff remarked. "We figure she might have buried her garbage out there."

The sheriff drove out to the farm and told his men, "Dig around in there and see if you can come up with anything. There may be nothing there, but at least this feller from South Dakota will quit pestering me."

So the shovelers put their spades to the "soft spots" in the barnyard, and before long they uncovered parts of a human body, dismembered and sewn into a gunny sack.

Asle Helgelein showed up at the farm just as the sack was being opened. Looking down at the grisly remains of the hacked-up corpse, he turned to Sheriff Smutzer and exclaimed, "That's Andy!"

The macabre confirmation that Andrew Helgelein had not gone back to Norway after all was only the first shock. By sundown four more bodies had been unearthed in Mrs. Gunness' innocent-looking chicken yard.

One of the partly decomposed corpses was identified as that of Jennie Olsen, the widow's fifteen-year-old adopted daughter. Jennie had not been seen in two years.

Whenever anyone inquired about her, Belle explained, "I sent her away to a Lutheran school in Los Angeles. She's such a bright child and the opportunities in California are so much greater than in a small town in Indiana."

The other bodies unearthed that dreadful day were those of two small children, and a tall man with a black mustache.

On day two of the digging the sheriff's astonished helpers exhumed four more bodies, and several days later, another, for a total of ten—not counting the decapitated woman and three children found earlier in the ruins of the fire.

As word spread throughout the countryside, morbid curiosity seekers gathered on the road bordering the farm and peered through the fence at the grim spadework going on in the chicken yard. The citizens of LaPorte were faced with the sudden realization that the poor widow Gunness had lived the secret life of a lady Bluebeard. "Bell the Butcher," was the name they hung on her.

And who were all those people the sheriff's men were finding under the dirt?

One of the chicken yard bodies turned out to have been that of John Moo, of Elbow Lake, Minnesota. Moo had gone to LaPorte two years earlier bearing $1,000 in cash to pay off the mortgage on the widow's farm as a wedding gift.

The mortgage was paid off, all right, but nobody ever heard of Mr. Moo again. "He went back home. The romance just didn't work out," Belle sadly explained.

Another of the corpses was identified as that of Ole Budsburg, of Iola, Wisconsin. Ole, the father of seven grown sons, left his home in Iola in April 1907 with a $3,000 bank draft, saying he was going to marry the Indiana widow who had advertised for a mate in a Scandinavian newspaper.

Strange. Ole never wrote to tell his boys how the wedding went. In fact, they never heard from him again. The sons finally wrote to the LaPorte Savings Bank, which had cashed the $3,000 note, asking for information.

A bank cashier made a few inquiries, and then wrote to tell the boys that Mrs. Gunness had advised him, "Ole didn't care for this part of the country. He decided to go out to Oregon to buy a farm."

With what? His $3,000 had gone to the widow Gunness. After the banker and the Budsburg boys began asking questions, the crafty Mrs. Gunness attempted to lay down a smoke screen by writing to the missing farmer in care of his Iola home. "Ole, what has become of you?" she wrote. "Please know that I am still willing to become your wife if you will reconsider and have me."

Ole Budsburg had indeed "bought the farm," as they say, but not in Oregon. He shared space under the chicken yard with Belle's other unfortunate victims.

Coroner Mack sent the stomachs of Andrew Helgelein and the four fire victims to Chicago where their contents were analyzed by Dr. Walter S. Haines of Rush Medical College.

Dr. Haines reported back: "Helgelein's stomach contained arsenic in abundance and a considerable quantity of strychnine." The same held true for the bodies of the woman and children found in the fire ruins—"an abundance of arsenic and a considerable amount of strychnine."

The victims had not died in the fire after all. They had been poisoned.

Another curious discovery: The four bodies in the ruins of the fire were found huddled on what remained of a mattress, causing authorities to assume that they had been in bed, and the bed had fallen through from the second floor to the cellar when the floors collapsed. In probing through the debris, however, workers found the remains of a piano on top of the bodies. This indicated that the four victims were already in the basement when the fire broke out, and the piano crashed through the burning first floor and landed on them.

As the sheriff's men continued to dig to see what else they might find, the town was buzzing with theories and rumors. Was that really Belle Gunness' headless body they found in the fire ruins, or yet another murder victim? And how about Belle's two legal husbands? Both died under rather suspicious circumstances, come to think about it.

Belle's first husband, Mads Albert Sorensen, had been insured for $8,500—an enormous sum in turn-of-the-century currency. Her second spouse, Peter Gunness, had a $3,500 policy on his life. Belle, of course, collected on them both.

For a time the widow Gunness had been considered somewhat of a local celebrity around LaPorte, after she let it be known that as a child she had performed as a tightrope walker with a circus in Norway, where her father was a sword swallower and contortionist.

The truth that came out as police dug into her background was that she had never been anything more than a cotter's daughter. She was born Brynhild Paulsdatter Storsetgjerde on November 11, 1859, in the village of Selbu. Her father, Paul Pedersen Storsetgjerde, was a dirt-poor tenant farmer married to Berit, sometimes known as Arabella. The child, Brynhild, who worked as a cattle girl, liked to call herself Bella, after her mother.

She was confirmed on June 21, 1874, and worked on neighboring farms until she was twenty-two. Then her married sister, Nellie Larson, who lived in Chicago, sent Brynhild boat fare to come to America and join her.

A sailing list from 1882 contains the following entry: Girl, Bronhild Paulsen, 22; date of registration; 8/9/1881, from Selbo [sic] to Chicago, paid in America.

Brynhild, who Americanized her name to Belle, lived with her sister and brother-in-law for about a year before marrying Sorensen, a Dane, who worked as a department store detective. They settled on the Northwest Side of Chicago, and in 1894 they opened a small candy store in the Austin neighborhood.

They had four children, but only two, Myrtle and Lucy (who would later be found in the LaPorte farm ashes) survived. The other two, Caroline, three months, and Alex, five years, were buried in the family plot in Forest Home Cemetery.

Belle and Mads adopted Jennie Olsen after the child's father, Anton, decided that the couple could give his baby daughter a better life than he could provide in those trying times. His mistake. Jennie would later be dug up in the LaPorte chicken yard.

The confectionary went up in flames in 1898. It was Belle, herself, who sounded the alarm when the fire broke out, and ran from the building with her children. Little Jennie was slightly burned in the blaze, which Belle told firemen started when a kerosene lamp exploded. Little significance was attached, at the time, to the fact that no glass from the lamp was found.

Belle, who had personally insured the little shop, collected on the policy. That appeared to have been the initial business transaction, so to speak, in which she discovered a whole new world of possibilities. From that day on, there was no stopping her.

Shortly after the candy store burned down the family moved to a new home at 620 Alma Street. Alas, that home, too, was the scene of a suspicious fire, after which Belle once again collected on the insurance.

Mads died in the West Side home two years later at the age of forty-six, after complaining that he didn't feel too good. By coincidence, his death occurred on the very day that his two insurance policies overlapped, enabling his grieving widow to collect on both of them.

Mad's death was attributed to "convulsions," but there was some gossip—unsubstantiated, of course—that he died of strychnine poisoning after enjoying a piece of Belle's home-made apple pie. He was buried alongside Alex and Caroline in the family plot, amidst rumors that the children might not have died of natural causes, either.

Such unkind speculation was enough to encourage Belle to move out of the neighborhood. With the $8,500 she had collected on Mads' two life insurance policies, and $5,000 more from the sale of the house, she bundled up the three surviving youngsters and headed for Indiana.

On November 9, 1901, according to local records, she purchased a fifteen-room mansion on McClung Road, a mile or so northwest of LaPorte. The two-story brick structure had been built in 1857 by one of the town's founding families. For a time, before Belle moved in with the kids, it had served as a bawdy house, to the displeasure of neighbors.

On April 1, 1902, less than four months after she arrived in LaPorte, Belle married Peter Gunness, the local hog butcher. Gunness brought into the union a seven-month-old daughter, Jennie, by a previous marriage.

Their honeymoon was cut short seven days later, however, by baby Jennie's untimely death. And by December, Peter Gunness would join his infant daughter in the grave.

The bereaved widow told authorities that her husband met his demise when a sausage grinder fell from a high shelf and crushed his skull as he sat in the cellar. Never mind that six-year-old Myrtle babbled to her little friends at school,

"Mamma brained papa with a meat cleaver. Don't tell a soul." Authorities dismissed it as childish prattle, and the coroner returned a verdict of accidental death.

Peter Gunness was buried by the same minister who had officiated at his marriage to Belle eight months earlier, the Reverend George C. Moore. And Belle found herself $3,000 richer, thanks to the life insurance policy of which Peter was thoughtful enough to make her the beneficiary.

Not long afterward her last child, Philip, was born. He was five when he died, with his two half-sisters, in the flaming farm house.

It was after Peter was killed by the free-falling sausage grinder, or mama's cleaver, if you care to believe little Myrtle, that Belle, a stout woman with a mannish appearance who stood nearly six-feet tall and weighed more than 225 pounds, began to advertise in lonely hearts columns in Scandinavian newspapers. "Triflers need not apply," the notices cautioned.

Olaf Lindboe, a Norwegian farm hand, arrived from Chicago with his life savings in hand to prove he was no trifler. Others who made tracks for LaPorte with their pockets bulging in answer to the ad were forty-eight-year-old John Lefgren and Herman Konitzberg of Chicago; George Berry of Tuscola, Illinois; Charles Ermond of New Castle, Pennsylvania; and Henry Gerhalt of Scandinavia, Wisconsin—all never to be seen again.

Only one hopeful bridegroom is known to have courted the buxom Indiana widow and lived to tell about it—George Anderson.

Anderson made the tactical error of showing up at Belle's farm without bringing *all* his money. "That isn't enough, George. I need more money than that to pay off the mortgage before I can marry you," Belle told him. So the gullible Anderson wired home to Tarkio, Missouri, for the rest of his money, and made himself comfortable in one of the guest rooms while waiting for the bank draft to arrive.

In the middle of the third night he awoke with a start to discover Belle leaning over the bed, peering into his face.

Anderson instinctively cried out in alarm, and Belle dashed out of the room. That was enough for the expectant groom, however. He pulled on his trousers and ran out of the house, keeping his bachelorhood—and his life—intact.

After Peter Gunness' bizarre death Belle hired Ray Lamphere, a French-Canadian carpenter and jack-of-all-trades, as a handyman about the farm. Lamphere, who was considered a local simpleton, became more than a little bit jealous over all the men Belle seemed to be entertaining. Belle eventually fired him, and hired Joseph Maxson to do the chores.

Which brings us to the night of the holocaust. Maxson, who lived in a wing of the house, escaped by jumping out the window in his underwear. "I woke up and smelled smoke. I pounded on Mrs. Gunness' door but got no answer," he told Sheriff Smutzer.

It was after the sheriff learned from attorney Leliter of Belle's remark that she was "afraid" of Lamphere, that the fired handyman was brought in for questioning. Lamphere's initial reaction was, "Did the Widow Gunness and the children get out?"

He denied any knowledge of the blaze, but the sheriff produced a witness, sixteen-year-old John Solyam, who said he had seen the handyman fleeing from the scene.

"You wouldn't say that looking me in the eye," Lamphere challenged.

"Yes I will," answered the boy. "You found me hiding behind a bush and told me you'd kill me if I didn't get out of there."

What the teen-ager was doing lurking behind a bush on the Gunness farm in the middle of the night was never explained. But what he claimed to have seen was enough for Sheriff Smutzer to book Lamphere for murder and arson.

The ne'er-do-well handyman was already under lock and key when the digging began in the chicken yard, and the sack containing Andrew Helgelein's dismembered remains was uncovered. When the grisly news reached the jailhouse,

Lamphere exclaimed, "Bodies! Murder! Helgelein! My God, that woman! Now I know what was going on!"

From what the sheriff was able to put together, however, Lamphere knew what was going on all along.

Another farmhand, William Slater, told the sheriff that Lamphere once confided to him, "Helgelein won't bother me. We've fixed him for keeps."

Coroner Mack, meanwhile, gave up trying to find Belle's missing head. At his direction Austin Cutler, the local mortician, shipped the remains of the woman and three children found in the fire ruins to Illinois for burial. Records of the century-old funeral parlor, now operated by Robert Cutler, show that four bodies, identified as those of Belle Gunness, forty-eight; Myrtle Sorensen, eleven; Lucy Sorensen, nine; and Philip Gunness, five, were placed aboard a train bound for Chicago, where they were to be met by Belle's sister, Nellie Larson.

But that was not the end of it as far as some of the townspeople were concerned. Austin Cutler, who knew Belle Gunness, insisted that the mutilated body he placed aboard the train was too small to have been that of the 225-pound widow who stood nearly six-feet tall, including her head. Maxson the farm hand, along with two of Belle's neighbors, Chris Christofferson and Swan Nicholson, agreed.

Furthermore, witnesses told Sheriff Smutzer that they had seen Mrs. Gunness drive a young woman to the farm on the Saturday before the fire. The woman, described as a slightly built brunette, was never seen again.

Four local doctors, J. Lucian Gray, J.H.W. Meyer, Franklin T. Wilcox, and Harry H. Long, who earlier had measured the charred remains of the headless woman at Cutler's funeral home at Coroner Mack's request, decided to settle the mystery for once and for all.

Between the four of them, they set up a chart comparing the known dimensions of the woman found in the fire to the approximate measurements of Belle Gunness. They drew up the comparative table of measurements:

	Fire Victim (inches)	Belle Gunness (inches)
Biceps	9	17
Bust................	36	46
Waist	26	37
Thigh	25	30
Hips	40	54
Calf	12½	14
Wrist	6	9

Making a generous allowance for the missing head and neck, they determined that the body found in the burned-out farmhouse had belonged to a woman about five-feet-three-inches tall, who weighed around 150 pounds. On May 9, Dr. Long, one of LaPorte's most respected physicians, declared that the reconstructed cadaver of the fire victim would have been a good five inches shorter than Mrs. Gunness, who outweighed the fire victim by nearly 100 pounds.

The evidence seemed irrefutable. The headless body taken from the cellar of the burned-out farmhouse, and buried in the family plot in Forest Home Cemetery in Chicago, could not have been Belle Gunness.

Dr. Ira P. Norton, the LaPorte dentist who had installed some of the widow's bridgework, said it was too bad the victim's head was missing, because if he could get a look at the teeth he would be able to "incontrovertibly" solve the troublesome riddle.

Enter Louis "Klondike" Schultz, a former gold miner, who happened to be in LaPorte at the moment. "Why don't we build a sluice, like we used to mine for for gold in Alaska, and sift the debris?" he suggested.

No sooner said than done. The sluice was built and Klondike was hired to operate it on a per diem basis, assisted by volunteer shovelers. The fire debris from the cellar, which had earlier been sifted, screened, and tossed about in a futile search for the missing head, was carried out into the yard and dumped into a pile. Spadeful by spadeful, the ashes, cinders, and bits of mortar were tossed into the sluice box and washed down the wooden slide, with no results.

A solemn Sheriff Smutzer presided over the operation, which attracted thousands of sightseers, some of whom traveled by rail all the way from Chicago to witness the historic event. Several times the sheriff had to leave town to check out leads, false sightings of Belle Gunness, and a phony confession by a New York man who claimed to have burned down the house. But the grim search continued.

On May 19 Klondike and his brigade of sluice miners had a remarkable piece of luck. As the water drained from the placer mine, there were Belle's elusive dentures—both upper and lower—along with the natural gold-capped teeth from the upper jaw to which the bridgework had been attached!

"They're found!" bellowed the jubilant sheriff, tossing his leather cap high into the air.

Jumping into his bright red police car he sped into town and presented the discovery to Dr. Norton. "This is my work, all right," the dentist declared, nodding his scholarly head. "These are the porcelain teeth I made for Mrs. Gunness. She is dead."

A local doubter, pointing out that the headless body taken from the ruins bore no resemblance to Belle Gunness in size, asked the beaming sheriff, "What is to have prevented the widow from removing her false teeth and throwing them into the fire before she left?"

"Well, this doesn't look much like it," scoffed Sheriff Smutzer, pointing to the teeth to which the dentures were attached. "Here is the tooth in place in this gold cap, showing where it was burned off. Could anything be more conclusive?"

Obviously, according to the sheriff's reasoning, the raging fire had somehow destroyed the woman's entire head, leaving only her bridgework and the teeth to which they were attached, without even melting the gold cap.

And what a remarkable miner Klondike Schultz must have been. Incredibly, he was able to flush out the upper and lower plates together as one unit, even after the basement debris had been raked, shoveled, sifted, and screened all over creation. Neither fire nor water nor the jarring shovels of his volunteer diggers as they scooped the debris into buckets and tumbled it into a waste heap had been able to separate them.

If such a drama had been played out in Chicago, somebody would have winked slyly and snickered, "The fix is in."

With the identification of the teeth Sheriff Smutzer declared that the fire victim had been Belle Gunness—the professional opinions of four physicians, and all other evidence, to the contrary. The woeful handyman, Ray Lamphere, went on trial for Belle's murder the following November. The trial produced some interesting testimony.

Dr. Norton, who had constructed the durable dental work, testified that, in his honest opinion, the teeth could not have been removed from Mrs. Gunness' mouth while she was alive without splitting the gold crowns.

He was unable to explain, however, how the gold caps could have survived the blaze without even being fused together. O. P. M. Squires, a local jeweler, revealed that the heat was so intense that the gold had been melted clean off several watches found in the debris.

The defense called Joe Maxson, who had succeeded Lamphere as Belle's handyman. He testified that both he and Isaac Andrapher were working around the yard on the morning of the discovery. He said Klondike Schultz fished the dentures out of his pocket somewhere around eight or nine o'clock and told them, "We've found what we've been looking for."

That was more than an hour before Sheriff Smutzer arrived and "discovered" them in the sluice. Andrapher corroborated Maxson's story.

Q. I will ask you to state when you first saw the teeth.

A. When I first saw them, he took them out of his right pocket.

Q. Who?

A. The sluice man.

Q. Was Mr. Smutzer there at the time?

A. No, sir.

Sheriff Smutzer hotly contradicted the two handymen's testimony. He swore under oath that the teeth were recovered on May 17 or 18. When prosecutor Ralph N. Smith refreshed the sheriff's memory, he changed his testimony to say the fortunate discovery took place May 19. The questioning continued:

Q. About what time of day?

A. About . . . the upper set were found about 10:30, I think, 10:30, 10:45.

Q. I now hand you that state's exhibit No. 16, purporting to be the lower set of teeth, and will ask you when those were found.

A. They were found in the sluice box at the Gunness farm about 11:30. I should think, 11:15 to 11:30.

Somebody was obviously lying. Klondike Schultz, who could have cleared up the mystery, was not called to testify by either side. He had long since left town in search of new adventure.

The contradictory evidence was enough to plant more than a little doubt in the minds of the jurors as to whether Belle had indeed died in the fire, or faked her demise with someone else's body. They found Lamphere innocent of murder, but declared him guilty of arson.

On December 30 the handyman was sent to the Indiana State Prison in Michigan City, where he died several months later of tuberculosis. In a deathbed statement in the prison hospital to an inmate nurse, Harry Myres, Lamphere confessed to being in cahoots with Belle Gunness all along. During his tenure as her assistant, he said, she lured no less than forty-two unsuspecting men to the murder farm.

"Belle drugged their coffee, then bashed in their heads while they lay in a stupor," he related. "Then she dissected their bodies in an operating room in the cellar, tied them in sacks, and I did the planting."

The only one who ever got away was the light-sleeping Anderson. Perhaps he had not drunk all his coffee. After Anderson's flight, Belle upgraded the process to include strychnine before applying the hammer for good measure, Lamphere explained.

He said money collected from Belle's would-be suitors, before they disappeared under the earth in the chicken yard, ranged from $300 to $23,000.

The murders were committed in a basement laboratory, which could be reached only through a single, well-oiled door, for which Belle carried the only key. The only illumination in the death chamber was provided by candle or lantern.

Belle methodically dismembered her victims on the table, and sometimes soaked their bodies in a large wooden vat containing a chloride of lime solution, according to Lamphere. The $23,000 man was beheaded to prevent identification, and his skull was buried separately. The rest of the victim was cut up, placed in sacks, and hauled on a farm rig to a neighbor's field for burial, "because Belle's chicken yard was getting filled up."

Lamphere confided to his prison nurse that folks who had argued that the burned body in the basement could not have been Belle's were right all along. "That was Mae O'Reilly. She was a servant girl Belle brought over from Chicago, telling her she needed help around the house."

It was Asle Helgelein's persistent inquiries about his missing brother, Andrew, that convinced Belle it was time to shut down her chamber of horrors and move on. But before she left, her three children had to die because, like their older sister, Jennie Olsen, "They were starting to ask questions," the handyman explained.

On Saturday, the day before the fire, Lamphere said he drove Belle in a horse-drawn wagon to a railroad station twelve miles from LaPorte and saw her safely aboard a southbound train. He returned to the farm that night, as per her instructions, placed the bodies of the three children and the decapitated Mae O'Reilly in the basement, buried Mae's head in the yard, and torched the farmhouse.

Despite Belle's charade of firing Lamphere and having nothing more to do with him, he insisted that he worked for her to the very end. "I guess I'm the only man Belle really loved, because she never killed me," he smiled proudly. Why bother? He had no money.

The widow Gunness got away with the macabre operation as long as she did, according to Lamphere, because a highly placed local official was taking hush money from her. On one occasion he said he walked into the house just as the unnamed official was pocketing a wad of bills. After the man had departed Belle remarked sarcastically, "I not only had to buy him an automobile, but I just gave him another thousand dollars."

To this day the LaPorte Public Library keeps a file on Belle Gunness, and the LaPorte County Historical Society maintains a period room in the museum, featuring a mannequin of the widow Gunness, along with photographs of the gruesome case and smears of red paint to simulate blood.

According to Dorothy Rowley, associate curator of the historical museum, the popular belief is that the unnamed "official" involved with Belle was none other than the local sheriff.

"Sheriff Smutzer was suspected because some believed he helped her get away," Rowley explained. "His car, a little red runabout, had been seen out there at the Gunness place quite a bit. People remembered seeing the car because of its bright color.

"Oh, Belle got out of town. No doubt about it. She had to have that fire to cover her escape. She wanted people to believe she had died in the fire."

If the sheriff was indeed in on the plot, that would account for the convenient appearance of Belle's dentures, and how they miraculously survived the fearful blaze in near-mint condition.

Local suspicion was that the sheriff delivered the teeth to Klondike Schultz to "discover" in the sluice bin after it became necessary to prove the identity of the headless corpse.

That would also explain why Sheriff Smutzer was so willing to accept the dentures as irrefutable evidence that the widow Gunness perished in the flames, despite the fact that the burned body was much smaller than Belle's.

The sheriff left LaPorte not long afterward and moved to Texas, where he suddenly came up with enough money to start his own grapefruit farm.

Also suspected of having a hand in the dark mystery was a neighboring black woman who indulged in voodoo, Elizabeth Smith, known locally as "Nigger Liz." She was a relic of slavery days and nobody, including Liz herself, knew how old she really was.

What was known, however, was that she was a friend of Belle Gunness, and Ray Lamphere was seen at her home—a fifteen-minute walk from Belle's farm—around 3:00 A.M. on the day of the fire.

"Three days after the fire a delivery boy walked into Liz' kitchen with groceries, and saw Belle Gunness standing there," Rowley said. "Well, he was scared to death of Belle and never told anyone until years afterward at a class reunion."

After the ageless voodoo woman died in 1916 workers, rummaging about in knee-deep debris in her tumbledown shack on Railroad Street, came upon a musty, cobwebby human skull. Could it have been the skull of the headless corpse found in the fire? Was that where Lamphere disposed of Mae O'Reilly's head? Or was it a prop used by the voodoo lady in her conjuring?

"When I feel that I am going to die I'll send for you and tell you everything," Liz once promised Lamphere's lawyer, Wirt Worden.

She tried to keep her end of the bargain. A few days before her death Liz sent for Worden, who had since become assistant prosecuting attorney for LaPorte County. Unfortunately, the lawyer was vacationing in Louisiana—by coincidence, the heart of America's voodoo land. By the time he was able to get back to LaPorte the voodoo woman had taken her secret to the grave.

In the years that followed there were occasional sightings of a woman believed to be Belle Gunness in various parts of the country. The local newspaper reported that authorities were often "summoned to far-off places to investigate." But by the time they got there, the mystery woman had flown the coop.

How many people did Belle Gunness butcher over the years before fire leveled her murder mansion in the wee hours of April 28, 1908? Enough to make the *Guiness Book of World Records,* but the exact number will never be known.

One published account, entitled "Norway's Mass Murderess," put the number at 180. Most observers agree that the body count could go well over 100, but this cannot be proved.

Belle's personal grave digger, Ray Lamphere, put the number of murdered suitors at forty-one, from the day he and his shovel entered the picture—not counting the one who got away. Add to that Belle's own three children and her adopted daughter, Jennie, plus the headless corpse of Mae O'Reilly, and you have forty-six. Then there were Belle's two well-insured husbands, Mads Sorensen and Peter Gunness. That would be forty-eight, that are known to historians.

And what about Belle's first two children, who died in Chicago? Considering their mother's frightful reputation, it is not outlandish to suspect that they, too, might not have gone to their graves due to natural causes.

But how many more were there in between? Who were the bodies of the children exhumed in the chicken yard, and where had they come from? Questions, questions that will never be answered in this world.

Once the story of Belle's basement dissecting lab got out, it became known locally as the "Chamber of Horrors" or "Bluebeard Hall."

And it was not long before someone composed a "Ballad of Belle Gunness" to commemorate the grotesque horror that had suddenly put LaPorte, Indiana, on the map. Sung to the tune of "Love, Oh Careless Love," the ballad ended with these lines:

> There's red upon the Hoosier moon,
> For Belle was strong and full of doom,
> And think of all them Norska men,
> Who'll never see St. Paul again.

EPILOGUE

And what of Belle Gunness, who disappeared into the night, leaving a trail of human bones behind her?

Historian Dorothy Rowley is convinced that an elderly woman who called herself Esther Carlson, arrested in Los Angeles in 1931 for fatally poisoning eighty-one-year-old August Lindstrom, a wealthy Scandinavian lumberman, was none other than seventy-one-year-old Belle Gunness, plying her trade to the bitter end.

LaPorte Sheriff's Deputy C. A. Fitzgerald, learning of the suspect's arrest, arranged for two former LaPorte residents who had moved to California to cooperate with authorities on the West Coast.

One of them, John A. Torkey, a former LaPorte liquor dealer who had known Belle personally, was shown a photograph of the woman, who had fallen seriously ill and could not have visitors. "Hmmm. That sure looks like Belle Gunness, except that Belle had a wart on her face and this lady doesn't," he mused.

Aware that commercial photographs were often retouched, Los Angeles police obtained a negative of the picture which showed that the woman did, indeed, have a wart on her face.

Before the identification could be confirmed, however, "Mrs. Carlson" died in jail on May 7, 1931, while awaiting trial for murdering Lindstrom to get her hands on his $2,000 bank account. Bear in mind that anyone who had $2,000 in the bank during the Great Depression was considered a wealthy man.

After the prisoner's death Torkey and John "Dennis" Daly, a seventy-year-old boilermaker who had also known Belle Gunness back in LaPorte, were escorted to the Los Angeles county morgue to view the body.

"I am positive she is Belle Gunness. I've talked to her hundreds of times," Daly asserted.

"Absolutely," Torkey agreed. "How do I know? Well, for one thing, her mouth. It has the same little twist to one side, just like Belle's. Her eyes are the same. Eyebrows not as dark as they were. Hair kind of faded, too, but it's Belle's hair. This is Belle!"

If the dead woman was, indeed, Belle, then we must add eighty-one-year-old August Lindstrom to her dreadful toll. His death fit her M.O. perfectly.

INDEX

ABOUT THE AUTHORS

Between them, Edward Baumann and John O'Brien have covered every major crime in Chicago and the Middle-West in the past four decades. They have worked together as a team since 1974.

Baumann, a native of Kenosha, Wisconsin, served with the Army Air Corps in the South Pacific during World War II. He worked as a reporter or editor on the *Waukegan News-Sun*, *Chicago Daily News*, *Chicago's American*, *Chicago Today*, and the *Chicago Tribune* before turning to free-lancing full time in 1988. He is a past president of the Chicago Press Club, former chairman of the Chicago Press Veterans Association, a director of the Chicago Newspaper Reporters Association, and winner of two Chicago Newspaper Guild Page One Awards for investigative reporting. In 1988, his peers honored him as Chicago Press Veteran of the Year.

O'Brien, who was born in Chicago, served with the U.S. Marine Corps before becoming a crime reporter for the *Chicago Tribune*. His assignments have taken him to police stations and county morgues from coast to coast. He has done in-depth stories on criminal justice in Michigan and California, exposes on child abuse in Texas and political dirty tricks in North Dakota, covered Mob Chief Tony Accardo in Florida, and joined investigators in tracking three suspects in a fortune in stolen cash all the way to the British West Indies. In 1989, he shared the *Tribune*'s Edward Scott Beck Award for investigative reporting.

Baumann and O'Brien are also the authors of *Chicago Heist,* the true story of America's biggest and most bizarre cash theft, *Getting Away with Murder* (Bonus Books, 1991) and more than 300 internationally published detective magazine articles. Baumann is also the coauthor, with Kenan Heise, of *Chicago Originals: A Cast of the City's Colorful Characters* (Bonus Books, 1990).

Other Books by the Authors

Getting Away with Murder
Edward Baumann and John O'Brien

Chicago Heist
John O'Brien and Edward Baumann

Chicago Originals
Edward Baumann with Kenan Heise